THE YEAR WE
DISAPPEARED

A *Publishers Weekly* Best Book of the Year
An IndieBound Next Pick

★ "Where John's chapters provide the grim facts, it is Cylin's authentically childlike perspective that, in revealing the cost to her innocence, renders the tragic experience most searingly." —*Publishers Weekly*, starred review

"A fascinating tale, making the costs of violence unequivocally clear. . . . John's hard-won conclusion about vengeance—violence needn't be perpetuated because it would only damage his family more—holds a striking lesson for everyone, not just teens." —*Chicago Sun-Times*

"A remarkable book. . . . Together, father and daughter weave a startling, heartbreaking tale." —*Barnstable Patriot*

"Riveting." —*Des Moines Register*

"Cylin's detailed account of her childhood is real and, though certainly full of danger and fear, is also a testament to the strength of the power of kids' resiliency. Although the shooter and his family remained on the run and after John Busby, the Busbys' drive to keep their family safe resonates with awe throughout the book. A fascinating true story." —*Copley News Service*

"The book flows seamlessly back and forth from father's to daughter's perspective, each jump between narrators providing further explanation and insight and pulling readers deeper into the story." —*VOYA*

"A drama that can suck readers in. Those who enjoyed Woodson's *Hush* may wish to pursue this real-life counterpart." —*BCCB*

"Both father and daughter have riveting stories to tell in this gritty memoir." —*The Horn Book*

THE YEAR WE DISAPPEARED

A Father-Daughter Memoir

CYLIN BUSBY & JOHN BUSBY

BLOOMSBURY

NEW YORK BERLIN LONDON

First published in the United States of America in September 2008
by Bloomsbury Books for Young Readers
Paperback edition published in April 2010
www.bloomsburyteens.com

For information about permission to reproduce selections from this book, write to
Permissions, Bloomsbury BFYR, 175 Fifth Avenue, New York, New York 10010

The Library of Congress has cataloged the hardcover edition as follows:
Busby, Cylin.
The year we disappeared: a father-daughter memoir / by Cylin Busby & John Busby—1st U.S. ed.
       p.   cm.
Includes bibliographical references
ISBN-13: 978-1-59990-141-1 • ISBN-10: 1-59990-141-2 (hardcover)
[1. Busby, Cylin. 2. Busby, John. 3. Police—Violence against—Massachusetts—Falmouth—Case studies.
4. Fathers and daughters—Massachusetts—Falmouth.]
I. Busby, John. II. Title.
HV8145.M42F343 2008   363.2092—dc22 [B]   2008017215

ISBN-13: 978-1-59990-454-2 (paperback)

Typeset by Westchester Book Composition
Printed in the U.S.A. by Worldcolor Fairfield, Pennsylvania
1 3 5 7 9 10 8 6 4 2

All papers used by Bloomsbury Publishing, Inc., are natural, recyclable products
made from wood grown in well-managed forests. The manufacturing processes
conform to the environmental regulations of the country of origin.

For Mom —C. B.

I dedicate this book to my family:
Polly, Eric, Shawn, and Cylin—the ultimate reason to keep on keeping on
—J. B.

All locations, dates, events, and people in this book are real.
Some names have been changed.

prologue

WHEN MY DAD DIES, HIS BODY will go to the Harvard Medical School at Massachusetts General Hospital in Boston, though I suspect they are mostly interested in his head. Before the surgeons there embarked on what was at the time experimental surgery to reconstruct his face, they asked Dad if he would sign a document bequeathing his body to the hospital. They explained that they would then be able to use his skull as a model to instruct medical students training in facial reconstruction. His was an interesting case—the lower half of his jaw was removed when he was shot in the head with a shotgun. His tongue was torn in half, his teeth and gums blown away, leaving a bit of bone that was once his chin connected with dangling flesh at the front of his face.

Dad saw the surgeons' request as a hopeful sign. During his hospital stays, he always had a yellow legal pad by his bedside to communicate. On this day he wrote a note to Mom: "They want my head after I'm gone, asked me to sign something to donate my body. Must think I'm going to live through the surgery."

The request also made me and my two older brothers feel somewhat better. We sat outside Dad's hospital room, playing Go Fish and War under the constant surveillance of the two Falmouth police officers who were on guard duty. "After Dad's dead, we'll get to see his skeleton," Shawn pointed out. "We could come visit it."

I wasn't so sure, but when I questioned him, Shawn snapped, "It's our *dad*—they'll let us come and hang out with his skeleton whenever we want to."

I also wasn't quite sure how they would get all the skin off of Dad, and what they would do with it. But I didn't like thinking about things like that; it reminded me of a scary comic book my oldest brother, Eric, had shown me once that had a creepy skeleton guy doing evil things and carrying around a big, huge sword. I just couldn't picture my dad like that.

· · ·

The series of surgeries needed to reconstruct Dad's face would be not only experimental but also incredibly expensive. And since Dad was a police officer, shot in the line of duty, the town of Falmouth would be responsible for the costs of reassembling his face—and his life. About two months after Dad's shooting, our hometown held a fund-raiser in the form of a bake sale and a somewhat inappropriately named "fun run."

The day of the fund-raiser was unseasonably warm and muggy, the November sky threatening rain. I wore blue shorts that were supposed to be saved for my school gym uniform, along with my winter coat and a pair of dressy sandals I'd gotten for Easter. Since Dad's shooting, Mom's rules about which clothes I could wear—and about everything else—didn't apply anymore, and I was pretty much free to do whatever I wanted.

I eyed the bake-sale table, wanting a chocolate chip cookie— my favorite dessert, and Dad's, too. I asked Mom for some money to get one. She looked at me like I'd lost my mind. "They're selling them to make money for *us*," she said, pointing out the obvious. "Just go get one if you want it." And she turned back to whomever she was talking to. I stood behind her for a second, wishing she'd step in and say, "Okay, I'll do it for you," like she used to do, knowing that even at the age of nine I was still painfully shy, but she didn't.

After a few minutes of standing around, I had worked up the courage. I approached the table and asked one of the women working there, "Can I have a cookie?"

"They're fifty cents for two," she responded before her coworker, a woman with long brown braids, said, "Do you know who this little girl is?"

"Tell her your name, honey," she said to me, and I did—my first name. "What's your *last* name?" the woman asked, giving her friend a knowing wink. When I told them my whole name, they both got this sad look—a look that I was getting used to seeing on adults whenever they talked about Dad. "Of *course* you can have a cookie, sweetheart. You take as many cookies as you want," the first woman said. The woman with the braids asked, "Can I give you a hug?"

After giving the woman an awkward hug, I sat on the curb to watch the runners cross the finish line. I had already eaten two huge cookies before my brothers found me, my face smeared with chocolate and crumbs. "Give it," my oldest brother said, motioning with his chin to the last remaining cookie in my hands.

"Go get your own," I said, pointing to the bake sale. "All you have to do is tell them your name and you get whatever you want," I whispered excitedly. Watching my brothers descend on the snacks and each get a big hug from the woman with the braided hair, I felt at once sick to my stomach. It was partly from stuffing myself with sweets, but also something else. We were just regular kids, suddenly thrust into a world of pity cookies and hugs from strangers. But with the small-town fame and all the public pleasantries came an unfortunate reality: someone wanted to kill our dad, and maybe us, too. It was a strange mix, being the most popular and most miserable at the same time. My older and wiser cousin summed it up best when she told me, "Everyone thinks your dad is going to die. But you're lucky—you don't have to go to school."

It wasn't until later, when my family had been relocated to an undisclosed address deep in the South—a tiny town where no one would try to hurt my dad or kill the rest of us—that I realized how "lucky" I had been, and how much I missed that notoriety and the distraction from reality that it afforded us. Instead of free cookies, there was just the waiting—waiting to see if Dad would pull through, waiting for whoever they were to find us or not find us, waiting to see what would happen next.

chapter 1

CYLIN

ON August 31, 1979, we were supposed to go see *The Muppet Movie*. Dad had promised us that when he woke up, he'd take us to the movie before he went in to work the night shift. He was a police officer on Cape Cod, in Falmouth, Massachusetts. He worked the 11:00 p.m. to 8:00 a.m. shift, then slept during the day for a few hours.

Usually, he'd come home from work right around the time I was sitting down with a bowl of Cocoa Puffs. Sometimes he'd hang out with me and my brothers until it was time for us to catch the bus, eating a piece of toast with raspberry jam, his favorite breakfast, or telling Mom about his night. But other days he'd go straight into the bedroom and change into his good suit, the dark brown one with the big lapels. He'd wear a cream-colored print shirt underneath, and a tie, too. I thought he looked like a movie star in his suit, with his strawberry blond hair, green eyes, and broad shoulders—like Robert Redford or Clint Eastwood. But as good as he looked in it, that suit always meant Dad was going to court to testify in a case. It also meant that he wasn't going to get much sleep, so we should be sure to stay out of his way when we got home from school in the afternoon.

During the summers when we didn't have school, Mom made sure to have us out of the house by 8:30 or 9:00 a.m., rain or shine. We'd go to the beach and have swim lessons in the morning. Then we'd spend the rest of the day there, eating bologna sandwiches that were a little too warm from sitting out in the sun and begging Mom for quarters so we could cross the hot sand to the ice-cream stand for a Nutty Buddy or some chocolate chip cookies. Mom usually brought a big bottle of something to drink and a few Styrofoam cups to keep us from asking for soda money, too. But on days when she was feeling generous, we could get a real soda in a cold can from the ice-cream guy. I loved the feeling of a freshly opened Orange Crush, so cold and fizzy it hurt my mouth to drink it fast.

As the afternoon wore on and my skin started to feel tight and hot from the salt and the sun, I would take my favorite towel, a white one with a bright rainbow arching across it, and wrap it around me, even covering my head. Then I'd lie in the sand by Mom and watch the sunlight filter through the stitches in the towel, transformed into my own private rainbow. Sometimes I'd fall asleep cocooned like that until it was time to go home.

On days when it rained, we still went to the beach for our swim lessons, and we'd stay for as long as we could take it. If it was a light rain, Mom would bring an umbrella and tell us to get out in the water. "What difference does a little rain matter, since you'll be getting wet anyhow?" she'd reason. She'd plant the umbrella in the sand, take out whatever paperback she was reading, and plunk down in a beach chair.

My two older brothers and I would come out of the ocean hours later, lips blue and shaking, only to wrap up in towels that were wet from being left on the beach in the rain. It's not like my mom or my family loved the beach—we weren't trying to break any records for being the biggest sand bums on the Cape. But Dad had to sleep, and when we were stuck at home there was no way that could happen.

Snow days were Mom's worst nightmare. We'd be sent out to go sledding for hours at a time, just to keep the house quiet. We'd come back in, soaked to the skin, and shuck off our snow-covered coats and boots with Mom whispering, "Your dad is sleeping, so keep it down." But we'd always want to watch TV or play records. And then the fighting would inevitably start. Maybe Eric, who was thirteen that year and totally into sci-fi, wanted to watch *Star Trek* while I wanted *Little House on the Prairie*. We'd end up yelling and chasing each other around the house, throwing Atari game cassettes at each other, Mom reminding us that Dad was sleeping, only to see him appear, bleary-eyed, groggy, and in his underwear, at the bedroom door. "Keep it down to a dull roar," he'd growl in his heavy Boston accent. Then he'd disappear back into the bedroom, and we'd try to be good for at least a half hour or so.

That summer I was nine years old—just turned nine that May. I loved the Muppets. I adored Kermit and Miss Piggy especially. The whole family watched the show religiously on Sunday nights, with my parents on the couch and the three of us on the rug right in front of the television. So that day at the beach, all I had been thinking about was how we were going to the movies that night, finally seeing the Muppets on the big screen. Dad would sneak in a big bag of peanut M&M'S for us all to share, and we'd get a huge tub of popcorn. But when we came back that Friday afternoon and found Dad at home, still in his suit, I knew that he had just gotten home from spending the day in court after working all night, and he hadn't had any sleep yet. We weren't going to the movies. I was crushed. While Mom went to make dinner, I laid on the bunk bed in my room, still in my sandy blue bathing suit, and cried.

The evening was a disaster in the making. Dad had to sleep, Mom was stuck in our two-bedroom house with three grouchy, hot, tired kids who couldn't face the disappointment of a canceled movie date. To cheer us up—and probably to get us out of the house for a few hours—Mom came up with a plan and pretended that it was something great. "We're painting Dad's car," she announced, and headed to the basement for paint and brushes.

Mom was really tired of Dad's car—a multicolored Franken-stein of a Volkswagen Beetle put together from spare parts. She was pretty tired of all Dad's other car "projects," too. We always had one or two VW Beetles sitting in our L-shaped driveway, either parked off to the side or up on blocks. Dad would buy them cheap and keep them around for spare parts for the one Bug that he actually kept running—most of the time. That sum-mer, he had a white MG parked in the yard too. The body of the car still looked good, but it didn't run. He had plans to fix it up when he had the time. Meanwhile, it made a great place for my brothers and me to play—messing with the radio knobs and jerking the stick shift around like we were driving. We weren't allowed to touch the emergency brake, after my brother Shawn accidentally sent the MG rolling backward down the driveway one day. But even with that off-limits, the cars in the driveway were the best toys we could have asked for.

The VW Bug that Dad was using as his main car that sum-mer had an okay engine and it ran, but it didn't look too pretty doing it. He had pieced together the body from three or four other VWs, so it had a red front fender and a blue front fender mismatched on either side of a faded red hood, along with a blue door on one side and a gray door on the other. The seats were split open in some spots, with rusty springs and tufts of coarse horsehair sticking out. This made riding in Dad's car a summer nightmare—sitting on the split seats, especially in the back, in shorts, or worse, a bathing suit, was torture unless you stuck a towel under you. Mom was on Dad's case about the car and how it looked. "It's embarrassing," she'd say. "Can't we at least paint it *one* color?" Dad would shrug. "Sure, knock yourself out."

I don't know why Mom picked that night to start in on her project, other than the need to get our butts out of the house for a few hours, but she did. She got out the only big paint can she could find in the basement—green paint—and a few extra paintbrushes. "We'll surprise your dad by painting his car while he's sleeping," she explained, and everyone joined in. It didn't take long to realize that painting a car with a paintbrush wasn't such a great idea. The brush left sticky lines on the car, and as the dusk rolled in, so did the gnats and mosquitoes, leaving streaks and spots where they landed in the gooey mess. Mom didn't want to give up, so she just kept on painting the door and one fender with the too-thick paint—paint that I think was actually for wood, not cars—until it grew too dark to see what she was doing.

I grew bored of the painting quickly, and opted to play with our new box turtle instead, while Mom and my brothers tackled the job. Dad had found the turtle on one of his runs up Hatchville Road—a sweet country street that wound its way around the corner from our house. Though it didn't run along the coast, Hatchville was one of the prettiest roads on the Cape; it cut through fields, past big houses, horse barns, and a famous organic farm. Sometimes, in the summer, Dad would take us running with him on the route, the three of us puffing behind him, trying to keep up. Shawn was the only one who had the steam to make it the full five miles, while Eric and I usually dropped out of the race around three. On evenings when I knew I couldn't keep up, I'd take my bike and race circles around Dad and my brothers. "Come on, slowpokes!" I'd shout, standing up on my pedals to push my bike faster than they could run.

With his better-than-20/20 vision and the instincts of a cop forever looking for clues, Dad always seemed to find stuff on the side of the road: a mangled pair of sunglasses or a beach hat. A piece of jewelry, cheap to start with and now run over a few times. A mangled baseball, rotted and brown. Usually the stuff Dad found was worthless, but one evening, he came home with a good-sized box turtle, about as big as my shoe. He didn't have any marks on him, except for a scuffed up shell; Dad thought he had probably been hit by a car since he couldn't seem to walk very well.

We put the turtle in a cardboard box and set him up against the house, in the shade. I brought him water in a little bowl, and some iceberg lettuce to eat. But he never even took a bite; the lettuce just turned brown and droopy. I tried fresh grass trimmings and leaves, too, but he just wasn't interested in eating. Late in the day, I would take him out of his box to give him some free time. If you waited a really long time, and you were very quiet, sometimes he would take a step or two in the driveway. But mostly he just sat there, blinking his big shutterbug eyelids and not doing much else.

When Mom was ready to put down her paintbrush for the night, she was so proud of the gooey half-painted car, she went inside to get the camera to record it, so we have a couple of pictures from that evening. In one photo, Mom is posing by her paint job. She looks petite and trim in shorts and a summer top. Her skin is tanned a honey brown, her dark hair in a pixie cut; she's smiling big. Another picture shows me, sitting in the driveway by the cardboard box with the turtle beside me. I'm painfully thin, all knees and elbows, and too shy to actually look into the camera, so I'm looking down instead, smiling a little. My long straight hair, parted in the middle, falls like curtains on either side of my freckled face.

There's one more picture, of my two brothers standing with their backs against our red-shingled house, squinting into the setting summer sun. Shawn, thin and darkly tanned like Mom, his brown hair cut in thick bangs over his eyes, his new braces crowding his mouth; Eric, big and broad like Dad, with the same strawberry blond hair and a splash of freckles over his nose. I'm glad we have this picture of them, taken on that night, before everything changed. I'm glad to have the picture of Mom, looking so happy and young. I'm even glad to have a picture of the turtle, though I don't know what happened to him—forgotten in his little cardboard box by our house while we were gone in Boston, where Dad was undergoing the emergency surgeries that would ultimately save his life.

But most of all, I'm happy to have the picture of Dad's car.

Because the next time I saw that car, it was in a black-and-white photo on the front page of the *Cape Cod Times*, shot full of holes. The front window was shattered, the driver-side window completely knocked out. And the driver-side door, freshly painted green, was riddled with shotgun pellets.

chapter 2

JOHN

AUGUST 31, 1979, was a Friday, the start of Labor Day weekend on the Cape. I'd worked the previous 11:00 p.m. to 8:00 a.m. shift, and then spent until late afternoon in court. After sitting around all day I didn't even get to testify, having only a minor backup role in the case. It was a major waste of time. I got home around five in the afternoon with no sleep, exhausted, and was supposed to take the kids to the movie theater.

I thought about calling in sick, spending some time with the kids before school started back up in a few days. But this was Labor Day weekend, and on the Cape that meant parties, drunk drivers, tourists having their last hurrah before heading back to New York and Boston and wherever else they came from. We needed extra cops on duty to handle this weekend—more of the real guys on the force, not just the "rent-a-cops" as we yearrounders called the summer guys. It would be an asshole move not to show up for my shift. So I told Polly I had to hit the sack and to wake me at 9:45 for work.

The kids were disappointed about the movie, but I told them we'd go tomorrow night instead. Polly got me up; I showered and trimmed my beard and had some coffee. I'd been wearing a beard for several years at this point. Came about as a result of a week-long vacation and fast-growing whiskers. We were working five days on and three days off, so right before my vacation, I skipped the shave for my last shift. That gave me twelve days to grow a beard, and it looked pretty good. So I went to work with it, and since there wasn't any official policy about facial hair, my sergeant said he'd talk with the chief. Next morning, Sergeant and I met with the "Grand Fubar"—our private name for the chief, "Fubar" meaning "fucked up beyond all reality." The chief approved beards as long as they were neat and trim. Within a month, a dozen bearded cops were saving copious bucks on razor blades.

Polly told me shortly after she woke me up that— surprise!—she'd painted half the car green. I took a look. She'd used a four-inch paintbrush and, under the circumstances, had done a credible job. But I was grumpy, still tired from getting only three hours of sleep, so I didn't give her any compliments. Instead, I pointed out that now I'd have to get a new registration due to the color change, just nit-picking. It was looking like it was going to be a tough night on the public indeed.

At about twenty of eleven, I fired up the newly painted Bug and headed in to work. As I drove down Sandwich Road, I noticed another Bug, a white VW, facing into Pinecrest Beach Drive and a full-sized light blue sedan facing out. The people seemed to be talking to each other. About half a mile south, a vehicle closed on me rapidly from the rear, hit high beams, and pulled out to pass. The speed limit on this stretch of road was thirty-five, and we were already doing a bit more than that.

But the car didn't pass. Instead, I heard this incredible roar and felt this tremendous punch in my nose. My head and upper body were thrown down, across the passenger seat. There was a second booming roar, and I started to sit back up. I noticed in the light from the radio that there was a pool of blood, bone, teeth, and hair lying in the passenger seat. Somehow I knew it was parts of me lying there, and I thought quite calmly, *Shit, now I'm going to have to go to the dentist.* I knew I'd been shot, that's what the booming sounds were. I'd probably been hit in the nose and mouth.

I sat up and stomped on the brakes, bringing the car to a screeching halt. A third boom went off and the passenger side of the front windshield filled with half-inch round holes. I could see the light blue sedan now, stopped about fifty feet in front of me, and I was thinking how easy it would be to shoot back through the windshield at it—the thing was already full of holes; it wouldn't do any more damage. But since I had kids at home, my stainless steel (to resist rusting in the salty Cape air) .357 revolver with its six-inch barrel was hanging in my locker and not in the shoulder harness that fellow officer Pauly Gonsalves had advised me to start wearing years earlier.

I decided there was only one way to get out of this alive, and that was to run for help. Whoever was in that other car wanted me dead, and they had come armed with a very effective weapon. I couldn't fight back, and suddenly I knew how it felt to be the other guy, like guys I'd arrested or pointed a gun at. I got an image in my head of the night Jack Coughlin and I pulled over a suspected drunk we'd gotten a call about from another cop. The perp was supposed to be carrying weapons in his car and on his person, so we weren't taking any chances. We had him put his hands out the window first, so we could see them, then when he was out of the car, hands up and on the roof.

"Spread your legs and step back to where your weight is on your hands," I told the guy—this so he couldn't pull anything out of a pocket. "Now listen carefully," I told him, and then I pumped a round into the shotgun and let him feel it on his back. "You move, I blow you away. Understood?" He was all, "Yes, yes, yes," so we asked him where his weapons were. He said, "I don't have any weapons." So Jack searched him while I held the shotgun on his spine. Nothing on him. We put him in the back of the cruiser and tossed his truck, meaning that we searched everywhere—seat cushions out, glove box emptied onto the street, even in the engine cavity—everywhere. Found nothing. We were red-faced, put this guy through hell for nothing, on a call from another cop.

We explained to the guy why we'd stopped him. His voice quivered as he repeated that he didn't have any weapons and also wasn't drunk. He said that when I had him against the car, he felt his arms weakening and shaking, and he was afraid that if he started to really shake, or if he passed out, I would shoot him. I felt like shit hearing that. Told him if he wanted to take any recourse, we would supply his lawyers with information about the search and why it happened. I was almost hoping he would sue, so the cop who had called this in—a real asshole—would have to answer in court. And so a lot of cops on the force who weren't doing their jobs right would have to answer too. But the guy just thanked us and drove off, like that.

Now I was the one in a gunfight, and what that guy told me, about being scared and feeling like he was a dead man, was suddenly coming back to me clearly. I'm a big fan of horror movies and Stephen King books, but this kind of scared didn't feel like that. "Scared" isn't the right word for it. There is no word for it. It's a gut feeling when you know you're about to die, and it's horrible. I put the car into reverse and backed into the oncoming lane, then put it into gear and just drove straight, at an angle, bouncing off the pavement and shooting across a lawn. I felt the car bump into, then drive over, a fence that I didn't realize was there, and almost crash into the front door of a house. As the car came to a halt, I tumbled out and ran to the door, fully expecting to hear a fourth boom and feel the bullets tear through the back of my head.

I reached the doorstep, and stopped. A large puddle of blood was pooling at my feet. It was a cool night so I'd worn the zip-in vest lining from my police jacket over my uniform shirt. I quickly took this puffy vest off and held it to where my lower jaw used to be, which was just now starting to hurt. I was doing two things—trying to control the bleeding and making my uniform visible so they would know I was a cop.

A young girl opened the door immediately—obviously they'd heard the gunshots and me driving up on their lawn. She took one look at me and ran screaming into the house. An older woman appeared—her mom, I guessed—and I somehow managed to indicate that I was police and I'd been injured. She led me into their kitchen and, in shock herself, started yelling for wet towels. I knew from my EMT training that I had to maintain my airway even though I might bleed to death anyhow, and this was a major fear as I watched the pool of blood spread slowly around my feet into a circle, and then across the entire kitchen floor. I had no way to tell her that dry towels would really be a lot better, so I just took what she gave me.

I had to lean over and let the blood flow out of my face, onto the floor, because to lean back or try to stop it in any way sent it down my throat, and I was literally drowning in it. Time slowed down, the wet towels being handed to me, the pool of blood on the floor creeping wider. I knew they had called to report a police officer shot; I heard them on the phone. Then, far away but growing louder, I heard the sirens coming. But it wasn't an ambulance; Tony Mello, a fairly new cop, was in the neighborhood and heard it over the radio. Once he saw me, the situation, he radioed in immediately, confirming that a cop had been shot and an ambulance was needed. Tony didn't know who shot me, what had happened, where the shooter or shooters were. He did know that EMTs won't enter until the scene is secure, so that's what he did, making the family sit together on the couch in the living room, away from me. Then he started pacing between the kitchen and front door with his gun out, keeping guard.

I was losing so much blood I could see it everywhere. No matter what, I just wanted to live long enough to describe the vehicle. Tony was walking a bloody trail into the carpet between the door and the kitchen, looking for that ambulance and telling me, "They're on their way, on their way." But I knew I was safe now from being shot again—they were going to have to go through Tony to get to me, and he had his weapon, so that was one worry off my mind. *They can't shoot me any more tonight*, I told myself, and just as I did, the pain caught up with me. Suddenly, I was hurting bad, with electric shooting pains radiating from my jaw and through my head, right into my brain, like I was being shocked, electrocuted. It's the feeling of touching a live wire, but in my face, my skull, and it wouldn't stop. I started shaking hard, going into shock.

Looking at the blood, the amount of it, I could tell I was going to either pass out or bleed to death before the EMTs arrived. I wanted them to know that I needed a transfusion of O positive blood. I wanted to let them know about the car, in case there wasn't time. This was all I could think about, that I had to write this down somehow. I always carried a small notebook and a pen in my shirt pocket when I was on the job, for anything I might need to write down to make a report on later—plate numbers on cars I wanted to run, you name it. I managed to hold the wet towel to my face with my left hand and to pull out my notebook and pen with my right. If I couldn't keep pressure on my face, I was definitely going to bleed out. But this was more important. Somehow, I scrawled the words "not an accident" on the paper, smearing blood on it as I wrote.

I heard more sirens, and Craig Clarkson—a fellow cop, good buddy, and also an EMT—ran into the house. I was so relieved to see he had the emergency kit from his cruiser; I was beyond happy to see this guy. Now Tony had the door covered and Craig was the best medical coverage I could have asked for. I shoved the notebook at him so he could read what I'd written, then I tried to write more while Craig was checking me out. I wrote the name "Ray Meyer." This is the only person I could think of who would want me dead, and I knew why. I also knew what this guy was capable of and how much he hated me. He was a convicted arsonist and a suspect in several murders and "disappearances," too. And if I was right, he was going to try to burn down my house and kill my family tonight, while the police department was distracted taking care of me. Last I wrote, "Polly and the kids—not safe."

Craig was looking in my eyes, and I noticed his pupils were huge. He was doing his best with what he had. He looked at the wound, then just put the towels back up to my face without saying anything. He didn't bother to even open the kit, there was nothing in there that could help me. Now he was the one applying the pressure, so I could write down more, about the car description; about the *boom, boom,* delay, third *boom;* about the light blue sedan with four headlights horizontal, not vertical. He kept telling me that I was going to be okay, but I knew I was dying, and I wanted him to have all the facts. I had to get this information to somebody. "You're gonna be okay," he kept saying, but I could always tell when Craig wasn't being straight. I knew the guy.

He was worried. So was I.

Everything slowed down more. It was quiet; everyone kept doing the same thing over and over. Craig checked my stats; Tony walked his bloody trail in the carpet, his police-issue black shoes making a swishing sound when he came near the kitchen. I wrote a note to Craig saying, "Where are the kids?" He said he was going to take care of that. "Don't worry about it now." I wrote more: "bone pain." My face was hurting in a deep, horrible way, but that's all I felt, besides the sensation of blood surging down my throat with every heartbeat, and even that was starting to slow way down. I could feel what was left of my face keeping time with the beats. Pump, pause, pump, pause, pump. Then

I heard more sirens, but these ones were different, they sounded so far away, like they were coming from underwater. I kept hearing them, but they didn't seem to get any closer. I kept hearing them, and hearing them, and hearing them. "They're coming," Craig said. "Hold on, Buzz. Hold on."

chapter 3

CYLIN

WE lived on a cul-de-sac called Decosta Circle, which was just off of Sandwich Road, on the border of Falmouth and a town called Hatchville. On our left were the Sullivans. They had only one kid, a daughter named Erin, who was in my grade at school. Erin was okay to play with when I was at home, but at school I thought hanging out with my neighbor just wasn't cool. I had other friends at school and I ignored Erin from the moment we got on the bus.

Mom was aware of this silent rule I had made and tried to talk to me about it, but I had my mind made up. Erin's parents were also aware of the way I treated their daughter, and they didn't like me very much. In fact, with their perfectly kept yard and prim white house, I don't think they were very fond of the big, loud Busby family next door, with all the cars rotting in the driveway, the unmowed lawn, and the barking beagle tied up outside. I saw the inside of their house twice, and it was perfect and clean, not anything like ours. Erin's mom was a bit older than my mom, and she stayed home all day, making Erin tuna-fish sandwiches with the crust cut off. My mom was a teacher, and she was in nursing school at night, so we mostly made our own sandwiches.

When my brothers and I tried to cut through the Sullivan yard to get over to our other friends' house, the Zylinskis, Mr. Sullivan would come out and yell at us. He was a big Irishman, with white hair and a high round belly that would have made him look like Santa Claus, except for the fact that he was always yelling. Mom told us that he had already had one heart attack and was "headed for another one," the way he got so worked up. "You're cutting a path through my grass! You're killing my yard, you Busby kids. Get out of my yard!" Never mind the fact that we really weren't cutting a path—we would walk along the fence at the edge of his property, where grass didn't grow anyhow. What really bothered him was the fact that we were cutting over to see the Zylinskis and we didn't invite Erin to come with us. But Mom would kill us if we walked down on Sandwich Road, so the only way to get there was by cutting through Mr. Sullivan's yard.

To our right, we didn't have neighbors, we had a church. It wasn't the kind of church that people went to on Sundays; in fact, we saw it open only a handful of times in the ten years that we lived in Falmouth. This church was rumored to have been built by descendants of the Pilgrims in the mid- to late 1700s, and it was known as the East End Meeting House. A big, three-story boxy Cape Cod building, its shingles had weathered to a dark, dry gray, and the windows were trimmed in white paint. On top sat a huge steeple, with a weathervane that you could barely see from the ground. There had once been a bell in the steeple, but it had been removed a hundred years ago and hung from a wooden post near the front door. The front of the building was not ornate. It had a barn-style door, white and flat, and no steps, just a slim granite slab to step up on, worn down in the center from the footsteps of hundreds of Pilgrims, or at least that's what I liked to imagine. And in back of the church was one of the oldest graveyards in New England. The gravestones—at least, the ones you could still read—dated back to the 1700s. This graveyard spanned an acre or so in back of the church, so while the building was our "neighbor," we really lived next door to a cemetery.

Our property was separated from the sloping green lawn of the church by a row of tall shrubs, intermixed with bamboo, about five feet wide. We called that area our "tree house" because of how dense the trees and bamboo had grown. It was dark and shady, a nice place to dig and build stuff on a hot summer day. When I was about six or seven, I was digging a hole in there and came across a long, flat stone. My brothers and I dug all around it, outlining the shape. It took us all afternoon.

When we showed it to Dad, he swore under his breath and got the shovel from the basement. He put the dirt we had dug up back over the stone and added some more for good measure, pounding it all down with the back of the shovel and pushing some fallen bamboo leaves over it. "Don't dig over here anymore," he told us. "Not ever." Though the border of the graveyard was a few feet away from our yard, some old stones had been forgotten when they drew the property lines, or they had been lost over the years in the trees that bordered the graveyard. After that, whenever we felt like being bad, we would creep to the back of the tree house, at the very end corner of our property, and dig, looking for more stones, bones, and whatever else we might find.

The graveyard and the graves in it were not scary to us. In our minds, this was our playground, with wide green lawns and old oak, pine, and weeping willow trees to climb. You had to go down to the very back of the graveyard to even see any head-stones that had legible markings on them. The ones up toward the front of the graveyard were old and weathered to the point of being mere markers. But some still had amazing engravings— swirling lines cut across the ornate tops into beautiful curlicues, ancient writing that had As and Es linked together as one letter. Mom would go to the graveyard with us around Halloween every year and we would do gravestone rubbings with her art supplies. The lines and letters on the stones that were invisible to the naked eye would come to life under paper with the help of a charcoal pencil. We would use the rubbings to decorate our house for Halloween, but still the spookiness of living next door to a graveyard never really got to us. It was just how we lived, and since we had never known anyone who had died, the concept of death, of ghosts or the afterlife, wasn't anything we had to grapple with.

One late-summer afternoon, as we played in the graveyard with the Zylinski kids, one of the older boys went to climb into an old oak and used a headstone near the base of the tree to get his footing. He pushed too hard, or maybe the stone wasn't firmly planted anymore. It slipped out from under his foot as he pushed up into the tree, and fell forward, hitting the ground with a loud, resonating thump. All of us tried to lift it back up, but it was surprisingly heavy, and we couldn't budge it. We knew we had done something wrong, and we told my mom later that night. Dad and one of his friends went over the next day and righted the stone, but we were in trouble.

"You cannot disrespect the people who are buried over there," Mom pointed out. "I'm sure they don't mind you playing and enjoying yourselves, but please remember to leave the stones alone, and let me know if you ever see anyone doing otherwise." I didn't really get what Mom was talking about, the "people" over there. Dad had told us that anyone buried in that graveyard was long gone. "Not even dust anymore," he'd say. I had seen the far back of the graveyard, a section that was still being used as the town cemetery. We had walked down that far a few times with Mom and Dad. One time we saw a pile of dirt and a little red plastic flag on a thin metal pole marking the spot. There were lots of wilted flowers and silky ribbons around. "This is a fresh one," Dad pointed out to my mom. I asked Mom about it, and she explained to me the basics about how people were buried, in a casket. Then she reminded my brothers and me that we should never disturb a grave with fresh dirt piled on top, and that we shouldn't be playing this far down in the graveyard anyhow.

. . .

That night, we went to bed late. Mom felt sorry that our movie plans had been canceled, so she let us watch TV until it was almost time for her to wake up Dad for his shift. I was asleep fast and didn't hear Dad leave, like I did on some nights if I was still awake.

I woke up in my dark room, hearing my mom crying and screaming. At first I thought she was just watching something loud on TV. But then I heard Kelly, my cousin, and I heard some men, too, talking low. Kelly was living with us that summer, before she started college. She and Mom were more like sisters than niece and aunt. They dieted together, sharing a grapefruit in the morning and watching each other's cottage cheese and Tab intake throughout the day. They'd lay on their towels and talk about the guys at the beach or the cute cops on the force. Kelly taught Mom some tanning tricks (add some iodine to your baby oil for a nice fake bake until you could build your own tan; lemon juice on your hair brought out highlights). Kelly was eighteen that summer, with sun-kissed auburn hair, light green eyes, and a killer tan. The younger cops on the force had definitely taken notice, and the ones who were single, or just there for the summer, probably would have asked her out more if it weren't for her overprotective uncle—my dad.

I knew something was wrong, but I was hoping that the voices were just some friends of Kelly's. She had been out to the movies that night—did her date come home with her? But why was Mom crying? I opened the door just a crack and saw Rick Smith, a big redheaded guy who was one of Dad's best friends on the force, standing in our living room. He was in his uniform, and I could hear the static sounds from the black walkie-talkie on his hip, the same kind that Dad carried, with the tinny voice of the dispatcher cutting through, saying something in a mysterious code of numbers and words I didn't understand.

Rick was holding Mom's arms down by her side, talking to her really quietly, and she was crying, saying, "No, no, no," over and over. I stepped out into the room. "Mom?" I asked, just as she shook her body free of Rick's hold. "Don't!" she yelled at him as he tried again to hold her, and she paced the floor a few times, walking into the kitchen. He stayed close behind her, saying, "It's okay, Polly, he's alive, he's alive."

I followed them into the kitchen, in my bare feet. I was wearing my summer nightgown, the white one with small pink flowers, and ruffles at the neck where the buttons were. I was glad I was wearing it that night and not my more babyish Winnie the Pooh pajamas, because I would have been embarrassed to have Rick and my dad's other friend see me in those. My mom was slumped down on the floor, like she had slid down the wall, and she was crying hard. "What happened to Dad?" I asked, and no one answered. Mom acted like I wasn't even there. "Are his eyes okay?" she asked. Rick crouched down beside her. "I think so," he said. Then Rick and the other cop, a guy I'd never seen before, looked over at me, then at my brothers, who had come in from their shared bedroom.

"It was like a BB gun, some kid shooting out streetlights or something. He's going to be fine, Polly," Rick said. He leaned in close to my mom and spoke quietly. "We need to go," he said, helping Mom up from the floor. "Let's go." Mom told Kelly to stay by the phone and that she would call from the hospital as soon as she knew more, and then she was gone, leaving me and my brothers with Kelly.

"Did Dad get shot?" Eric asked as Kelly locked the door behind them. He was standing very straight, with his hands clenched into tight fists down at his sides.

"I think your dad just had an accident," Kelly said. "You know how tired he's been, and he just drove off the road into a ditch, but he's fine. He's going to be okay."

"Rick said he got shot, I heard him," Shawn said.

"Maybe his car got shot or something. You guys, he's going to be fine," Kelly said, but we could all tell she had no idea what was really going on. "Let's go in the living room and wait for your mom to call." Kelly had us sit on the couch and she put on a record that she was into that summer. It was a James Taylor album, in a brightly colored jacket that reminded me of a flag I'd seen on a boat in the Falmouth Harbor. As we listened to James sing his cover of "Day Tripper," I was thinking about what would happen if Dad died. I didn't want him to be buried and for other kids to use his gravestone to climb trees. I decided then that I would sit at his grave all day, guarding it so that other kids wouldn't play there. I would bring rocks and I would sharpen sticks to keep them away.

While I was busy making my silent plans, Kelly was on the phone, calling my uncle Joe in Boston to tell him that Dad had been in an accident. That's when we heard a car pull into the cul-de-sac and saw the car lights swing around into our driveway. Kelly put the phone back into the cradle on the wall and told us to go into the kitchen, where it was dark. My brother Shawn and I peeked through the shutters of the kitchen window at the car, which was sitting in our driveway with its lights on, still running. It wasn't a police cruiser, but an old hot rod–style car. I'd never seen it before.

Eric started to say something, and Kelly said, "Be quiet, you guys," and she watched through the shutters. After what seemed like a long time, the car turned off and the door opened. We could see in the streetlight as a guy got out. He was not in a uniform. Then he reached back in the car and pulled something out. It was a long gun—a rifle.

"Jesus Christ!" Kelly yelled. "Into the back. Get in there." We ran to my parents' bedroom at the other side of the house, and Kelly turned off all the lights in the living room. She slammed the door to my parents' room behind us. "In the closet, now," she ordered. The closet wasn't quite big enough for all three of us, but I crouched down, trying to keep my balance while standing on my mom's shoes. We weren't allowed to play in here, and Mom was going to be pissed that we had crushed her shoes and knocked down some dresses. The clothes smelled like Mom and her Givenchy perfume. That smell always made me think of when she went out with Dad and we would be left with a babysitter. On those nights, I would lie in my bed half-awake until I heard them come home, and only then could I really fall asleep. When were they coming back tonight? How long would they be gone? Eric tried to close the closet door, but it wouldn't work with all three of us in there, so we just crouched like that, in my parents' clothes and shoes, barely breathing, with Kelly sitting on the floor just beside the door.

There was a hard knock on the back door. "Oh my God," Kelly whispered. "Oh Jesus, okay. You guys just don't move, be quiet." We were all silent. I could still hear James Taylor singing in the living room. Even though Kelly had turned off all the lights, she had forgotten the album and left it playing. The knocking came again, over the soft sounds of "Up on the Roof." Whoever was out there knew we were here.

"Oh my God," Kelly kept whispering over and over again. She was sitting on the floor beside the closet, her back to the wall. She had her hands over her mouth, and I think she was crying because she was sniffling quietly. The knocking stopped for a few minutes. I started to think that whoever it was had left, although we didn't hear a car start up. The song ended and a new one came on. The phone rang a few times, then stopped. Another song started. Eric and Shawn were whispering. They had a plan. "You stay in the closet," Eric said to me, then he turned to Shawn. "I have a big rock in our room. We'll tackle this guy and hit him in the head with it. Then we all climb out the window and run through the graveyard."

I didn't want to go into the graveyard at night, and I didn't have my shoes. Shawn said we should run up Hatchville Road, the route he and Dad did when they went jogging. "I can do seven miles, and I'll get help," he explained. That seemed like a good idea; I knew Shawn was a fast runner. Then the knocking started again, harder this time. Then it stopped. Someone was at the front door now, right by my parents' room, and ringing the doorbell.

Kelly took a deep breath. She whispered, "Okay, you guys, listen to me. I need you to go upstairs." Only my brothers' room was upstairs, and the attic.

"When you're up there, I'm going to open the door. If you hear anyone come into the house, you go into the crawlspace up there, hide, and do not make a sound. Not a sound. And don't come out until your mom comes home or it's morning." I could barely see her eyes in the dark room, but I could see enough to tell that her face was deadly serious. This wasn't like Kelly at all. I thought about telling her not to open the door, to come with us to the attic, but I knew, all three of us knew, she had made up her mind.

We tumbled out of the closet and ran to the stairs, glad to be doing something, taking action. We crossed through the dark house, afraid to stop and look out the windows, and scrambled up the steep ladder. We didn't hide in my brothers' room or wait to hear what happened to Kelly when she opened the door. Without talking, without making a plan, Eric opened the small door that led into the crawl space. We made our way across the rafters in our pajamas on prickly sharp insulation, and we hid, silently, in the pitch black.

chapter 4

JOHN

SOMETHING was wrapped around my neck—a collarlike pad—to hold up my head and apply pressure to my face. I was surrounded by ambulance and fire department paramedics. When did they get here? Time had slowed down to a heartbeat, now everything was fast: an IV was inserted in one arm, then another in the other arm. I was swiftly loaded onto a gurney sitting up— the way I was bleeding, I'd drown in my own blood if I laid down.

The guys carried me out into the yard. The area was lit with rotating blue, red, and white lights from all the emergency vehicles flashing off the quiet neighborhood houses. They carried me past my own car, the VW, driven up into the yard, close to the door of the house. It looked awkward there, parked sideways on their lawn. I tried to get someone's attention to tell them to turn off my lights before the battery died. This was all I could think about as I was loaded into the ambulance.

Minutes later, we arrived at the Falmouth ER and were met by the attending physician and an oral surgeon they'd called in. I was in and out but somewhat aware of what was happening, and as they tried to examine my face, the pain was excruciating. "About an inch here," one doctor said. "Lucky." He wasn't talking to me, but I followed the conversation. "Okay, we've got the left jawbone shattered, and right jawbone," one of the doctors said. He had a pencil near my face and pointed something out to the other people in the room. "We've got something up in this sinus cavity below the right eye. Tissue, bone, bullets—maybe all three."

The other doctor was taking notes. "Could be some teeth were pushed up there," he said without taking his eyes off his pad.

"Close to the eye socket," the nurse said.

"And brain," the other doctor said. The way they were examining me made me nervous. They were talking about me like I was dead already—like this was an autopsy.

Both doctors quickly agreed that they couldn't treat me in Falmouth; I'd have to be transported to Massachusetts General Hospital in Boston ASAP. Another doctor entered my vision. He'd heard about the shooting over the police scanner, and although he wasn't on duty tonight, he got to the hospital to see if he could help. "I was in a mobile army surgical hospital in Korea," he told me confidently. "I've seen injuries like this before."

The MASH doc, Dr. Gibbons, took over for the other two

doctors and offered to ride in the ambulance to Boston. Everyone agreed. Dr. Gibbons was the only one who talked directly to me; the other doctors spoke as if I were a stump sitting between them to be examined. As he looked over my wounds, Dr. Gibbons leaned in close. "It's all up to you whether you live or die tonight," he told me, looking right in my eyes.

I motioned for pen and paper to write another note. This one I gave to Craig, pressing it into his hand. I told him who I thought shot me. I told him if I died he had to avenge me. He had to protect my family. This was laying it heavy on a good friend, but I could tell by the way the doctors were talking about me—around me—that they thought I was a goner.

Before they loaded me into the ambulance again, Polly arrived with Rick Smith. She was in her second year of nursing school, so the blood didn't bother her—the fact that it was my blood did. The doctors were trying to get enough morphine into me to calm me down so they could insert a breathing tube. But the second I saw Polly, I had to let her know this wasn't an accident. A nurse saw me motioning that I wanted to write something, and she brought me a clipboard.

"He wants to write," she said to the doctor.

"He also wants to breathe." The doctor brushed her off. "Not right now."

But she found a way around him a minute later and gave me the board and a pen anyhow. I wrote, "Not an accident. Who is with kids?" Polly just looked at me, and I could tell she was in shock. She hadn't said anything since she walked in. She couldn't even read what I'd written down. I hadn't seen myself yet, but I could tell by the look on her face that I must look bad. I hit the board three times with the pen, demanding an answer. Rick Smith looked over her shoulder at the note. "They're covered; we've got someone at the house already," he told me. Then I sat back and let the doctors slide a plastic tube down my throat and we headed for the ambulance. Polly got into the ambulance too, along with another nurse and two EMTs.

The doctor told me to raise my hand when I needed suctioning, when the blood blocked my airway. We moved fast, it was late and we had a blue light escort by the state police up Route 3, where they handed us over to the Norwell staties, who took us to the Southeast Expressway, where the MDC—Metropolitan District Commission—took us to Mass General. A trip that usually takes an hour and a half done in about forty minutes. Fastest ride to Boston I've ever had.

I needed suctioning several times—the fluid they were putting into me through the IV was just pumping out of my face and down my throat. In the IV was something called ringer lactate fluid to prevent me from going into shock from the blood loss. Everyone was trying to keep me aware, breathing, and stable until we reached the hospital. But I had swallowed so much blood that I started throwing up. I threw up my airway tube a couple of times; the doctor had to keep reinserting it so I could breathe. Once we got to MGH, I entered as a trauma case, so things moved at lightning speed. They had been warned that I was on the way, and even though they were ready for me, the outlook wasn't so good.

"We've got a shooting injury to the head, neck, face," someone was yelling. "It's a police officer." The last thing I heard was a man's voice saying, "We're losing him, let's go!"

Then the pain stopped at once.

It's dark and I hear this beautiful music playing. My eyes are closed, but there is light, like a calm blueness. More a sensation than a light. And the sensation is good; I want for nothing. It's warm and calm and peaceful. All I can think is that I want to stay here. Everything is okay now. The worry and fear I've been feeling about my family—*Are they safe? Am I safe?*—the anger about being shot, it all melts away. I just want to stay here.

Then suddenly I'm whacked in the face. And I'm not in the hospital anymore.

I'm in the Hyde Park Police Station.

It's 1961. I'm eighteen.

I've just been punched in the face by the station chief. We'd been brought in for questioning, but he came in swinging. It was my good fortune to be the closest to the door, and the first one hit. He smacked a couple of the other guys, too, but by now they were ready and blocking. He couldn't punch for shit, it was just a surprise to get whacked in the face by this big cop.

I rub the side of my face, my jaw aches. *Why does it hurt so bad?* The chief starts yelling, "How many points do I get? How many?" This is not good—it means he knows all about the points system.

At my high school, we had a loosely associated gang, with a core of maybe twenty members. No name, no dues, no colors, just East Dedham guys—the neighborhood just south of Boston where I grew up. Dedham was then—and still is—a slum. I didn't know it until years later, after I'd already moved away, when I read a *Boston Globe* article about the East Dedham Square slums being torn down. Slums in the ghetto of Boston. News to me.

East Dedhams were white, Irish Catholic, and dirt poor. And we thought we were bad. Sharpened Garrison belt buckles and chain dog collars—you could swing these or wrap them around your fist for punching, also snap the chain quick on an opponent's head. We'd fight with just about anybody who wasn't from Dedham, and had set to with guys from Natick, Norwood (our archenemies), and Malden. The Malden fight happened during a hockey game and that was where I acquired the nickname "Strangler" for choking some loser. He passed out and we took off before he came to. I read the paper the next day, fearing I'd killed him, but there wasn't anything about it—a great relief to me. We'd also invaded a house party in an upper-class section of town—we left the birthday cake spinning around on the phono and a couple of pretty college boys with lumps and abrasions.

Every time you got into a fight, you got a "point" for each guy you punched. It was strictly honor system because you were too busy defending yourself to observe anything else. Word of our point system got around. Maybe it made other guys more afraid, or maybe it just made them hate us more. One night I was riding around with my car full of friends when we saw another friend, Mike, with his car full of guys and decided to trail them. Turns out they're going to Sunnyside, a section of Hyde Park. The Sunnyside boys and the group from East Dedham didn't get along. We'd ride through their turf yelling insults at them, and they'd return the favor.

Mike's car stops and his guys pile out, grabbing three Sunnysider locals and laying some lumps on them. Before my crew can get into action, Mike's running back to the car and we all leave the scene. We're hanging out at Dave's Sub Shop about an hour later when the Boston Police arrive in force, backed up by our local fuzz, and they grab us all. They search my car and find a huge butcher knife in the trunk that I've never seen before (it took me years to realize they'd dropped it on me). Possession of a deadly weapon. So we're off to Hyde Park district station for questioning. It's not my first time there.

After the chief gives us all a few knocks, he rants at us about the "point" system, assault and battery charges, the deadly weapon they found in my car. Turns out they don't really care about the Sunnyside fight, they want to shake us for names of some guys in West Roxbury who may or may not have been involved in a more serious crime. We don't even know the guys, and besides, we won't talk. So it's off to court we go.

We show up in suits and ties, the Sunnyside victims in

engineer boots, jeans, and muscle shirts showing off their tattoos. The prosecutor takes a look at his little lambs and gets a continuance—moving the court date to another day so that he can get his clients in order. Next date, everybody shows up in their Sunday Mass duds and the tragic facts are presented by their side. Mike and his guys hire an attorney who will later become the lieutenant governor of Massachusetts. I hire a guy who's done some real estate law for my parents. Cost fifty dollars—my life savings at the time. He puts me on the stand to defend myself. I'm sweating bullets but somehow get through it. Swear the knife isn't mine, and I mean it.

The judge finds Mike and his friends guilty, me and my crew not guilty. But the judge has seen me in here twice before and has something to say to me personally before we're led out of the courtroom. "Join the service, boy," he says. "Your next appearance before me, you're headed to Village Avenue"—the address of the local jail. I go home that night and think about what he said. It wasn't really a choice. I went down to enlist in the Air Force the next day.

. . .

When I woke up, I didn't know what day it was. I knew I was in a hospital. Polly was there. Then I remembered being shot. I looked at all the tubes, IVs, hoses, and machines attached to me. There were tubes going in and out of my stomach and chest for some reason too. Was I shot there? I couldn't remember, couldn't figure it out. Polly started talking to me.

"You're okay. You were in surgery for twelve hours, now you're in the ICU." I remembered seeing parts of my face and my teeth in the passenger seat of the car. I remembered the doctors talking about me at Falmouth. I motioned for paper and wrote Polly a note: "Don't let me live like this."

Polly just gave me this look and didn't say a word. I knew she couldn't pull the plug. Later I learned that when Rick Smith got to the house the previous evening to bring her to the Falmouth ER, he'd told her I'd been shot but not badly. He was trying to ease her into it. When she arrived at the hospital, she thought I would be wearing an eye patch or something. She couldn't believe that my chin was hanging down onto my chest. The bones on both sides of the lower jaw had been discontinued— not broken or fractured; they were gone. Most of my teeth were gone, or broken off at the root. My tongue was nearly severed. I had metal fragments from the lead and from the car and glass fragments from the side and front windows in my face and eyes.

I'd been lucky to be hit where I was. Had the bullets passed an inch higher or an inch farther back, I would have bled to death or died from brain damage. It seemed the idiots who tried to kill me were pretty amateurish. First of all, it's almost impossible to aim accurately from a moving vehicle, and this becomes a lot harder when you're shooting at another moving vehicle. Second, they got too close. They used a shotgun loaded with double-O buckshot. Inside the casing for each shot are nine 32-caliber copper-plated lead pellets. The object of double-O buckshot is that, once fired, the nine pellets will spread out into an ever-widening pattern. If they'd been six feet away, the bullets would have spread sufficiently enough to literally blow my head apart. Instead, they pushed the gun almost to the window of my car and the nine bullets followed a two-inch-wide path through my face.

Had those rounds been an inch lower, I would have suffered from little more than a singed beard and a busted-up car. But then I guess the second blast that came through the top of the door and the roof might have hit me since I wouldn't have been knocked over into the passenger seat. I could have gone around and around with these kinds of thoughts, but it wouldn't have gotten me anywhere. I was still faced with the simple facts: Someone shot me. They wanted to kill me. And here I was, still alive.

chapter 5

CYLIN

FROM our hiding spot in the attic, we couldn't hear anything going on downstairs, but we waited like Kelly had told us to do. The insulation pricked my skin, and I was careful to balance my bare feet on a wooden rafter so it wouldn't touch me. After a few minutes I was tired of hiding and wanted to know what was going on. My feet were numb and tingly from crouching down and not moving too much. But I knew Eric and Shawn would kill me if I made a sound, so I stayed quiet.

Finally Kelly called up to us. "You can come down, it's okay," she said. We climbed down the ladder and stood in the kitchen, watching her face. "He's a cop," she explained. "He's going to wait outside the house all night, so you don't have to be afraid."

Something wasn't right. Who was this guy who had come to our house in the middle of the night? And if he was really a cop, like Dad, where was his uniform? How come we'd never seen him before? And why was he going to be outside all night?

"Okay, you guys have to go to bed now," Kelly said. She seemed scared, and it was making me nervous. Eric and Shawn looked at each other, then back at Kelly. She couldn't tell us what to do, not unless Mom said it was okay. "Tomorrow morning, we're going to the beach early. Your mom wants us to be in public so nobody can mess with us."

I didn't understand what she was talking about. "When's Dad coming home?" Shawn asked.

"I don't know," Kelly told him. She sat at the kitchen table and put her hands down on the wooden top. She moved her palms over the table, as if cleaning off imaginary crumbs. "Your uncle Joe will meet us at the beach tomorrow, and then we'll go see your mom and dad, okay?" She looked like she was going to cry. "You all need to go back to bed, this guy is going to be here all night, and we'll leave for the beach early." It sounded more like she was talking to herself.

"What if Mom comes home and he accidentally shoots her?" Eric asked. "Does he know that Mom is coming home?"

"He's not going to shoot her!" Kelly snapped. "She's not coming home tonight, so don't worry about it."

Eric and Shawn went back up to their bedroom and I went into mine without asking any more questions. During her stay with us, Kelly had been sleeping in my room on the bottom bunk of my bunk bed. I climbed up the little wooden ladder and lay down on the top bunk, pulling the covers up tight under my chin. I listened to Kelly in the living room, walking around, and watched as car lights came and went down the street. How did she know Mom wasn't coming home? I hadn't heard the phone ring.

It was after one in the morning. I was never allowed to be up this late unless I was really sick. Something about that was thrilling, but I also felt bad. I knew it was important to try to go to sleep quickly. If my mom came home now, I would have to pretend to be asleep or Kelly would get in trouble. As I drifted off, I thought about what Kelly had said about going to the beach early the next day. So no one could mess with us.

.   .   .

The next morning, I heard people talking. It was early. As I climbed down from the top bunk, I noticed that Kelly's bed was still made. I could smell cigarette smoke. In the kitchen, my uncle Joe was sitting at the table. He was a big guy, with sandy auburn hair and eyes so light blue, it seemed there was no way that he and my dark-eyed, dark-haired mom could possibly be brother and sister.

"Hey, kiddo," he said, exhaling smoke from his cigarette. Eric and Shawn were already sitting there, eating cereal, and Kelly was there too, still wearing the clothes she had on the night before. I looked out the window and saw the hot rod car was still there, and one police car, too.

"Is that Dad?" I asked.

"What?" Kelly said, looking out the window. "No, that's someone else."

"Whose car is that?" I pointed to a new light brown two-door car parked in our driveway.

"That's mine," Uncle Joe said. He was drinking coffee and looked tired.

Kelly poured me a bowl of cereal and put in too much milk. I didn't like it that way, and milk made my stomach hurt, but I sat down anyhow. "Where are Lauren and Cassie?" Shawn asked about our two cousins.

"They couldn't come," Uncle Joe explained. It was very strange for him to be here without Aunt Kate and without Lauren and Cassie. Why was he here anyhow?

"Are we still going to the beach?" I asked, trying to eat the soggy cereal.

"You guys are coming to Boston with me, and we'll go see your dad," Uncle Joe said. He was tapping his pack of cigarettes on the table, then took out another one and lit it.

"Is he going to be at your house?" Eric asked, confused.

"I think they'll still be at the hospital," Uncle Joe said.

"You're coming too?" I asked Kelly.

"I'll be there later. Lucky's coming to pick me up," she explained. Lucky was her older brother, one of our favorite cousins, who lived up in Maine. I wondered why he would drive all the way down here to pick her up when she could just go with us in Uncle Joe's car.

"When you're done eating, you need to go pack," she added, looking at my brothers. "You need to take your sleeping bags."

"We're staying over?" I asked. I loved having a sleepover at my cousins' house. Lauren, who was a year and a half older than me, was really pretty and always had expensive clothes that she gave me as hand-me-downs. Cassie was three years younger than I was, so she was the baby of the family but still fun to hang out with.

"You're going to stay over." Uncle Joe took another sip of his coffee.

"When are we going?" Eric asked, putting his cereal bowl into the sink.

"As soon as you can get dressed and packed," Uncle Joe said. He gave me a weak smile, but his eyes didn't get all crinkled up like they did when he was really happy or laughing. I put my cereal bowl into the sink and ran some water into it like mom always made us do. I wondered when she would wash the dishes, when we would come back home. When I broke my arm the summer before, it took forever to get the cast put on at the emergency room—X-rays and doctors and waiting. We were there all day and into the night before we could go home. I wondered if Dad was getting a cast put on, how long it might take. Then I went into my room and started to pack.

I took out the new dark red corduroys that Mom had bought me for school; they still had the tags on them. Kelly came into the room and sat on the bottom bunk. "Should I take these?" I asked her, holding up the pants. I had never worn them, but I wanted to show them to my cousin with the new sweater my mom had also picked out. Lauren would think they were so cool.

"I don't know," Kelly said. I laid the pants on the bed and Kelly touched the price tag gently with her fingers. "You still wear a size slim?" she asked, looking me up and down. "Jesus." She shook her head. I didn't know what to say.

I opened my drawers and took out a bathing suit. Uncle Joe and Aunt Kate had a pool. They were rich. I put in some shorts, a couple of halter tops, then I looked at my suitcase. It looked really empty, so I put in my other bathing suit, too. "When are we coming back?" I asked Kelly.

"I'm not sure." She folded the cords up carefully and laid them in the suitcase on top of everything else. "Maybe you should take these," she said quietly.

I loved staying at my aunt and uncle's house, except for the food. Aunt Kate liked to cook "gourmet," which Mom thought was so amazing. She had all kinds of beautiful pots and pans and an expensive Cuisinart that Mom was sort of jealous of. Whenever we went to visit, Aunt Kate would try out new recipes and spend hours in the kitchen cooking things like chicken breast stuffed with blue cheese or a huge roast with some weird orange sauce. It was disgusting, and I usually ended up eating nothing for dinner when we were there. I know it used to make my aunt unhappy that I wouldn't try some of her dishes, especially since she worked so hard on them and everyone else loved her cooking, but most of it was just too gross for me.

"Let's go, gang," Uncle Joe said. I picked up my suitcase and took it outside.

"I'm starving. What do you guys say we go to McDonald's?" he asked as he loaded our sleeping bags into the car. We had just eaten cereal, but we weren't about to turn down a trip to McDonald's.

Shawn nodded and I realized that I hadn't heard him speak all morning. His brown eyes were big; he looked really scared. I got into the front seat before my brothers could call it. But they just climbed in the backseat without a word.

"I like your new car," I told Uncle Joe as he got into the driver's seat. "It's really nice." The seats were soft and clean, and the radio was pretty fancy.

"It's not that new," Uncle Joe said, like he was embarrassed. Still, it was the nicest car I'd ever been in. I felt small and dirty in the shorts I'd worn the day before. I probably should have dressed better to be sitting in this car, to be going to his house.

After we all had pancakes at McDonald's, we started the drive to Boston, about an hour and a half from the Cape. Uncle Joe was quiet on the way there, and Eric and Shawn didn't talk either. I played with the radio until I found some of our favorite songs. "Don't Bring Me Down," by ELO. And "Sad Eyes" by Robert John. The music sounded great on the radio in Uncle Joe's car.

"I wish Dad would get the radio in his car fixed," I said, but no one said anything. "Don't you guys?" I said to my brothers in the backseat. Shawn was looking out the window, and Eric just gave me a blank stare, so I gave him one back for a second, but he didn't flinch.

When Uncle Joe was ready for another cigarette, he let me push in the special button in his car that heated the lighter. When the lighter popped back out, the end of it was fiery hot and glowing red, like coals in the barbecue. After he lit his cigarette, he cleared his throat. "Here's the thing," he finally said, turning down the volume on the radio. "Your dad is alive, and he's going to make it. He's a strong man."

Uncle Joe was acting weird, so serious, so tired. I was used to him always joking around, so I didn't like him like this. Maybe, I thought, I just don't like him when Lauren and Cassie aren't around.

We were quiet. No one wanted to ask any questions; we didn't really want to know what he was talking about. "My dad died when I was a kid, when your mom was only nine years old," Uncle Joe reminded us. "And we turned out okay. Just remember that." He kept his eyes on the road. I kind of had to pee, but I didn't want to tell my uncle. It seemed like he was in a bad mood. Besides, we would be there soon.

chapter 6

JOHN

THE second time I regained consciousness, I was looking at an aluminum ceiling with thousands of tiny holes in it. I knew I'd been shot and I'd had surgery. I didn't know what day it was. I couldn't figure out why my stomach hurt so badly. Slowly I began tracing where the lines went from all the bottles and bags hanging around the bed. A few of them were smaller tubes— IVs with blood, water, meds. I found a big tube, about a half-inch in diameter, that went under the sheet. It looked like it had milk in it.

I inched the sheet down and saw that this tube ran into my stomach. I realized that they had inserted this tube to feed me since I had no mouth to eat with. A machine rumbling next to the bed was connected to hoses attached to my trachea tube—it was mixing the right amount of H_2O vapor with the air I was breathing.

Polly was there and gave me a kiss on my forehead and welcomed me back into the land of the living. She held a pad of paper for me so I could write her a note. With all the needles and tape in my hand, it hurt to hold a pen, and my writing was shaky. I wrote that my stomach incision hurt, and that my throat where the trachea went in was burning. Polly, with her own nursing training, quickly figured out that the stuff the nurses were using to clean my incisions didn't agree with me—she guessed I was probably allergic to it. Polly said she would make them use something else.

She told me that two MDC officers who were formerly on the Falmouth PD responded to Mass General the night before—Paul Stone and Mitch Morgan—and they stayed through the night so Craig could go home. Two officers would be stationed outside my hospital room around the clock. "Don't worry about anything, it's all taken care of," she said. She also told me that Joe had picked up the kids, and that they were safe at his house; that my parents were here too. That I should rest. And I did.

She didn't tell me what the doctors had said to her about my prognosis. That I might never talk again due to the damage to my larynx. That I would never be able to eat food, smell, or breathe through my mouth or nose. That I would probably need a permanent trachea tube.

When I opened my eyes again, it was another day. Sunday. The doctors needed me to do a breathing exercise, to cough through the trachea hole in my throat. Polly explained that I needed to do this to clear the airway, keep my lungs clear, especially since I was immobile. But the coughing raised holy hell with the stomach incision. I found that by holding a pillow down hard against my abdomen, I could cough without pushing at the incision.

Next time I was conscious, Joe and his wife, Kate, were in the room. Kate was a surgical nurse at Brigham & Women's Hospital in Boston. "He's reached the maximum swelling now," she said, looking at what was left of my face. "Now it will start to go down and we'll see what we have here."

Polly joked that with my face so swollen and distorted, I looked like Chip and Dale, the cartoon chipmunks. I was glad to hear a joke, see a smile. Maybe things weren't so bad after all. I had drainage tubes inserted in my face that the nurses changed every so often, and when they did, they kept shooting heparin into an IV lock, which I could taste. Polly and Kate explained that this was to keep the IV locks open so they wouldn't clot and need to be changed, which would be extremely painful.

Even with people in the room whom I wanted to see, I got tired quickly and drifted in and out of consciousness. I hurt all over, but my face was the worst. The bone pain was excruciating—my jawbone had been pulverized, and there are so many nerves in the face, sometimes it just felt like I was on fire. I was on an IV of Demerol, a strong narcotic, for the pain, but the medication wore off every four hours. When the nurses came to inject more Demerol, it would take about fifteen minutes to start working. I would break out into a cold sweat, followed by a warm tingling sensation all over. Then the pain would slip away, but so would I. I wasn't sure what was really happening and what I was imagining.

A doctor came in to see me from the Harvard Maxillofacial clinic—Dr. David Keith. He had headed up the medical team that did my emergency surgery, but this was my first time meeting him. He told Polly that they needed to remove the metal from my nose and face—metal not from the bullets, but from the car's roof. When the bullets went through the car's frame, they were carrying some fragments that got embedded in my face.

So the next time I was awake, I was being wheeled to the Harvard Maxillofacial Unit at Mass General. Maybe they thought that since I was already on so many heavy painkillers, they didn't need to use a local anesthesia for the procedure (and here's when not having a mouth can be a real problem). As they started slicing into my nose and upper cheek to remove the pieces of metal, I could feel everything, but I had no way to tell them. I didn't want to motion too much because they had a scalpel next to my face. So I just waited for it to be over. And besides, everything else hurt so much that on a scale of one to ten, this felt like a three. They stitched me up and sent me back to my room.

Afterward, Dr. Keith had some good news for Polly—that

maybe it wasn't as bad as the other oral surgeons thought. "He's lost a lot of blood, and his body needs to recover from the trauma, but he will recover," Dr. Keith told her. He also said that he wanted to take on my case, and that he believed he could reconstruct my face with some other surgeons from Harvard Medical. He even thought that I would be able to talk and eat and breathe again. But, he warned her, it would take years of surgery and need to be done in steps. Polly was so happy to hear that I might have some semblance of a normal life that she didn't care about the timeline. I was only thirty-six, what was a few years?

When I was wheeled back to my room after the surgery to remove the metal fragments, there was a visitor waiting for me. Sergeant Don Price. He was the first cop I rode with when I started on the Falmouth Police Department and a good friend.

Don was a spic-and-span, spit-and-polish officer. His voice was deep and gravelly and reminded me of James Coburn's, an actor who was popular at the time. He was a little over six feet tall, two hundred pounds or so. He'd been on the force almost ten years when I met him and was studying to be a sergeant. We were assigned to the same cruiser, the so-called party car.

Falmouth was a beautiful town, on the tip of Cape Cod— long sandy beaches; a warm, calm oceanfront; great weather; lots of nice places to eat and drink. In the summer, when the weather was good, our shore town drew all types of tourists: kids on break from college, rich folks from Boston, New York, New

England. And, on occasion, some not so lovely folks from South Boston, looking to party and have fun. The town had passed a noise ordinance designed to keep those summer celebrations from getting out of control and to keep Falmouth from getting a reputation as a party town. The ordinance stated that any noise emitted from a dwelling or property that was harsh and/or objectionable at a distance of one hundred feet was in violation of the bylaw. Hence the "party" car—an unmarked Ford we used to roll around town and check out noise complaints.

The first night I met Don was in early July 1970, a few days before the Fourth—a major party week on the Cape. College-aged kids by the thousands would be pouring onto the beach for a good time. And youthful exuberance being what it is, we were going to be busy.

Polly and I hadn't even bought our house on the Cape yet. I had been on duty only a few days or so. It was just starting to dawn on me how precarious my position as a cop was. I didn't know how to do the job, couldn't understand half of what the other cops were saying, where the streets were, who the bad guys were. And I didn't know how long it was going to take me to learn these things, to get some confidence in the job.

"You're going to help me study, rookie," Don told me as we went out to the car. "Maybe you'll learn something yourself." He handed me the books he was using to study for his sergeant's exam and off we went in the line captain's unmarked Ford to save the residents of Falmouth from the party-loving tourists. It was only 6:30 p.m., parties wouldn't get going until 11:00 or later, so Don drove and I read question after question. He got them right for the most part. The only answer I remember still is that you can't have a battery without an assault. I must have been a pretty good instructor; Don passed the exam a couple of months later.

As the night wore on, calls began coming over the radio, and wonder of wonders, I began to understand some of them. It was also my job to write our calls in the logbook kept in the car. Time in, complaint, location, finding, action taken. About nine o'clock, Don heard a call that I didn't totally follow. He put me out at Maravista Avenue, southern end, telling me to divert traffic from entering. So I directed cars away, responding to questions with the answer that there had been an accident, but really I didn't know more than that. About midnight, Don comes back to pick me up. By then, I'd waved my arms to exhaustion trying to imitate traffic cops I'd seen in the movies and on TV. Seems two people on a motorcycle had been killed up the street—that was the radio call I hadn't understood.

We headed down to the Pizza Shack, where Don knew some guys in the kitchen, who gave us pepperoni slices. By 4:00 a.m., we had been to a few noise complaints, but all were unfounded. In any event, I got a chance to watch how Don approached a house, talked to people, and took action like the authority law figure that he was. By the night's end, I was feeling a lot better about the job. I'd be spending at least another month with Don, a good guy and experienced cop. Maybe things wouldn't be so bad after all.

And so there I was, nine years later, in a hospital room with all kinds of tubes and machines keeping me alive. And it was Sergeant Don Price, along with a Falmouth police detective named Leno and another cop whose name I didn't catch, asking me questions about the vehicle the shooter was in. I wrote out my answers for them, everything I could remember about the car, type, and color.

I wrote them a note telling them I'd had a run-in with Raymond Meyer shortly before this—and was supposed to go to court to testify against his brother, James Meyer. Had either of them been questioned?

Leno told me that they were aware of that. "No one has seen Raymond Meyer since the shooting."

"Maybe one of your guys already took care of him, if you know what I mean," the other cop chimed in, and gave Don a knowing look. Cops looked out for cops. At least, that's how it was supposed to be.

When they were done with their questions, I was so exhausted, I drifted off. When I came to again, there were more cops in my room. Paul Stone, Mitch Morgan, John Ayoub, and Jack Coughlin. Don was still there, and he was organizing the police security detail assigned to protect me. This was part of the police contract: any officer who was threatened was entitled to protection at the town's expense. There would be two guys on duty at all times, twenty-four hours a day. Paul had been a tight end on the BU football team. Jack, a body builder. Both with

Hollywood good looks. I noticed that the nurses started coming by my room more often after the security detail kicked in.

As part of the security detail, anyone who wanted to visit me had to be cleared by the Falmouth Police Department first. This was not a major issue in the first few days, as most of my visitors were cops anyhow. I was visited by just about every officer in the department while in the intensive care unit. A lot of the guys made the trip all the way to Boston just to donate blood, even if they weren't my blood type, even if I couldn't see visitors because I was still in surgery. The only notable absences were two cops who I knew were tight with Meyer: Larry Mitchell and Arthur Monteiro. The fact that they didn't show their faces made me more certain that it was Meyer who wanted me dead, if there had ever been any doubt. And of course there was the rather glaring absence of our chief of police, John Ferreira, who was kind enough, when he heard I might survive, to send me an insurance form that I'd have to fill out pronto or the medical bills were mine. In all the weeks that I would later spend in the hospital, he never once made the trip to Mass General. In fact, I don't think he even sent a card.

chapter 7

CYLIN

WHEN we got to Natick and Uncle Joe's house, it was the middle of the day on Saturday. Lauren and Cassie were there with Aunt Kate. They were all in their bathing suits and had already been in the pool. "Where's Mom?" I asked.

"She's at the hospital with your dad," Aunt Kate told us. "Why don't you change into your swimsuit and come outside?"

I went upstairs to Lauren's room, and Eric and Shawn used Cassie's room. After I had changed into my blue one-piece, I sat on the floor by Lauren's bookshelf for a minute to check out her Nancy Drew collection and see if she had gotten any new ones since the last time I'd been over. There was one with a cool-looking cover called *The Secret of the Old Clock* that I hadn't read. I wondered if she would let me borrow it.

"Cylin?" I heard my aunt calling me from downstairs. I put

the book back in its place—Lauren didn't like anyone touching her stuff—and went down to join them all by the pool.

My aunt was in the kitchen, fixing lunch for us. I watched as she cut the sandwiches and put each one on a plate. From outside, I could hear Eric and Shawn already in the pool with my cousins, screaming and laughing and splashing. I looked at Aunt Kate's face while she focused on lunch. She was tall and blond and very pretty. I liked just looking at her. I waited for her to say something to me, about my dad or anything, but she didn't. It felt funny to be at her house without Mom and Dad there. "Take these outside, okay?" she finally said, handing me the sandwiches.

The afternoon went by and before we knew it, Uncle Joe was back from the hospital. "Who wants hamburgers?" he said. We never got to have food like that over at their house. But tonight was special. "And after that, we have ice cream and jimmies," Aunt Kate added—this was what they called sprinkles there. I was pretty excited. It sounded like we were having a party. Uncle Joe fired up the grill, and we ate hamburgers and potato chips out by the pool, our bathing suits still dripping wet. When it started to get dark, Aunt Kate got out the popcorn maker and we melted butter to put on top. "You guys can stay up tonight and watch *Love Boat* and *Fantasy Island*, okay?" Aunt Kate told us.

"Even Cassie?" Lauren asked. Cassie was only about six, so it would be pretty late for her.

"Everybody," Aunt Kate said. So we all piled into the den and ate popcorn and watched *Love Boat*. I fell asleep somewhere in the middle of *Fantasy Island*, which was probably a good thing, since the show sometimes scared me.

Eric and Shawn and I slept in our sleeping bags in Lauren and Cassie's playroom, which Uncle Joe had built in the basement. It was a big room, about half the size of their house, and had a soft, shaggy blue carpet. This is where Lauren and Cassie kept most of their toys, and we spent hours in this room playing when we came to visit. That first night, Lauren and Cassie wanted to join the slumber party, but I could tell from the look on Aunt Kate's face that she wasn't too happy about it. "Go get your sleeping bags," she said finally after Lauren and Cassie begged and whined.

I woke up late the next morning, and everyone was already upstairs. I went up and found Uncle Joe and Aunt Kate in the kitchen with Mom—it was the first time I'd seen her in two days. "There's my girl," she said, and I went over to sit on her lap. "You better brush this hair today," she told me, pushing my long, tangled hair back from my face. It was all snarled from being in the pool yesterday and not brushing it out afterward. Without Mom there, I had forgotten to take care of it.

Mom looked tired and her eyes were red. "How's Dad?" I asked.

"Your dad's doing real good," Uncle Joe said quickly.

"He had an operation. And he's in a part of the hospital right now where kids aren't allowed," Mom explained. "But as soon as they move him, you guys can come visit, okay?"

I nodded and looked closely at Mom's face. She was telling the truth. So he must be okay. "Is it like when he had his tonsils out?" I asked. My dad had to go in for surgery once a few years before, and I remember that he had to rest on the couch for a day or so afterward.

"Tonsils?" Uncle Joe asked, looking at Mom.

"Oh my God, I had forgotten all about that." Mom laughed. "I'll explain later," she told Uncle Joe quietly.

"The kids are in the den watching cartoons," Aunt Kate told me. "Why don't you grab some cereal and go in there?"

I could tell they wanted to talk without me, so I got some Lucky Charms and went in to watch TV with my brothers and cousins.

"You guys remember when Dad had his tonsils out?" I asked my brothers.

Shawn snorted a laugh. "You're such a retard; he was getting fixed. They just told you that."

"What do you mean, 'fixed'?" Cassie asked.

"It's like when they cut a dog's balls off," Eric said, not taking his eyes off the TV screen, where superheroes were battling it out.

"Ewww, that's gross." Lauren made a face.

"Don't you remember how dad had to sit on the couch with a bag of frozen peas between his legs?" Shawn asked me. I vaguely remembered, but I didn't really know what he was talking about. I pretended that I didn't care.

"Well, what about that time when Dad had that bump cut off his side and had stitches?" I asked them.

"Yeah," Shawn said. "And he went and played handball the next day and tore the stitches out."

"Mom was so mad," Eric said.

"And when he came home, his shirt was all bloody," I added. Seeing Dad covered in blood, I had been horrified and started crying. I was sure he was going to die, but it didn't seem to bother him too much. Mom also wasn't worried; instead she was pissed. "Just what the hell were you thinking?" she yelled at him when he got home.

"The stitches tore right after the first serve, so I figured I might as well just keep going," Dad explained. "Gonna have to have them redone anyhow, right?"

Mom lifted his shirt to see the spot where he'd had a tumor removed two days before, beneath his right arm. As she lifted his arm, the incision opened and blood poured down his side and into the waist of his running shorts. It looked horrible. "You have to go to the hospital," she said, wrapping a towel around his middle and pressing his arm down against it to hold it in place. It was decided that he would drive himself, since he really was fine. After he left, Mom took the bloody shirt and threw it into the sink, talking under her breath about how she had married a crazy man.

"Is Dad going to be okay?" I had asked her, sniffling back tears.

"He's going to be fine, he just doesn't think sometimes," she said angrily. She lifted the bloody shirt from the sink and looked at it for a second. "Damn it, John!" she said to no one, and dropped the shirt into the kitchen garbage.

"What'd you throw my shirt out for?" Dad asked her a few days later.

She just shook her head. "You're unbelievable," she replied. But Dad was fine later, just like he knew he would be. Just like he said he would be.

"I remember that day," Eric said, turning away from the cartoons for a second. "He was dripping blood all over the carpet in the living room."

"You better stop being gross, or I'm telling my mom," Lauren threatened.

"I'm just saying, Mom said he had an operation—like before, but that we can't go see him yet," I explained. I liked being the one in the know.

"Yeah, right," Shawn mumbled sarcastically. Eric didn't say anything. I felt like they were keeping a secret from me, so I decided to go and ask my mom. But when I went out to the kitchen, Aunt Kate was the only one there, and she was doing dishes.

I handed her my cereal bowl. "Where'd Mom go?" I asked.

"They went back to the hospital," Aunt Kate said without looking at me. "Go get on your suit and go out to the pool." I did as I was told, and we spent another day swimming and eating all the junk food we wanted and staying up late. And then another day the same way. Mom was usually there in the early morning, but we never saw her at night. She was always wearing the same pair of jeans and always looked tired.

On Monday—Labor Day—I sat at the edge of pool with Lauren as we both dangled our feet in the deep end. We watched as Eric and Shawn did a competition to see who could do the most underwater somersaults without coming up for air. Shawn was winning.

"I heard my mom say that your dad is in a coma," Lauren told me.

"What does that mean?" I asked her.

"It means that he's almost dead but he's not dead yet." Lauren kicked her legs in the water, trying to splash big enough to hit Eric and Shawn, but they didn't even notice. "After you're in a coma, you always die," Lauren explained.

I was getting pretty tired of Lauren thinking that she knew everything. I didn't think Dad was in a coma, so she must be wrong. Even if he was, he wasn't going to die. Not my dad.

I thought again about the day that he tore his stitches out and came home in a shirt drenched in blood. Even though things had looked really bad, he just went to the hospital for a few hours and then he came home. He healed up and had hardly any scar. That's what would happen again this time. Lauren would be wrong.

chapter 8

JOHN

BY my fourth day in the hospital, I was awake long enough at one point to notice that I was having trouble seeing. I couldn't see the signs out in the hall without squinting, and I used to have better than 20/20 vision, so something was wrong. I wrote a note to one of the oral surgeons, and they sent someone up from the Eye and Ear Infirmary, who found glass fragments stuck in my eyes—probably from the second shotgun blast through the windshield. So Eye and Ear decided that I needed to visit their clinic, and my guards wheeled me down with all my IVs and tubes but without the breathing machine. (I was able to breathe through the trachea now for short periods without being hooked up all the time.)

The female doctor in the clinic set me up, sprayed something into my eyes, and shined a light from the side onto my eye's surface. She then began trying to pull glass slivers from my eyes

with some fine tweezers. I don't know if you've ever had somebody poke something at your eye and tell you to sit still, but I
couldn't do it. As soon as she would touch my eye, I'd blink and
flinch no matter how hard I tried not to.

Another doctor walked in during the procedure and gave the
woman a dressing down. "You never do that!" he yelled at her.
"Now let's see what we've got here . . ." and he leaned in and moved
the light around to get a look at the glass too. After his examina-
tion, I was set up with a full operating theater procedure. This is a
surgery done in an operating room surrounded with glass windows, and behind the windows are chairs set up for the audience—
other doctors. I guess the eye doctor decided that if this woman
didn't know how to extract glass from someone's eyeball, maybe the
other docs didn't either, and he was going to demonstrate. On me.

I was conscious for the procedure, but they numbed my eyes
with a special anesthetic. I could see but not feel anything, even
the urge to blink. They managed to get all the glass out. When
they were done, my right eye needed a patch over it, and the next
morning, I woke up with two black eyes. The oral surgeon crew
came in to see me, including Dr. Keith. "I want that eye patch off,"
he told the other doctor. "It makes us look bad, like we missed
the glass." They were taking me into another surgical theater that
day, but not for a procedure, just show and tell. They wanted to
show the other doctors at the hospital, especially those in the
oral surgery department, what they had done on me so far. I
guess they didn't want the Eye and Ear guys to get all the credit.

Before taking me out of my room for anything, my security guys always checked out where I was going, what path we would take, and how best to get me there safely. John Ayoub, a Falmouth policeman who also grew up in Dedham, was the senior officer running my security detail the day of the show and tell, so he had to approve moving me anywhere the security wasn't as good as my room. John checked out the space. It was a big amphitheater in Mass General called the "Ether Dome"—the location of the first successful demonstration of ether as an anesthesia back in the mid-1800s. Historical significance aside, the place was big and open and all the doctors at the hospital were invited to come and check out my face, so security was an issue. John called in for more guards, and they added a couple of guys at each entrance to check hospital IDs on anyone coming and going.

Once the security was set up, a couple of guards and order-lies wheeled me down to the Ether Dome. It's actually a beautiful space, with stadium seating along one side and a center stage lit by a stained-glass dome overhead. It feels almost more like a church than a hospital. The seats quickly filled with doctors. My doctors brought my X-rays and displayed them on a big lighted board. They talked about what they'd done so far and how they planned to rebuild my face. When they got to the part about future surgeries, one doctor said that it would take years to do the type of reconstruction they wanted to attempt. I felt my chest tighten up at the mention of years—who knew how I was going to eat, talk, or even breathe between now and then.

I noticed one older-looking doctor in the audience nodding off, and by midlecture, he was heavily asleep. Made me nervous to think that this guy might be taking care of other patients in the hospital, and I hoped that he wouldn't be in charge of anything involving my care.

When they were done with me, it was back to my bed, tubes, breathing machine, eye patch, and pain meds. The room was starting to look a little bit like a shrine—my Catholic mother was a true believer and thought that if she attached enough saints' medals and prayers to my hospital bed that I would survive. She had even added a signed photo of the Pope on my bedside table.

On my fifth day in the hospital, I was holding my own when two good friends and former fellow officers, Arthur Pina and Mickey Mangum, came in to see me for a serious talk. The Falmouth Police Department was probably similar to a lot of other small-town police departments in that a great deal of the regular officers were doing part-time work as something else—some of them were school bus drivers/operators and a few worked in construction. Working as a cop didn't pay great, so it was nice to have something else on the side.

Some of the guys were what we called RACs: rent-a-cops, or "summer specials," since the population of the town—and the crime rate—swelled in the summertime. Most of our RACs were guys who had full-time gigs in law enforcement, local government, or just about anything else from carpentry to bus driving and took on the part-time police work during the summers.

About the time I came on the force in 1970, the town had grown enough that it needed to start hiring so-called "outsiders" to be on the force. Even though I'd grown up just outside Boston, I would be considered an outsider because I wasn't a Falmouth boy. So we started getting full-time cops on the force who, like myself, came from outside Falmouth and wanted to do police work—not part-time police work. Some lines were drawn in the department, unspoken but still there. For the most part, I got along with everyone on the force—I didn't care where you were from as long as you were doing your job.

But even with new blood, the majority of the cops on the Falmouth force were still locals, especially the senior guys and the brass—all the way to the top—and they definitely believed in selective law enforcement. We could ticket, arrest, and hassle the tourists and Southie bums all we wanted, but there were some locals who were untouchable. No matter what they were guilty of, we were supposed to look the other way. That's just how it was done.

Mickey Mangum had been a North Carolina state trooper who started as a summer RAC and then became a full-time regular shortly after I started on the force. But Mickey didn't quite get the unspoken rules when he joined the force and was so gung-ho arresting and ticketing locals that they took him off the street and put him on permanent desk duty. He was allowed to use a cruiser only to go home to supper with his wife and kids. That is, until a rookie whom he had trained arrested a "connected" local for DUI. The next day, her ticket was cleared by the chief and removed from the log book. Mickey complained to the chief, but nothing came of it. Except for the fact that after that, Mickey had to bring his supper or have it delivered—he was now officially a troublemaker, and they didn't want him out in a patrol car if they could help it. Two years before I was shot he resigned from the force, but not before writing a nice long letter to the town officials, letting them know all about the issues and cronyism in the police department. Didn't make a difference. At the time of my shooting, he was working for the community college, teaching law enforcement.

Arthur Pina was a local guy from West Falmouth, worked full time for the Department of Motor Vehicles and part time as a cop in the summers. Nicknamed "the Bear," Arthur was six foot five and around three hundred pounds. His size came in handy on party raids—when the first cop on the scene completely fills the doorway, things have a tendency to quiet down quickly. But for his size, Arthur didn't have a mean bone in his body—a good guy with a good heart. Before long, Polly and I were spending time with Arthur and his wife, Cynthia, and our kids were playing with their two daughters.

I worked with Arthur and Mickey for years, both of them good guys on the right side of the law, so when the two of them came to see me, I knew they weren't there to talk about the weather. Mickey got right to it and told me that he'd heard the following story: the morning after my shooting, Raymond

Meyer shows up at the back of the police station to empty the Dumpster. Meyer is a local character running Falmouth's garbage disposal under contract, but he's got a bunch of guys who work for him. There's no reason for him to personally pick up the trash outside the station, unless he wants to be there.

"And guess who climbs right up into the truck with him?" Mickey asked me. I wrote the name "Monty" on my notebook and showed it to him, referring to a cop on the force who we all knew was dirty. But Mickey shook his head. "Nope, Larry Mitchell. And they're having a good chat. After that, Ray leaves and no one has seen him since." Mitchell is a cop and also a friend of Meyer's, so this came as no surprise to me. But the thought of a fellow officer casually chatting with the chief suspect in my shooting wasn't just troubling, it was infuriating. I felt my heart beating faster, the machine monitoring my heart rate by the bed keeping time with the blips.

I wrote, "Has he been questioned?" Arthur explained that the district attorney, Philip Rollins, was away on vacation until Tuesday and was just now getting back into his office. He's the one who had to order the investigation.

I was confused. No one had asked Meyer anything yet? It had been about five days since I was shot. I'd told everyone—or rather, I'd written notes to every cop who had been in to visit me—that I knew who wanted me dead. Maybe Meyer didn't shoot me himself, but if he didn't, then he hired whoever did. This was simple cut-and-dried police work. I was shot. I told my fellow officers that there was only one person I suspected. And no one had even talked to this dirtbag yet?

I wanted to ask our chief of police, John Ferreira, what the hell was going on, but he still hadn't found the time to visit the hospital. Then it dawned on me that he wasn't going to. He didn't want to see me, to have to face me. He didn't want to answer my questions. There was a big difference between looking the other way when a town selectman is caught driving drunk and looking the other way when an attempt is made on a police officer's life.

While I was figuring this out, Mickey was still talking, all heated up about the force, about who was connected to whom, and how pissed he was. But I was only half listening. In my head, I was already making plans. I didn't have the time to wait for the police detectives to botch the investigation like I knew they would. Even if they did their jobs and linked my shooting to Meyer, I had a sinking feeling that he would never pay a high enough price for it.

Since the shooting, I'd been focused on survival. My survival, my family's survival. But now I was mad—beyond that, I was consumed with hatred for this guy. It was clear to me that as soon as I was well enough to leave the hospital, I needed to get a gun, one that couldn't be traced, and go after Meyer myself.

Mickey asked me if I knew who I could trust on the force. He asked who was watching my family, who did they have on detail guarding my room. He was trying to ease me into some harsh facts: someone on the force knew my work schedule; someone told Meyer where I lived and exactly when I would be driving to work. Mickey was a smart guy. He was thinking like I was thinking. Meyer wasn't the only one involved. This wasn't over. It was just beginning.

chapter 9

CYLIN

ON Tuesday morning, Lauren and Cassie went back to school. My brothers and I went swimming and watched TV and hung out. Aunt Kate had taken time off from work to be at home with us, and when she wasn't there, Uncle Joe was.

In the afternoon, we got out our cousins' art supplies and made a few more cards for Dad. We had been making cards every day for Mom to take to him in the hospital. I used crayons to draw a picture of our house on Cape Cod, the little red house with a big yellow sun over it, and I added some colorful flowers in our front yard that weren't really there but I thought they looked nice.

Eric drew a mini comic book of an imaginary superhero he had invented years ago called "Super Hippo." Super Hippo was wearing a red cape with the letters "SH" on it and doing feats with his super strength. The drawings were pretty good.

Shawn was the real artist, though. Like Mom, he could draw

anything. So he did a picture of Spider-Man, using a comic book to get it just right. It looked like a store-bought card when he was done with it. We left the cards for Mom so she could take them to Dad the next day.

Around the time that Lauren and Cassie came home from school, my grammie showed up at the house along with our uncle Brian, my mom's other brother. They had been to the hospital to visit my dad. Uncle Brian sat down on the couch and put his head in his hands like he had a bad headache. It seemed like Grammie couldn't stop crying. Uncle Joe helped her to sit down, and she asked me to sit next to her so she could put her arm around me. I'd never seen her cry, so it was a little scary. I didn't know what to do to make her feel better, so I just sat there. "You're so young," she kept saying, hugging me tighter. She took off her glasses and wiped the tears off them. "You're just a little girl, nine years old. You're the same age your mother was when my Floyd died."

I knew that she was talking about my grandfather, Floyd, my mom's father, who had died a long time ago in a canoe accident in Maine. After diving in to help rescue a drowning friend, he struck his head on a rock and never came back up—they didn't find his body until days later, miles downriver. Grammie always said that he was the love of her life, and I guess it was true because she never even went on so much as a date with another man after he died. "Your poor mother, to have to go through what I went through . . . ," Grammie said, sobbing.

Uncle Brian didn't say anything, but sometimes he would look over at me and shake his head like I had done something bad. Eventually Uncle Joe told us kids to go down to the playroom and stay down there until Grammie felt better.

When we got downstairs, Cassie and Lauren got out their Barbie playhouse and gave me a Barbie doll to use. I never played with Barbies; I didn't have any at home. Having two older brothers around meant that I mostly did what they did: riding bikes, skateboarding, playing Atari and *Star Wars* make-believe. It was nice to have two girls to play with, and to play dress up with their dolls.

"You know why Grammie is crying?" Lauren asked me. "Because your dad is going to die," she said, putting a form-fitting sparkly gold dress on her Barbie. She held up her doll and started brushing its hair. "But you're lucky," she pointed out, "because at least you don't have to go to school."

I looked down at the doll in my hands and tried to find an outfit for her. But I felt sick to my stomach. Why would Mom tell us that Dad was okay if he was really going to die? I tried to tell myself that Lauren was just a bossy know-it-all, because she was older than me. She wasn't always right.

Later that night, Mom came back to Uncle Joe's house after Grammie and Uncle Brian had left. Lauren and Cassie were already in bed. Ever since school had started for Lauren and Cassie, the slumber party in the playroom had ended. Now Eric and Shawn and I slept downstairs while Lauren and Cassie were in their own rooms.

I could hear Mom talking and walking around in the kitchen, then she came down the stairs. "You guys still up?" she asked softly.

"Grammie was here," Shawn told her. He had been sitting up in his sleeping bag, reading MAD magazine.

"I know," she said. "Grammie came to see your dad today."

Then, before I could stop myself, I blurted out, "Lauren said Grammie was crying because Dad is going to die."

"God!" Eric rolled his eyes. I wasn't sure if he was mad at Lauren or me.

Mom shook her head. "Your dad is not going to die. In fact, you guys can see him tomorrow," she said. "If you want to." She looked at us and we all nodded.

"Then I need to tell you some things so that you're ready to see him," Mom said. She sat Indian-style on the rug by our sleeping bags. "Your dad will have a lot of bandages on his head. You might see some blood on the gauze, but that's nothing, he's fine," she told us.

My brothers and I were silent as she went on. "He can't talk, but he is able to write notes if you have anything you want to ask him. He's also really tired. He might be asleep when we get there, we'll see." Mom took a deep breath. "The worst thing you're going to see tomorrow are the tubes. There are a lot of tubes going in and out of your dad—on both of his arms, his stomach, his face, and his throat. I don't want you to be scared," Mom said, looking directly at me. "Okay? There are going to be a lot of tubes and machines. The machines make a lot of noise, so you have to speak up so that he can hear you."

"Okay," Eric said, nodding. When Grammie had been at the house earlier, I overheard her telling Eric that he was the man of the family now, and that he had to be there for my mom, be someone she could lean on. His face was like stone now—strong, no emotion.

Shawn's eyes were big and his feet were moving around in the sleeping bag like they did when he got nervous and agitated. "Did his face get hurt from driving off the road or from getting shot?" he asked.

"Well . . ." Mom started to say something, then stopped herself. "It was probably both, but mostly getting shot," she finally said. I could tell she was about to cry. If he was going to be okay, then why was she so sad? "It's going to take some getting used to, how Dad looks now," Mom went on. "So you have to give yourself some time to get used to it."

Something wasn't right with what she was telling us, and I knew it. She was lying. He wasn't going to be okay. That's why Grammie was crying, why Uncle Brian wouldn't talk to us. Lauren was right. I started crying

"Cee, it's okay to cry now, but don't cry tomorrow. You'll make your dad feel bad, and we need him to feel good so that he can get better, okay?" I could tell she was done talking to us for the night. "Now go up to the bathroom and wash your face," she told me. "You'll feel better."

I went upstairs to the bathroom crying so hard I couldn't catch my breath. When I tried to breathe in, the air caught in my throat. I hated Lauren for being right. Tubes and bandages and machines—my dad *was* going to die, and even Mom was lying about it. I hated everyone, everyone, everyone.

I went into the bathroom and slammed the door hard. Then I opened it all the way and slammed it again, harder. I sat on the floor and cried, waiting for my aunt or uncle or mom to come yell at me for slamming the door, but no one did. After a few minutes, I looked in the mirror over the sink at my blotchy face and red eyes. I stared at my face for a long time. I was still freckled from the summer sun, and my skin was brown, my hair bleached blond. I looked just like the girl I had been last week, but I felt so different. I didn't understand why the anger I felt didn't show on my face. I wanted to scratch myself and put a mark somewhere. I ran my fingernails down one cheek, but my nails were too short to leave a mark. After staring at myself for a few more minutes, I splashed some water on my face and went back downstairs.

The room was dark, and Eric and Shawn weren't talking so I guessed they were asleep. I laid in my sleeping bag and sniffled back tears until I drifted off.

When I woke up the next morning, Lauren and Cassie had already gone to school. It was the day that we would see Dad. I was feeling better, but when I went upstairs and into the bathroom, I saw my red, puffy eyes and I remembered crying myself to sleep. I felt a little babyish and ashamed of myself, and I hoped no one else would notice. I went into the kitchen and found Mom sitting with Eric and Shawn at the table. "Hey, lazybones," Mom said to me. She was drinking a cup of coffee. Her skin looked gray.

"Do you have any money?" Eric asked me.

I said no. I hadn't thought to bring any when we came to my uncle's house a few days before. "We're going to put our money together and buy Dad an *OMNI* magazine," Shawn said. "And maybe some other stuff, too." *OMNI* was a science fiction magazine that Dad loved. It had lots of weird illustrations and creepy stories in it.

I felt bad that I didn't have any money to chip in. "That's okay," Mom said. "I have to give you guys your allowance anyhow." She looked around for her purse. We hadn't done our chores—like making our beds and cleaning up the yard—in almost a week, and that was the way we usually earned allowance. But Mom seemed not to care.

We drove to the hospital in Uncle Joe's car, the three of us kids crammed into the backseat, where I had to sit in the middle. My uncle took us to a store where we could buy Dad his favorite magazine. I picked up a bag of M&M'S and put those on the counter too.

Shawn grabbed the bag. "He can't eat those, didn't you hear Mom? His face is all messed up!" He stuffed the M&M'S back under the counter before the cashier could ring them up. I had forgotten that Mom told us Dad couldn't eat for a while. But I was too embarrassed to admit it. I reached down and picked up the bag again. "They're for me." I scowled at Shawn as I put them back on the counter.

"Nice, really nice. We're supposed to be getting stuff for Dad," Shawn pointed out. I felt tears stinging my eyes, but I wasn't about to let him see me cry again today. After we paid for our presents, I stuffed the bag of M&M'S into my jeans pocket. I was going to give it to Dad anyhow and just tell him that he could hold on to it until he could eat again. The other stuff we had gotten him was from the three of us, but this would be from just me to him, and I knew Dad would like that.

chapter 10

JOHN

RIDING with Don Price in the summer of 1970, I was advised about local politics, local untouchables, local bad guys, and other pains in the ass I'd be interfacing with if I was going to make a career as a local cop. There was a guy in Falmouth Heights who was a lawyer known as "the Suer." He parked his car wherever he wanted. "You leave this one alone," Don said, pointing out the guy's car to me. If a police officer ticketed or towed his car, the Suer would immediately bring a personal lawsuit against that officer. He might lose the suit—in fact, he always did, or it was dismissed outright—but until then you were tied up legally until it was settled, which was just an annoyance. I didn't see how this could affect me—I was a cop doing my job; this guy was parked illegally and should pay the consequences. Don said, "Some hornets' nests are better left undisturbed, but you do what you want," and left it like that.

Don also pointed out local deadbeats, bad actors, and the fray—guys who were likely to be involved when we had a theft, fight, or drugs. One we'll call Artie L. had worked out a scheme in the mall. He'd step behind a car backing out of a parking spot and get knocked down. Then he'd put on a limp and ask for twenty dollars just to cover getting his clothes clean. Quite a few tourists paid the bum to avoid the legal and insurance headaches involved in a pedestrian accident. Artie was stopped for a traffic violation early one morning with a glove box full of bottles of Valium with no prescription. He was eventually put away on charges of being a "habitual criminal"—a title reserved for those stupid enough to get caught so often that the court just sends them away permanently.

We had a town drunk, Jimmy Agardy. Jimmy spent a night or so every week with us, then went to court the next day, paid his fine, and went on with his drunkenness. On one occasion, I was in court on another case when Jimmy was brought up on his usual charge. The clerk pointed out that it was his two hundredth appearance. In honor of the occasion, the judge waived the fine. I saw Jimmy frequently during my nine years on the force and never saw the guy eat anything. Somehow he lived on booze. He was never belligerent or violent, just falling-down drunk all the time. We actually kept a pint bottle in a locker for him. In the morning before taking him to court, he'd shake like a dog shitting razor blades, so a little bit would get him stable enough to make his court appearance.

There was also an unspoken rule that you didn't mess with anyone related to a police officer or a city official. Unless they'd done something you couldn't overlook, they were pretty much untouchable. But it would take me a while to get to know all the names and faces, as I learned pretty quickly one night that summer. I was patrolling town in a cruiser and saw a fight going on outside a diner—a group of maybe four or five guys. I grabbed one perp and caged him in the back of the cruiser, during which time a few others managed to run off. When I went to cuff the guy who was left behind, he started yelling, "Get the guns!" to his friends, who had run off. Naturally, I radioed for help, and when backup arrived, it was made clear to me that the guy yelling for the guns also happened to be related to someone on the force, so he walked. But I still had this other guy cuffed in the cage, and he's yelling, "Monty! Help me! Get Monty!"

Monty was one of the cops on the force, a huge Cape Verdean guy, about six foot two, two hundred and thirty pounds, with enormous hands. An amateur boxer in the service, he was about forty when I met him and had gone a little soft, but not much. Monty was a local and had the local attitude, which meant keeping an eye on the Southy bums and letting everyone else get away with everything else. This was a problem because it seemed that Monty knew or was related to just about everybody in town. There was a rumor that he retired with the same motor vehicle citation book he'd been given as a rookie cop. Since you could normally expect to write at least one citation per shift, the idea that Monty still had his original book suggested he was heavy into things other than traffic tickets.

I told the guy in the cage to shut up and he could see Monty down at the station, where I brought him and booked him on disorderly conduct. By then my shift was over, so I went home to sleep. Polly knew that I had to work again that night, and I'd told her before not to wake me unless Jesus Christ himself came to the door. Well, on this day she woke me up at noon, when I'd had about three hours of sleep, and said, "Monty's at the door for you." She looked scared.

I threw on some sweatpants and a T-shirt and went to the door. Monty was there in civvies, even though I thought he was on duty at the time. "I want you to talk to my brother," he said. "You arrested his son last night and he wants to know why." Monty didn't look happy. Now, I was no shrimp. I'd had my fair share of fighting—I'd boxed with prisoners at Norfolk Prison when I was in high school and taken a little karate. But Monty was a big guy—he had forty pounds on me. So I didn't trifle with him, just stayed calm and said, "Let's go." I was pissed that I had to defend my actions, but surprisingly when we got there, both Monty and his brother listened to my side of the story and agreed that the nephew was in need of a little straightening out. He was about to head to UMass, where he had a basketball scholarship, and his dad was hoping that maybe this arrest would scare him straight and keep him in line when he left home.

Later that day, Monty was back at my house. He had a

bunch of clothes with him—nice stuff—suits, coats, pants—things that fit him a few years ago. He said, "You remind me of myself about twenty years back, so I thought maybe these things would fit you." He left the clothes, most of which turned out to be too big for me.

Monty knew or owed favors to so many people in town that when you pulled over a local, they would say, "So, you know Monty?" This was supposed to convey to the officer that you shouldn't issue a citation—they were connected to Monty, and you didn't want to piss off Monty. But since I'd staked my ground with Monty early, and held firm, this didn't really work with me.

Back then, the regular officers on duty wore what we called our "Smokey the Bear" hats—a ranger-style hat with a wide brim. The RACs wore a military-type cap with a short bill at the front. The chief of police, John Ferreira, had a standing order for years to "don your chapeau" upon exiting the vehicle (the hat was too tall to wear in the cruiser). Who knows why this was important to him; I guess he thought it gave his officers a more official look.

When you pulled over a local, they knew the difference between a full-time "real" officer and a temporary summer special by the hat you were wearing. The first couple of years I was on the force, I'd carry an extra hat in my cruiser, the kind worn by the summer specials, and sometimes pretend to be an RAC so I could plead ignorant and wouldn't have to give in to favoritism. That, and I actually enjoyed wearing the RAC hat and listening to some of the ranting and raving the locals would give a summer special. "What the hell are you doing pulling me over? Do you know who I am? Why don't you go grab some tourist and leave us alone? You're only a RAC—where are you from, Southy? Don't you know Monty? You might want to ask Monty before you write that ticket, son."

But pretending to be an ignorant summer special only worked for so long. After a couple of years, I'd become quite well known to the local residents and couldn't play the RAC any-more. Instead, when I took out my citation book, they'd look at me knowingly and say, "Hey, do you know Monty?" I'd just say, "Yes, I know Monty. And I'd like to see your license and registra-tion for this vehicle." Which usually brought a good deal of hem-ming and hawing. When I was done with the official business, I'd close with, "You have a nice day now, and please tell Monty I said hello next time you see him." Always trying to promote good relations with the public.

But all of these locals, bums, deadbeats, and half-assed cops like Monty were small-time compared to our resident ex-con Raymond Meyer. He was the real deal, pointed out to me early on by my fellow officers. When I started on the force, Ray had already served a few years in Walpole Prison for burglary and arson—he'd burgle a place, then burn it to the ground. No one knows what's missing, right? The only problem being that he was selling all kinds of stuff, some of which was recognized by the former owners. He was also a bit of a firebug—his conviction on

arson included some fires he'd set purely for intimidation pur-
poses. Burning someone's house or torching their car right in
their driveway worked well for keeping most folks quiet.

In 1968, during a three-week arson spree, Meyer burned
twelve buildings and a car. The Shorehaven Motor Lodge on
Shore Street. The Wood Lumber fire was so big, it could be seen
across the bay in New Bedford. The Pomeroy Day estate on Fay
Road, and seven other palatial summer homes. And for icing on
the cake: the police chief's car was burned in his own driveway.

A seventeen-year-old kid employed by Meyer's trash-hauling
business finally testified against him. Meyer was found guilty
and given five to eight hard time in Walpole, of which he served
only a year and a half. The teenager knew Meyer was out of jail
when he found his new car, a Pontiac convertible, torched in his
driveway. He got out of town quick.

The year I started on the force, the detective branch was
looking for a missing woman, Brenda Meyer, Raymond's wife.
Ray had been out of jail a year or so, and the trash hauling business he'd set up was growing pretty quickly. Word was that he'd
made a few connections on the inside, because he started doing
really well for himself, with a whole fleet of trucks and employees
to drive them.

According to Ray, he and his wife had an argument, and
she'd taken three hundred dollars and disappeared. But then he
changed his story and said that she had asked him to drop her at
the bus station so she could go visit a cousin of hers in Wareham.

Trouble was that the family said they have no relatives in Wareham. And there weren't any buses to Wareham from that station anyhow. The seventeen-year-old babysitter, Laverne Linton, who was left at home with Brenda's two little boys, aged four and seven, said Brenda went to visit her mom. Brenda's mom said no chance—that her daughter never went anywhere without her kids. Most unusual.

It wasn't long after this that the babysitter, Laverne, moved in with Ray and family—to help take care of the kids, of course. When Laverne turned eighteen, she became more than the babysitter and officially took on the role of girlfriend. Ray was the chief suspect in his wife's disappearance, but no one was really questioning him. The town dump was searched since Ray was in garbage disposal and could have easily put her body into a truck, compressed it into a load, and put her out to be plowed under the rest of the city's trash. Ray was also in construction and it seemed that he had recently poured a new cement floor in his garage. So the state and local detectives got a search warrant to look for "stolen goods," but really it was a ruse to check out the newly poured concrete. When they got there, they decided to start digging. They didn't get far before Ray came out and reminded them that their search warrant didn't cover digging up a cement floor. Ray had been on the wrong side of the law for so long, he really knew his loopholes. The guys backed off; they never did find Brenda or her body.

All this was going on right around the time I joined the

force. So here was someone to really look out for. Meyer was building a power base with his garbage company, he employed a number of bad actors—some guys he met in jail, some on the outside—and kept them loyal with threats and intimidation. His power base spread to include relatives—legit and not. Ray was similar to Monty—you could stop a car and hear all about "Uncle Ray." Again this was to impress on the cop that if he didn't want trouble, he'd ignore whatever he'd stopped the perp for. This worked with some of the force then, and as far as I know, it works to some extent even now.

Falmouth was a lot like many other small towns, I imagine. I never worked as a cop anywhere else, so I have no proof. Just a feeling there's politics, untouchables, bad guys, and assholes in all towns, no matter what size. And then there are power bases built by certain people, the kind of people who like to be in charge and have folks working under them, who run the big-time scams, not just petty crimes. Who bring in the city contracts, bid rigging, construction deals, plus a few legit businesses to clean the profits made elsewhere. Our town was small enough that we had only one guy running a game like that. And that guy was Raymond Meyer.

chapter 11

CYLIN

WHEN we got back into Uncle Joe's car to drive to the hospital, Mom turned around and looked at the three of us in the backseat. "Some of your dad's friends from the force will probably be at the hospital today," she said. "If they ask you where we're staying, don't tell them." Then she turned back around in her seat.

"Why?" Shawn asked.

"We just don't want anyone to know where we're staying . . . ," Mom started to explain.

"It's nobody's business," Uncle Joe said in a gruff voice. He sounded mad, but I didn't understand who he was mad at.

"What about Don, or Arthur, what if they ask us?" Shawn said, mentioning two of Dad's best friends on the force.

"I don't know," Mom said, and looked over at Uncle Joe. He shook his head. "Let's just keep it to ourselves for now, from everyone. It's just easier that way," she finally said.

We parked the car in an underground lot, then took a series of elevators to get to the floor where Dad was staying. Mom and Uncle Joe seemed to know the hospital pretty well—where all the elevators were and exactly where we needed to go. We rounded a corner and saw a guy in a Falmouth Police uniform sitting on a folding chair in the hallway. It felt funny to see someone in that uniform, the same one Dad always wore. "Polly," the man said, standing up. "He's gonna be happy to see these guys!" He gave me and Eric and Shawn a huge grin, then grabbed a clipboard from a hook on the wall and started writing something on it.

We walked into the room, and there was a man lying on a big white bed. Around him on both sides were lots of machines and poles with plastic bags hanging from them. There were cards and flowers all over the room. The man on the bed did not look like Dad. His head looked funny; it was all wrapped up in gauze, like a mummy's. And it looked smaller; his head didn't look right, like his eyes were in the wrong place or his face was shorter. Maybe they had just wrapped him up too tightly, I thought. The guy in the bed lifted one hand and gave us a thumb's-up sign. Mom went over and kissed him on the forehead, then held up a clipboard for him. He had a tube going into the back of his hand, which was held in place with a big piece of white tape. He wrote, "Thanks for the cards." It did look like Dad's small, angular writing. I was trying really hard to believe that this person in the bed was him, but I just couldn't.

"Do you want to say anything to your dad?" Mom asked us.

"That's not my dad," I heard myself say quietly, before I could stop it from coming out of my mouth. Then Shawn turned and darted from the room before Uncle Joe could grab him. I heard his sneakers screech as he tore down the tiled hallway. Uncle Joe took off after him while Eric and I just stood there.

Mom let out a weak laugh. "This is your dad, he's just bandaged up right now. I told you that, remember?"

Dad waved me over to show me the board. "I love you. I'm OKAY," he had written in capital letters. Once I read it, he motioned to Mom. "I'm scaring them. Do I look that bad?" he wrote, and looked at her. I took the bag of M&M'S out of my pocket and put it on the table next to his bed without a word. Uncle Joe walked in with Shawn, who looked like he had been crying. That made me start crying. Eric just stood at the foot of the bed; his face was blank but I could tell he was chewing the inside of his mouth like he did when he was really mad.

"I think it's time to get these kids some lunch," Uncle Joe announced, and I saw Mom nod. "Let's go, you guys. Say goodbye to your dad."

"Bye," I said, but I didn't look up from the floor. I didn't want to look at whoever that was in the bed, even if it was my dad. We walked out of the room and made our way back to the elevator.

"Oh, aren't you pretty. Look at that hair, would you?" I heard one nurse say to another about my long honey blond hair as we walked by them.

"Wow, I'd love to have hair like that," the other nurse said, trying to meet my eyes.

I wondered if they were just being nice to me because they felt sorry for me, so I kept walking.

"You should say thank you," Uncle Joe reminded me, then murmured under his breath, "Aw, who gives a damn, right?" He had his pack of cigarettes out as we got into the elevator and lit one up the second we reached the parking garage.

"Your dad isn't like Baretta, you know," Uncle Joe said, blowing out some cigarette smoke. "That guy gets shot up one week and he's back the next week. That's fake. When you get shot, it takes time to get better. Your dad is going to need some time."

We were silent as we walked over to the car. The three of us climbed into the backseat together, even though one of us could have sat in the front.

When Uncle Joe started the car, Shawn turned to me. "I don't think that was actually Dad, do you?" he asked.

I shook my head. But part of me knew the truth: that *was* Dad. That was how Dad looked now. I couldn't even imagine a time when he wouldn't be lying in that bed attached to all those machines. How could he come home again, go to work again, go to the beach with us? And what was wrong with his face under all those bandages? I didn't want to think about it, how his head looked too small.

When we got home, Lauren and Cassie were still at school, so Uncle Joe made us some sandwiches and told us we could go swimming if we wanted to. He sat outside by the pool and drank a Tab and smoked another cigarette. We took our sandwiches into the den and put on the TV, but there wasn't a lot on, just soap operas and some dumb science fiction movie that was in black and white.

"Do you think Mom will remember to give him the OMNI?" Eric asked suddenly, eating some potato chips. I had forgotten all about our gifts. I hoped that Mom would remember it—she had been carrying the bag. It made me sad to think that we wouldn't get to see Dad's face when he opened the present, but then I realized that even if we had been there, it would have been hard to tell what was going on under all those bandages, so what did it matter?

Lauren and Cassie came home from school, and then Aunt Kate came back too. Uncle Joe left to pick up Mom from the hospital. Even though they got back in time to eat dinner with us, Mom went straight up to the guest bedroom and went to sleep without seeing us. I wondered if she was mad about what I'd said at the hospital, about that not being Dad. Uncle Joe said she didn't feel well, and we should try to keep it down.

I had been in Mom's room earlier that day, and it was very messy—clothes that she had borrowed from Aunt Kate were all over the place, and an old bra was hanging over the back of the chair. By the bed was a beautiful crystal vase with one perfect red rose in it. The rose was a few days old now; Uncle Joe had bought it for her over the weekend. The tips of the petals were turning a little bit brown, but they were still velvety soft.

That night, Aunt Kate made something for dinner that smelled horrible. "You like meatballs in spaghetti, right?" she said to me. "This is just like a meatball, a big meatball," she explained, putting some on my plate. It was meat and some kind of a red sauce. The meat had all kinds of things in it, like ground up leaves or something. Everyone else was eating it, but even the smell made me feel sick.

"Oh, Cylin, you're skin and bones. Eat something," Aunt Kate finally said.

I looked over at Eric and Shawn and saw them happily eating the meat and pasta on their plates. I put my fork down and sat quietly, trying not to breathe through my nose. "How about a bowl of cereal?" Uncle Joe asked, and I nodded. As he got up to fix my cereal, Lauren said, "That's not fair! Why does she get to eat Cocoa Puffs?"

"She had to see her dad in the hospital today. Leave her alone!" Uncle Joe snapped. But I didn't want cereal because of Dad—I wasn't even thinking about him. I just hated my aunt's cooking. Still, it made me feel special that I was getting my way without even trying.

After dinner, I helped Aunt Kate clean up and load the dishwasher, just like I always did at home. I liked cleaning up; I got some satisfaction from scraping the leftovers into the garbage, where they belonged. I was glad the battle over this meal was done. When I was finished helping my aunt, I went into the TV room where Lauren and Cassie were watching TV with my brothers. "Your mother has had a nervous breakdown," I heard Lauren tell Shawn.

"I know," Shawn said. He looked very serious. We had a priest at our church back on the Cape named Father Mark. He was my favorite—he was everyone's favorite. When he first came to Saint Patrick's, it was like he woke the place up. Sunday was no longer boring. He would ask the kids to all come and sit up front during Mass. He really talked to us about God and Jesus and religion and made it seem like it was actually something to care about. He had a nice face, but he wasn't so handsome that you were scared of him—brown eyes, dark hair, a trimmed dark beard. And sometimes, when it wasn't Sunday, we would see him in town wearing jeans with his shirt and collar. This was totally unheard of for the other priests at our church. Dad liked Father Mark too, and he especially liked that we now had doughnuts and coffee after church in the basement—Father Mark's idea of "building community."

We all came to count on Father Mark for a lot. Then one day, he just wasn't there. Everyone in the congregation was whispering about him. "Where's Father Mark?" I asked Dad.

"He's sick," Dad said. But when we got home, he told Mom a different story. Father Mark had had a "nervous breakdown," and according to some folks in the church, it wasn't the first time. There was something wrong with him, and he had to go away to get better. I asked about him every Sunday for a few weeks after that. The old priest who took his place was crusty and dull, and he quickly did away with the coffee and doughnuts, saying that it was too expensive. After a while, we just stopped going to church.

*   *   *

The next morning when we got up, Mom was sitting at the kitchen table and she looked fine. She had taken a shower and put on a clean pair of jeans that she borrowed from Aunt Kate. She hadn't had a nervous breakdown! I couldn't wait for the chance to tell Lauren that she had been wrong.

I went into the den while everyone else was still eating breakfast and got out some art supplies to make another card for Dad. I pictured the man lying in the hospital bed and how he had written "I love you." I drew a big red heart, then put a happy face on it and arms and legs. Then I added some running shoes and some flowing hair. It was a jogging heart. I thought it was pretty creative, especially since Dad liked to go jogging. "I love you, too," I wrote over the heart. "Get well soon," I wrote under it.

chapter 12

JOHN

THE kids came for a visit and were terrified of me. Eric was stone-faced the whole ten minutes, Cee cried, Shawn couldn't even stay in the room and instead ran up and down the hallway until Joe grabbed him. I could tell from the look on Joe's face that there was no way he would bring his daughters here to see me; he seemed to think the whole thing was a huge mistake. But Polly had been saying that the kids thought I was dead, or about to die, and she wanted them to see that wasn't the case. I don't know if her plan worked exactly; now the three of them were in shock after seeing their dear old dad hooked up like Frankenstein. I didn't expect they'd be back anytime soon.

About five days after the shooting, the pain level dropped markedly. I was suddenly more aware, could stay awake for longer periods, understand what people were saying, and actually remember conversations. My blood oxygen level was returning to normal after all the blood I'd lost, and that was helping me to get my bearings and feel more like myself.

Around this time I had a visit from Joe Urcini, a guy I went to high school with, who was working in the ballistics lab of the Mass State Police. He came in one afternoon and held up a small plastic bag that contained a shotgun round. "Dug this out of the house across the street from where you were shot," Joe explained. The slugs went through me, out the passenger side of the car, and straight into the side of a house across the street.

"It's double-O," Joe went on. "Impossible to trace. I'm sorry, John." He looked pretty glum, but I didn't need ballistic evidence to know whose weapon of choice that was.

A few years back, I'd heard a story from a fellow officer—a good buddy of mine, someone I trusted. He was in the east on the four to one shift one night and had picked up a kid—around sixteen or seventeen years old—for loitering. He was talking to the kid in the cruiser when a truck from Ray's garbage company rolled by. Suddenly, the kid hit the floor, hiding under the dash, scared shitless. My buddy wanted to know what was up. The kid told him that he was afraid of Ray and said that if Ray got his hands on him, he would be dead. "Did he threaten you?" my friend asked. The kid said yes, then said no, and generally looked terrified. He probably knew that Meyer had some guys on the police force under his sway, and wondered if this cop could even be trusted. Finally the kid admitted that he had just heard some stuff through the grapevine, innuendo, that Meyer didn't like him. My friend told the kid to either get things straightened out with Ray or split to somewhere else, somewhere he'd be safe. But the kid did neither and was found floating facedown in the cranberry bogs across the street from Meyer's house not long after.

The kid's name was Jeff Flanagan, and when his body was pulled out of the bogs, it appeared that he had been shot at point-blank range, execution-style. From the autopsy, it was clear that the bullets had entered his head at the right cheek and exited from his upper back, severing his spinal cord and killing him instantly. A 20-gauge shotgun had been used, the ammo untraceable.

In his final hours, Jeff had gone to a movie with some friends. He was last seen getting into a car with Raymond Meyer and Laverne Linton, who were giving him a ride home. According to Jeff's mom, the boy had been dating Laverne. He had even given her his class ring. At the time of his death, Jeff was sixteen years old, just a few days away from his seventeenth birthday.

Meyer was obviously the chief suspect, but there were no witnesses, no evidence. The day police found Jeff's body in the bogs, Raymond's girlfriend, Laverne, had been seen in the yard thoroughly cleaning his Cadillac, inside and out.

. . .

About a week after my shooting, I noticed that people stopped referring to it as an "accident"—even the staff of the hospital. It had become clear to everyone there, especially with the heavy police presence, that something bad was up. The nurses and doctors treating me had caught up with the stories in the Boston and

Falmouth newspapers. The staff of the hospital had been put on notice to look out for any suspicious activity or unusual visitors. I had survived the shooting, and that was bad news for somebody—whoever had wanted me dead. The questions that remained were: How badly did they want to kill me? Would they be back? And when?

As I slowly stabilized, I was able to see more visitors. Friends and family alike stopped in as soon as they were approved by the two officers on security detail. It was tiring trying to converse by writing—I found myself just skipping a lot of details and cutting right to the point. And I couldn't count the number of times someone took my pad and wrote their responses back to me. I had to constantly point out that while I couldn't speak, I could hear just fine.

The note writing was also a pain in the ass for the hospital staff, I'm sure. All of my interaction with doctors and nurses had to take place in writing, even the small stuff like changing the sheets and bed pan—everything. This only became a major issue, though, during medical procedures, like when they changed my heparin locks. These were the IV locks that my meds were pushed through, and they would reach a point where the vein started to close up and they had to be changed. A pretty simple but still painful process—a new vein was selected and the IV lock was pushed in. It wasn't fun for two reasons: one, getting a needle pulled out of one vein just meant it was going to be pushed into another one, and two, since the locks were held down with adhesive tape, I lost lots of arm hair every time they ripped them off. I was getting my locks changed every couple of days at that point, and to say I didn't look forward to it would be a massive understatement.

A member of the IV team came in at one point to put in a new series of locks. She put a rubber band around one upper arm and selected a candidate vein, then stuck the needle in. "Oops, went right through that one!" I heard her say as she pulled it back out. She tried again. And again. And again. She finally got it on the fifth try. "Thanks for being so patient with me," she said when she was taping the new needle down. "Most people start bitching if you miss once or twice." I guess she didn't notice that I was a neck breather and couldn't say shit if my life depended on it.

About ten days later, this same IV nurse was back again, looking to change my locks. I'd removed my hospital wristband ID because it was bothering me. "Are you Busby?" she asked me, looking at my arms for ID. She was about to rip the tape off my arm when I grabbed my pad and quickly wrote, "He died and was removed."

"Oh," she said, looking at her paperwork. "I'm here to see Busby, so let me find out what is going on." She put down her Little Red Riding Hood basket of pain tools and went out to the nurses' station. When I knew she was gone, I took her basket and hid it under the bed. A few minutes later, the head nurse came back in with her and ID'd me as Busby. So the Stabber started looking around for her needle cart. "Now where did I put that?" she said to herself, wandering around. She went back to the nurses' station to look for it. Then back into my room. Then down the hall into the room of the last patient she'd stuck. Then back into my room. Then back down to the nurses' station.

While she was gone the last time, I reached down and pulled the basket back up and put it on the tray next to my bed, in plain view. When she came back in, she said, "How long has that been there?" I wrote her a note saying, "What?"

"The basket," she told me as she began to prep my arm. I wrote back to her, "The whole time," and gave her a shrug. Now she must have thought she was losing her mind. Or maybe from her viewpoint I was just a royal pain in the ass. In any event, I'd call us even.

About a week and a half after the shooting they let me get up and try to walk. The doctors thought I might need a little more time, but I thought I was ready and I was determined to try. The breathing and feeding tubes were disconnected, and I was given a wheeled IV pole that my meds could hang on. I stood and started shuffling with my entourage around me—a nurse who had made me her pet project and two guys from the police force who were on security detail. I was wobbly as soon as my feet touched the ground, but my mind was made up. I was gonna show the bastards who did this to me they couldn't keep me down. I got about twenty feet and felt woozy. The room started to turn on its side and I felt myself sliding with it, but someone had my arm and held me up. I turned around and made my way back to the bed, little black spots dancing into the corners of my eyes like I was going to hit the deck—that look boxers get right before they totally check out. When I got back in the horizontal position, I was sweating bullets. I'd gone from running seven miles a day to walking a few feet. Now I knew how much I had to recover. The team of surgeons who wanted to reconstruct my face wouldn't even start on me until I was stable, until the tissue from the first surgery had time to heal. I had a long road in front of me. Very long. But I knew that I could make it. Tomorrow I would take a few more steps, and a few more after that. I had nothing but time. I would get there. On this, I was resolved.

The strange thing was, I wasn't thinking about getting well so I could see my family, so I could go on with my life, so the surgeons could get to work on my new face. I had a singular mission: I wanted to get well enough to get out of there, to track down Meyer and kill him. I had to get well so I could get him.

It was as simple as that.

chapter 13

CYLIN

ABOUT a week after our first visit to the hospital to see Dad, Mom said we could go back. He was doing better now, she told us. He was able to walk around a little bit and didn't need to be on oxygen all the time.

The night before the visit, we were all a little nervous about what he might look like, but not really scared. I got out my cousins' art supplies and started making a card. I was in the den coloring when Lauren walked in. "What are you wearing to the hospital tomorrow?" she asked me. I was embarrassed to tell her that I hadn't really thought about it.

"I have a dress that's too small for me, maybe you'd want it," Lauren said casually.

I looked up from my card. "Really?" Lauren had the most beautiful clothes I had ever seen—she and Aunt Kate both dressed really well and their things were expensive.

"Come upstairs, try it on." Lauren smiled. We'd been having a hard time all living together, and I had honestly forgotten how nice she could be.

The dress was black silk and cut in a Chinese design, buttoning over one shoulder. It was long and sleek and beautifully embroidered. I looked like a princess in it. "It's not quite right for the hospital," Lauren said knowingly, "but you can still have it. Wear it when you get home, like to a party or something." The way she said it, it sounded like she knew we would go home eventually—to our old lives where everything would be normal. It implied there would even be parties to go to, and that I could wear this dress like nothing bad had ever happened. It made me feel good.

"Here, try this on." Lauren handed me a pink shirt with a tiny alligator on the front. "This won't fit Cassie for ages, so you should take it."

I slid off the silky dress and put on the shirt. It was pretty and preppy, like stuff that the rich kids at school wore. "Wear your jeans with that tomorrow; your dad will say you look nice," Lauren told me. I wanted to make Dad happy, so I decided to wear the shirt.

When we saw Dad the next day, I was disappointed that he looked the same. His face was still wrapped up in bandages, and there were lots of tubes and wires connected to him. I had pictured him really being better, like Mom had said, looking more normal somehow. But he did seem more awake; he was sitting up and writing a lot of notes to us on his board. There were handmade cards all over the room, taped to every wall and surface, probably fifty or more—and they weren't all from us. "Who made those?" I asked Mom, looking at the cards on Dad's bedside table.

"The kids from your school," Mom answered. "They all made cards and sent a big package. Actually, there were too many to hang up." She showed me a huge envelope stuffed with construction-paper cards. There must have been more than a hundred. I looked at a few of them. "Get Better Soon, Officer Busby!" one read, signed by Matt. "Hope you feel better," another one said, with a really good drawing on the front of a brown dog with round pink ears.

I didn't even know these kids. They went to my school? I studied the envelope and looked at the careful handwriting on the outside, and all the stamps. They must have had every class at school make cards. For *my* dad. We had been in Boston so long I had almost forgotten that school had started back home a couple of weeks ago, that my friends were there, that they knew what had happened to us.

While I looked through the cards, my brothers stood close to the bed and watched as Dad wrote on his board. I saw Shawn studying Dad's face, his eyes, as he wrote, and I knew he was trying to make sure this really was Dad. By the end of the visit, we hadn't seen him get up and walk, but I was pretty sure that it was him. His notes to us sounded like our old dad.

"You guys are going back home and going to school," he wrote in his familiar block letters. "I'll be home soon, too."

Looking at what Dad had written, Mom nodded. "Next week, we're going home. I have school, you guys have school. Your dad will stay here a little bit longer, but as soon as he can eat, they'll let him come home too. Right, honey?" she said, pushing some hair back from Dad's forehead. It still seemed weird that Dad couldn't say anything. How could he come back and live in our house? Where would all his machines and tubes go? I couldn't picture it.

On the way back to Uncle Joe's house, Shawn asked how Dad was going to eat.

Without turning around in her seat, Mom said, "He's going to have special food for a while."

"Yeah, but *how* is he going to eat it?" Shawn asked again.

At first, I didn't get what Shawn was asking. But then I did: Dad had no mouth. Where was the food going to go?

Uncle Joe laughed a little. "Good question," he said.

"Well, he's going to have a liquid diet. They're going to show us how to insert it using a syringe," Mom said.

"Insert it where?" Eric asked. "That tube in his stomach?"

"Yes, it's called a GI tube," Mom explained. "We'll put a special type of liquid food in there." Mom made it sound like this was all very normal, so we just nodded like we thought it was too.

When we got back to Uncle Joe's house, I asked Mom when we would go back home. I liked the idea of going back to school and seeing my friends. Now that they all knew about what had happened to Dad, I was sure they would want to ask me questions, and I would feel very important. I also wanted a chance to wear the new clothes that Lauren had given me. I would be going back to school a whole new girl.

"A few more days," Mom said, but she looked sad. "And then Dad will come as soon as he's stable."

That night, Mom and Uncle Joe made dinner for us because Aunt Kate was at work. I was happy to sit in the kitchen and help, especially since I knew we were having something normal, not gourmet food. "He might as well recover at home; I'm practically a nurse now anyhow," Mom said as she cut up some vegetables for the spaghetti sauce. "After the trachea heals up, they can close his GI tube and then he should be fine until it's time for his surgeries. He'll do better at home."

"I don't think it's his recovery they're worried about," Uncle Joe said. "It's his safety—and yours." They seemed to forget that I was sitting there. "At the hospital they've got him covered twenty-four hours a day, and no one knows where you guys are," Uncle Joe pointed out. "If you're all under one roof . . . I don't know, Polly." He looked over at her and stopped stirring the pot on the stove. "I just don't know."

Mom didn't say anything, just kept chopping up the vegetables like she hadn't heard him.

By the end of the week, we had packed up our stuff, rolled up our sleeping bags, and put everything into the back of the old brown Pinto that Uncle Joe had given Mom. Dad's car was ruined, they said, and couldn't be driven anyhow because the police detectives had it, so we needed something to drive. I had carefully packed the hand-me-downs that Lauren had given me—I couldn't wait to show them off at school, especially the new Izod shirt and the silk dress.

"Here," Lauren said, handing me a book as we stood in the driveway saying our good-byes. It was one of her Nancy Drews. I couldn't believe it. They were numbered on the spine, a real series, she couldn't just give one away!

"But it will be missing from the set," I told her, looking at the cover. It was the one about the clock that I had wanted to read.

"Just bring it when you come back," Lauren said, looking down. I could tell she was sad we were leaving. We hugged my aunt and uncle and climbed into the car to go. As we backed out of the driveway, waving, I realized that it was the first time we had been together, just us four, in almost a month. It felt good to be on our own, even though Dad wasn't there. It felt normal. I looked down at the book in my lap and thought about my new clothes in the trunk, the fact that we would be home soon. When we got close to the Bourne Bridge, I held my breath—the way you do when you drive by a graveyard. I told myself if I could hold it until we reached the other side, everything would be okay.

Dad would come home soon, and he would be fine. As we crossed the bridge, I could see the cranberry bogs, the berries already getting fat and ripe in the fall sunshine.

"We're home," Mom said quietly. I took a deep breath and was happy for the first time in a long time.

chapter 14

JOHN

POLLY and the kids went back to the Cape while I was still in the hospital. We both felt the kids had been through enough, missed enough school, and it was time for them to get back to a normal life. Though how normal things could be with a cop or two sitting in the yard all day and night and a police escort to school, I don't know. I wanted to be updated about who was on duty at all times at the house, and the guys who were guarding me kept me informed about that.

Rick Smith was one of the guys on the force I was tight with. He was the one who went to the house to get Polly on the night I was shot, and he came to see me on a regular basis. After I'd been in the hospital about three weeks, I was able to sit up and play a little chess when he or Don Price dropped by. It was a way to kill some time without too much talking, and it felt good to use my mind again, just to reassure myself that even though I'd been shot in the head, I was still all there. I'd been having some short-term memory problems—people's names, stuff like that, but no major brain damage, which was a big relief for me.

Chess had been a hobby of mine since I was in the Air Force. Learned it while in the brig serving time for "inciting a riot"— that was the charge, anyway. If you didn't know better, it might sound like I went from a life of crime on the streets of Boston to a life of crime in the service. But there are two sides to every story. This time I was going to fight one guy I had a problem with, but when he showed up at the appointed place and time, he had five other guys with him. So my guys got into it, and next thing you know, it was an all-out brawl. When we were finally pulled apart, I was thrown into the brig for a month, along with him and all five of his guys. This was the so-called "riot" that I incited; guilty as charged.

During our confinement, this guy and I started playing a lot of basketball and eventually became friends. One of his friends, another inmate, was a pretty damn good chess player and taught me the game. I'd never played anything like it, and I took to it. It was a long month, and we played a lot of chess and basketball. I lost two stripes (Airman Second Class) because of the fight but learned chess and made a couple of good friends out of former enemies. Later, I earned the stripes back, and had I managed to be a good boy, probably would have made sergeant before my discharge.

Chess wasn't Polly's game, but I did find a couple of guys on the force who liked to play, so I usually carried a travel chess set in my cruiser. It was something to do to stay awake on slow nights, and I enjoyed the fact that I learned something new from every opponent—the more I played, the better I got.

When I was in the hospital, one of the guys brought me a chess set, remembering how much I liked to play. So when Rick dropped by one afternoon and found me awake and feeling pretty good, we started in on a game. As we were playing, he told me about the investigation into my shooting, what he had been hearing back at the department. It seemed that on the night I was shot, there was a group of cops in town on vacation from New York City. These guys got wind of what had happened and went into our local PD to report for duty. "They said they'd do whatever we needed, investigate, question people, even do street duty to reroute traffic from the scene," Rick told me. "One of the guys even said he'd just hang around to get us coffee."

At first, this story made me proud. Brothers in arms, indeed. I wanted to think I'd do the same if I was ever in a similar situation. I wrote a note on my board and showed it to Rick: "What happened?"

Rick looked down and shook his head. "I wasn't there, but some of the guys told me that the chief turned them down, said we had it covered. Detective department was going to handle the investigation." Rick gave me a knowing look.

I had also heard that the chief turned down an offer of assistance from the nearby Fall River Police Department and a couple of other offers. He didn't want anybody going through his garbage. Those NYC cops probably would have solved this thing in one night. They would have questioned Meyer, arrested his ass, and still had time to go out for a beer. State police, too, though there was talk that Meyer had some pull there as well.

None of this was a surprise to me, but it still pissed me off. I was lying there watching liquid nutrition get pumped through a tube into my gut, half my face was blown off, and the brass of the Falmouth Police Department was still running scared of Meyer.

After Rick left, I told my nurse that I wanted to try walking again. I'd been getting up a couple of times a day and wheeling myself through the hallways. *I've got to build up my stamina; it's the only way I'm getting out of here*, I thought. I walked into the hallway with her help and made it a few steps farther before I had to rest against the wall, using my IV pole to hold me up.

"You're doing great!" the nurse said, smiling. "I honestly can't believe that you're even out of bed already." I would have said something back to her, but I didn't have my board to write on, and besides, I needed my strength for walking. *It is amazing what you can do*, I wanted to tell her, *when you get angry enough.*

. . .

Don Price had told me years before that Meyer's game was psychological. He didn't threaten; he never said anything that could come back to haunt him. Instead, he'd use taunts, hints. The most famous of these was "I smell smoke." Ray would say this to let you know you were on his shit list. Smelling smoke meant that something, most likely your house or your car, was going to burn—maybe with you in it. And we knew from his past record that this wasn't an idle threat. He would do it. And he would get away with it. Meyer had learned to be a wiser perp—probably something he picked up in prison. You can't arrest someone for saying he smells smoke. But saying it was enough to get people to back off, and most of the time, Meyer didn't actually have to do anything.

I had heard so many horror stories about Meyer that by the time I actually met the guy, I was in for a surprise. We had a shopping plaza in town anchored by a Stop & Shop grocery store. In 1972, when I'd been on the force a couple of years, the stores there started having problems with young punks gathering in large groups of vehicles in the parking lot. This usually happened in the evenings, on the weekends, but the kids were taking up most of the parking places and being obnoxious, loud, and general pains in the ass. The plaza manager wanted to hire an off-duty policeman to patrol the parking areas to the front and rear to prevent this accumulation of riffraff on Friday and Saturday nights. It was an outside detail but short hours, and once the word got out, it should have been a cakewalk. I volunteered for it and started rousting the personae non grata. I conducted a lot of vehicle inspections and issued expensive citations for any faults found. Anyone who got one, and the fine that went along with it, wouldn't come back to this hangout spot anytime soon.

One evening, I told a teenage kid in his souped-up hot rod to go park someplace else. He did so by peeling out, burning rubber on the pavement of the parking lot. I took notice of his car and plates so I could discuss it with him if ever we were to meet again.

About an hour later, Meyer pulled into the lot in one of his huge garbage trucks. And right behind his truck was the hot rod. Obviously, this kid was someone Meyer knew. I approached the car and asked the kid for his license and registration.

"What for?" he huffed.

"For the purpose of issuing a citation," I told him.

"What for? What did I do?" the kid asked.

"You'll know when I give it to you," I said. I could hear the rev of Meyer's garbage truck as he pressed down on the gas, just idling beside us. He was like an angry bull, stamping his feet and snorting. I knew he was watching my back, but he probably couldn't hear anything I was saying.

"That's my uncle—maybe you want to talk to him before you write me a ticket," the kid said snidely.

I kept my mouth shut and slowly wrote out the citation: "Failing to use care and caution in starting, stopping, and turning a vehicle." As I handed it to him I said, "Anytime you want some more, just come back to this parking lot. I'll be happy to oblige."

Meyer was still there in his dump truck, the big compressor kind with the prongs on the front used to lift and empty Dumpsters into the crusher compartment. The thing smelled, not just of burning fuel but of garbage. It probably wasn't full right now, but that was a stink you couldn't get rid of. I found myself wondering if Meyer went home to his young girlfriend and his two kids smelling like that every night.

"Hey, cop!" he yelled at me. "What are you giving him a ticket for? He didn't do anything!" I turned and walked around the truck to the driver's side, then climbed up on the running board so we could talk face-to-face. This was the first time I had seen Meyer close up and personal, and I almost had to laugh. Here was this small, greasy-looking dude who had everyone in town scared to death. He looked like a real nobody: his ears stuck out from beneath his pomade-slicked black hair. He had a scrawny build, maybe five foot nothing, and the posture of a man twice his age. All of this combined with his sharp, pinched features reminded me of a troll.

"What'd you say?" I asked him.

Ray sniffed the air close to my face. "I said I smell smoke." He grinned at me, deep lines cutting into his sharp face.

"You're right," I told him, pretending to sniff. "Kind of like the candles at somebody's funeral, right?"

Two could play that game.

Ray looked startled—he wasn't used to anyone standing up to him. Before he could say anything, I added, "So, Ray, if you're planning to do some shopping here tonight, no problem. But if you're not a customer, you're gonna need to move out." I climbed down from the truck and stood there looking at him. He stared back at me for a few minutes before slamming his truck into gear and roaring out of the lot at top speed, his nephew following behind him.

I'd been contrary since I was a teenager. Always wanted to tackle the biggest guy on the football team, bodycheck the biggest hockey player, etc. It didn't matter if I came out second best in the collision; I wanted him to know I wasn't running scared of contact, and I'd be back to whack him again as soon as the opportunity presented itself. I was building my own little power base as somebody you didn't fuck with. If you messed with the bull, you'd get the horns. I had my turf and nobody—Monty, Ray, or even the privileged locals—nobody influenced my behavior. I was either too dumb to feel fear or too proud to show any.

My theory about Meyer back then was that he might come across as a menace to a teenage kid or his wife, but he was really just a blowhard, a bully who'd throw his weight around where he could. And I suspected that, just as fast, he'd pull his horns in when a bigger bull was present. I was quite proud of myself—I'd faced Meyer down. He'd lost turf and I'd gained some. Most important, though, I'd sent him a warning: his power base didn't extend to me; he and his supporters were fair game where I was concerned.

chapter 15

CYLIN

WHEN we pulled into our driveway, I noticed a police car parked there. And as soon as Mom stopped the car, another cruiser pulled in behind us. Mom got out and said hi to the officer. I didn't know who he was. My brothers and I got our stuff from the car and went into the house. The door was unlocked and two cops were sitting in our living room. The TV was on, but one of them quickly turned it off.

"That's okay," Mom said, following us into the house. "You guys can keep watching whatever you had on."

"We'll just be outside if you need us," one of the cops said. He was tall and had dark hair; I had seen him at a cookout earlier in the summer. I'd never seen the other guy before. What were they doing in our house? And why did the kitchen smell funny, like someone had been cooking something—meat and onions?

"Go unpack your bags and bring me anything you need washed," Mom told us as she started in on the dishes that the guys must have left in the sink. My room looked the same way it had before we left, except that Kelly had made the bed for me. Everything was neat and put away. I unpacked my clothes and put everything back into the drawers. I hung up my new silk dress and brought the pink Izod shirt to my mom.

"I think this needs to be ironed; I want to wear it to school tomorrow."

Mom looked at the shirt. "It looks fine to me," she said. But then she looked at me for a second. "Leave it on the table, I'll do it tonight."

Later, when Mom needed to go to the grocery store, she made us all come with her. Usually we could stay home as long as Eric was there. He was thirteen. But not today. "Into the car," Mom said.

"We're going to Stop & Shop," she told one of the cops as she went to lock the back door. She stopped with the key half-turned in the lock. "I guess I don't really need to do that, do I?" She laughed, unlocking the door again.

The dark-haired cop laughed too. "I think we've got it covered," he said. As we drove out of the driveway, I watched as his partner got into the police cruiser and pulled out behind us. The cruiser followed closely behind as we reached the stop sign down the street.

"Why is he following us?" I finally asked Mom.

"They just want to keep an eye on us, keep us safe," she explained.

"Like the guys sitting outside Dad's hospital room," Eric added. It was clear that Eric and Shawn had been told that we would have police guarding us, even though no one had bothered to explain it to me. Maybe they thought I wouldn't notice.

That night during dinner, one of the officers came to the door to use the bathroom and check in on Mom. She gave him a cup of coffee, and they talked on the steps for a couple of minutes about Dad and how he was doing. Later I was nervous to get into the tub for my bath. "What if that guy needs to use the bathroom again?" I whispered to Mom.

"Don't worry about that; take your bath. If one of the guys needs the bathroom, they can wait." She made me feel like I was being silly so I got into the tub, but I took the fastest bath ever.

After I had gotten into my PJs, there was a knock on the door again. "We're just changing shifts, wanted to let you know," the dark-haired cop told Mom. "The Teixeira brothers will be on tonight." He pointed to two cops sitting in a cruiser in our drive-way. I peeked through the shutters in the kitchen window to check them out, but it was too dark. I couldn't tell if I knew them or not.

"You on tomorrow?" Mom asked the dark-haired cop.

"In the afternoon," he told her. "The Bear will be here in the morning with Don to take over for these guys."

In the morning, I was excited to get to school and see all my friends. I dressed very carefully in my new corduroys and Lauren's Izod. Mom had forgotten to iron my shirt, but it looked fine. It wasn't until I was standing at the front door that I remembered lunch—we had forgotten to get me a new lunch box!

"I'll just pack something in a paper bag," Mom said, looking through the cabinets.

"I'm gonna miss the bus!" I yelled at her. How could she totally forget about lunch? She was going to ruin my first day back at school.

"Here." She handed me a dollar. "Just buy lunch today, okay? We'll get you a new lunch box after school."

Mom knew I was a picky eater; I couldn't eat the school lunch. But I took the dollar and stuffed it in my pocket as I headed out the door. I was alone; Eric and Shawn had already left for their bus stop to the middle school, which was down by the Zylinskis' house.

"All ready?" someone asked as I was walking down our front steps. I stopped. It was Dad's friend Arthur; he wasn't wearing his uniform. "Let's head on out, don't want to be late." Arthur was a huge guy—so tall he had to duck to get into the doorway of our house. His hands were about as big as my torso. We mostly just called him by his nickname: the Bear.

I turned and saw that Mom was watching us from the window. She waved like it was no big deal that Arthur was walking me to the bus stop.

"Where do you catch the bus?" the Bear asked me.

"In front of the church next door," I told him, and we walked over together.

"So you happy to get back to school?" He seemed uncomfortable as we waited for the bus to come. I noticed a cruiser had pulled into the church's dirt driveway.

"Who's that?" I asked, pointing to the car.

"That's a friend of mine. We're just gonna make sure you get to school okay today. That all right with you?"

"Sure," I lied. All I could think about was that the kids on the bus were going to see the cop car and how embarrassed I would be about it. I thought about asking him to stand farther away from me, but I was too shy.

We stood there in silence until the bus showed up. When I climbed on, Arthur got on the bus behind me. I went to find a seat while he talked to Mr. Arnold, the bus driver, for a minute. I didn't know what Arthur was saying, but I saw Mr. Arnold glance up at the big rearview mirror over his head and look at me while Arthur was talking to him. Then Arthur shook the bus driver's hand and turned to leave the bus, but before he went down the stairs he waved back at me. "Okay, Cece, have a great day." My face burned red. He had used Dad's nickname for me. Maybe no one had noticed. Mr. Arnold closed the door and the bus continued down the road to where we would pick up my friend Meg at one stop, and then Amelia two stops after that. I tried to put the morning out of my mind and focus on how surprised my friends were going to be when they saw me. I wondered what they would think about my new outfit.

"Hey, Mr. Arnold, that cop car is following us!" a boy from the back yelled up to the bus driver.

"I know," Mr. Arnold said, and I caught his eye in the big rearview mirror again. His face looked sad. I turned around in my seat and looked out the back window. Sure enough, Arthur and the other cop were following the bus. Were they going to tail us the whole way to school?

When we got to Meg's stop, she got on and sat with a group of girls in the front, like she didn't even see me. At Amelia's stop, she wasn't there, and I just shrugged down into my seat and put my forehead against the window. I was almost relieved that no one sat with me the whole way to school. Maybe no one knew that the cops were there for me.

I got off the bus and went into school. Mom had told me to go to the principal's office first thing to let them know I was back. The principal wasn't there, but the secretary told me that I could go to my new classroom. I had a teacher named Ms. Williams. Shawn had had her two years before, and she was supposed to be really tough. I always did well in school, so I wasn't too worried about it.

As soon as I walked into the classroom, I was shocked to see Arthur and the other cop talking to my teacher. They stopped talking the second they saw me, and Arthur looked down like he was feeling uncomfortable again. Our family was pretty close to Arthur's family; he had been a friend of Dad's since I was a baby. But suddenly I felt like I didn't know him at all, like he didn't know me. I didn't understand why he was acting so strange, so serious. I wanted him to just be the Bear again and not be standing in my class talking to my new teacher. Everything was wrong.

"Cylin, this is your desk, up front, close to me," Ms. Williams said. I could tell she was putting on a fake nice act for the officers. I sat down without talking to anyone.

"Let's move this conversation to the hallway, shall we?" Ms. Williams said to them. They went outside and closed the door, but I could see them through the glass window. After a few minutes, Ms. Williams came back and started class like nothing had happened. She laid a stack of books on my desk. "Write your name in those and take them all home tonight and have them covered by tomorrow." She really *was* mean.

I was so busy trying to keep up in class that I didn't really get to talk to any of my friends. Besides, Ms. Williams made it clear that there was no talking during class. By lunchtime, I was ready for a break; I hadn't used my brain so much in months. When Ms. Williams led us out of the classroom to go downstairs, the uniformed cop from this morning was standing outside our door! Had he been there the whole time? When our class went down the stairs, he did too. And then he followed us into the lunchroom and stood just inside the door. He never took his eyes off of me.

I went through the lunch line pretending that I didn't notice him. The food looked terrible, and I felt like everyone was staring at me. I finally picked up a piece of pizza—it was cut into a square, not a triangle like pizza was supposed to be, and the cheese they had used on it smelled like throw-up to me. I sat at the table with my friends and everything seemed normal enough. Amelia gave me a big hug and told me how much she loved my new shirt. Her mom had driven her to school, but she said tomorrow she would be on the bus. I hoped that Arthur wouldn't walk me to my stop again. We talked about Ms. Williams and how awful she was. I was so glad they hadn't noticed the cop standing off to the side. Maybe things weren't so bad. I ate a few saltines and drank some juice.

A boy I'd never seen before leaned over our table. "You know why that cop is in here?" he asked.

"Go away, Richie," Amelia said, rolling her eyes at me.

"Because somebody wants to kill her!" he said, pointing at me. Then he whispered, "Maybe they'll come to school and shoot you, too, that's why the cop is here."

Amelia stood up. "Mrs. Maseda," she yelled over to the teacher who was monitoring the lunchroom.

"Tattletale," the boy said under his breath. As he walked away, he turned and made a gun with his fingers, pointed at me, and said, "Pow, pow." When Mrs. Maseda got to our table, Amelia told her what had happened. I saw her walk over to talk to him.

"We're not supposed to say anything to you about your dad or about the cops at school," Amelia confessed, looking at the cop out of the corner of her eye.

"The principal told us not to," another friend whispered.

"It's okay," I said. "I don't really care."

But I did care. I was still shaking from what Richie had said. I thought about my dad and his face all bandaged up, all those tubes and machines going into his body. *Pow, pow.* Did someone really want to kill me too?

I looked over at the cop on the other side of the room, and he was staring right at me. It must be true, why else would he be here? Why else would Arthur follow my school bus, talk to my teacher? I looked down at the pizza on my tray—the puddles of grease had started to congeal and turn waxy. It made me feel sick just looking at it.

. . .

Two days later, I was running late trying to get ready for school. I couldn't find anything to wear and almost decided on the new silk dress Lauren had given me. "That's not for school," Mom said when I asked if I could wear it. She looked tired and grouchy, so I didn't push it. When I finally found something, I heard Mom yell, "You better hurry up! You're about to miss the bus!" I came out of my room and grabbed my stuff.

"If I miss the bus, the cops can just drive me to school," I pointed out.

"They aren't here to drive you to school," Mom said. "They're here to protect you. You better not miss that bus." She looked angry.

"What's the difference? They're going to drive behind the bus anyhow!" I yelled back at her. "It's embarrassing!"

"Embarrassing?" Mom stopped what she was doing and shot me a look. "Don't you dare say that. Those guys are risking their lives to keep you and your brothers safe."

Mom had as much as admitted it: Richie was right. Someone did want to shoot me.

"You get on that bus," Mom said, turning away from me. "Now!"

I stormed out of the house with an officer trailing behind me. Just like I thought, a cruiser was waiting in the church driveway, and the bus was there too, idling by the side of road. The other cop was up in the bus talking to the driver. When I reached the stairs, he stepped down and headed back to his car without saying a word to me. I climbed on and Mr. Arnold gave me a weak smile. "A little late this morning, huh?" I scowled at him. "Don't you worry about it, sweetheart," he said. "Take a seat."

I didn't know what he was so happy about. Normally, if you were late for the bus, he would leave you. He wasn't the type of driver to honk and wait a minute. I sat down and looked out the window at the brightly colored leaves on the trees. It was already fall; I hadn't even noticed it was happening. Soon it would be Halloween; then the snow would start. I wondered if we would be allowed to go trick-or-treating this year.

The bus went right by Meg's house—no one had been waiting there for the past few days; Mr. Arnold didn't even slow down. I wondered if maybe she was sick or something. It didn't really matter; the few times she had seen me, she just acted like I wasn't there anyhow. I closed my eyes and decided to see if I could hold my breath until we got to Amelia's house. If I could hold my breath that long, something good was going to happen.

chapter 16

JOHN

ONCE the kids and Polly were back home on the Cape, I had even more reason to get well and get out of the hospital. It looked like it was going to be at least three months before the next stage of surgery; the muscle and tissue in my face needed time to heal completely. The jawbone on both sides of my face had been discontinued. I had temporomandibular joints (TMJs) and a piece of my chinbone left—all of this was wired shut to heal. Once the soft tissue had healed, the plan was to insert a steel bar to connect my TMJs to what was left of my chin. The experimental part of the reconstruction would come next. They would hang a micromesh stainless steel net from the steel bar and pack it with osteoblast cells—these are the marrow cells from which bone develops. The hope was that, in time, I would "grow" enough new bone in my face to have a working jaw again. To be able to eat and breathe, at least. Would I be able to talk? The doctors said, "Let's not get ahead of ourselves."

I was facing months before they could go in and start the rebuilding work. But there was no way I could stay in the hospital until Christmas. I had to show them pronto that I could walk, use the bathroom, and feed myself if I wanted to go home.

I'd lost about thirty pounds or so but was building up strength every day—walking the halls with my IV pole, keeping my mind sharp with chess and science fiction books. There were still days when I would get blinding headaches and couldn't seem to keep a thought in my head. I just wanted the pain to stop. These were some kind of injury-related migraines that no medication could touch; they had to pass. When the pain finally went away I felt like I had a new lease on life. There was still discomfort, but it could be managed with meds—nothing like the pain of those headaches.

It was especially hard to be an invalid since I'd spent so long on the force marking my place as a guy who could handle anything physically. I was confident, had done some boxing and enough karate to defend myself, and knew that I could take any call without needing to bring in backup from a big guy like Arthur the Bear or Monty. The sergeants felt the same way about me and sent me out one night to bring in a felon named Danny Mannis—an ex-con and ex–pro boxer on parole from a federal mental prison in St. Louis. A convicted bank robber,

Danny had lost it while doing time and finished his sentence in the mental lockup. Who knows what happened to him in there, but he wasn't a well man, obviously.

Danny was living back in Falmouth and one night tore the locked door off of a Dunkin Donuts (never did figure out why—maybe he was pissed they were closed). Two federal marshals were there to get him but they needed local backup, and I was their guy. The marshals had heard that Danny was bad news—and one look at the door confirmed it. He'd torn it clean off—aluminum metal frame with the dead bolt and everything. He was a formidable physical specimen—a bit taller than me, he'd spent his time in the can running, lifting weights, and doing boxing workouts. He wore a World War II aviator's cap and rode a bicycle when going anywhere in town. Nobody messed with him, with good reason. He was a deadly combination of really crazy and really strong. The marshals wanted nothing to do with him.

When we got to the scene, I explained to Danny why he had to go with them, that he had to let them chain, cuff, and manacle him. "I don't want to have to fight you," I explained. "They don't want to have to fight you either. But if push comes to shove, I will bundle you, and you will have to go with them anyway, so let's do this the way you want to." He went willingly. I don't know if his choice had anything to do with the fact that I was ready to take him on physically, but it doesn't really matter. The job got done, and it got done because I was ready to handle it any way I had to, which is why it was my call and no one else's. I wasn't exactly

Dirty Harry, but not bad. After a few years on the force, karate training plus tactical squad training and good old common sense had turned me from a know-nothing rookie to a very competent officer of the law.

I loved being a cop, but after my shooting I found myself wishing I had applied to the fire department like I wanted to when I was younger. Lord knows I had the opportunities, and I'd thought it through, too, even talked to Polly about it. The pay was the same, and with training I could have worked my way up to paramedic within a year. I was certainly exposed to the same risks on occasion. I'd spent a few calls crawling through houses as they burned, looking for occupants, and even sifting through ashes after fires, looking for victims, then loading them onto stretchers and transporting them. There was one guy who was burned so badly that when we picked up the stretcher, he flew up into the air. We were expecting him to weigh his living weight, which had been reduced drastically in the fire. Most embarrassing to have to reload his corpse and buckle it down.

I spent a lot of time in the hospital thinking about what could have been, how things might have been different. It's hard to believe the old saying that "things happen for a reason" when the things happening to you are god-awful and you just want them to be over with. No matter how I looked at it, I just couldn't wrap my head around the idea that this had happened for some reason that made any sense.

My last week in the hospital was spent with Polly and me

both learning how to care for my wounds and keep me fed and watered. Polly felt okay leaving the kids in Falmouth for the day with Kelly and the guards to come up for a couple of visits. I got the distinct feeling that the only reason the doctors were letting me go home was because of Polly's nursing training, so thank God for that.

Once I was ready to go, my trachea hole would be covered with gauze. I didn't need the respirator anymore; I could breathe fine through my nose. But with what was left of my jaw fused shut with wires, there would be a lot of fluid in my throat that we'd need to remove, so they were giving us a suction machine. They'd been using suction on me in the hospital, but this was a portable device, a small metal box that you plugged in. It had a gauge on it to adjust the amount of suction you needed from the attachment on the end of the tube—kind of like a vacuum cleaner, only smaller. After they showed us how to use it, my favorite nurse on the floor explained that we'd need to do this at least three times a day, and I would need to try to cough up anything I could and suction that out as well.

"I would recommend keeping these pieces of equipment away from the children, as it might scare them," Nurse Kathy pointed out. Polly and I both nodded in agreement. *Might also scare us a little*, I thought, looking at the odd contraption plus all the gauze, ointments, extra tubing, and formula cans they were sending home with us.

Feeding was a whole different process, but equally unpleasant.

Every two to three hours, Polly or I would need to withdraw whatever liquid was in my stomach through the GI tube using a syringe. This was to measure how much residual was there to determine how much I needed for my next feeding. But then, so I didn't remove the enzyme needed for digestion from my stomach, I had to return the contents of what I'd drawn out back in, then add more fresh stuff to level it off. The whole process was pretty bad, and the smell was truly horrible. How Polly could stand it, I don't know. The stuff we had to draw out of my stomach was basically puke, and smelled like it. And then I had to put it back in. It's a wonder I didn't just vomit, but I tried to distract myself by mixing up the can of formula for my next meal and just getting on with it. When it was feeding time, I would hook the container up to my GI tube and sit there watching the fluid go in. When it was gone, I was done. We flushed the GI tube with water to keep it clean, clamped it to keep it from dripping, then used medical tape to secure it off to the side until my next feeding, and that was it. Bon appétit.

I would also need a special bed, since I couldn't lie flat until the trachea hole was healed, so a bed was ordered and shipped to the house from a medical supply store. It was a lounge bed chair that I could sit up in like a hospital bed. With two pillows or so propped under my head, I found that I could breathe just fine.

Dr. Keith came in to see me before my discharge to explain the next steps. I could tell he wasn't entirely comfortable with me leaving the hospital, maybe because I was his pet project and he didn't want me getting more body parts blown off before he could try rebuilding my face. "You need to come back in three days for a checkup. If your health is satisfactory at that point, you can go home. But then you need to be back in three more days for another checkup," he told me. "That's a lot of driving," he added, after a beat, eyeing me. I think he was waiting for me to say that I'd changed my mind and that I'd rather just stay in the hospital. Instead, I wrote on my pad, "Then what?"

"Then you come back in a week. And eventually, when you're stable, you can come in every two weeks for us to check on your progress." He looked down at my file for a second. "If all goes well, we'll do the next surgery on December twenty-sixth," he finally said. "How does that sound?"

"Great," I wrote on my pad. "And Merry Christmas to you too." I was just so happy to be going home, I would have agreed to almost anything.

chapter 17

CYLIN

ONE afternoon when I got home from school, Kelly was sitting at our kitchen table, just like she had never left—like nothing had ever happened. Mom was back in nursing school full time, and with Dad gone, it was hard to do everything in the house by herself, so she'd asked Kelly to come back and help out. Kelly had brought our family pets back with her, too—our cat, Pyewacket, and dog, Tigger. She'd taken them up to Maine with her while we were gone in Boston. I was so glad to see Tigs and Pye that for the first few minutes, I didn't even care that Kelly was back.

My dad's friend Don was there, drinking coffee with another cop named Stoney—his real name was Paul Stone. He and Dad were considered to be two of the most handsome cops on the force—both tall and blond, with classic good looks. Stoney was a bit taller than Dad, about six foot two or so, and had been a football player for Boston University before becoming a cop, and he and Dad both had the same broad shoulders and strong builds. Stoney had left the force and gone to work for the MDC, Metropolitan District Commission, a couple of years before Dad was shot, but he still hung out with all the Falmouth cops, especially Dad, and they played a lot of handball. I noticed that Kelly usually took a little extra time to look nice when he came around.

My brothers and I suspected that Kelly might have a little crush on Stoney, so when I first got home from school that day, I thought for a second maybe she had come over because she'd heard he was going to be there. But it turned out that she was actually moving back in with us for good.

Mom was home too, sorting laundry in the kitchen. She had just gotten home from one of her nursing classes. "We got another basket today, from the Cheese House," she told me, pointing to a huge gift basket on the table. We had been getting a lot of these—local places sending over big baskets and boxes of goodies for us and for the officers guarding us. Every night for dinner we had a covered dish that someone had dropped off. Usually one of the officer's wives would make us a lasagna or a casserole or two, enough for our whole family, visitors, and the guys guarding us outside.

I dug into the basket, bypassing the pretty cellophane-wrapped apples and oranges for the good stuff that I knew was underneath. "Can I have this?" I asked Mom, holding up a giant chocolate bar.

She gave me a look and I just smiled. "Please?" I begged, but she just shook her head. "Okay, how about this?" I held up a bag of some granola mix that had chocolate chips in it. "This is practically health food!"

"Fine," Mom said with a smile. "Not too much. Arthur and Cynthia sent over a whole turkey for dinner and . . ." I was busy opening the granola bag, so it took me a second to notice that mom had stopped talking. When I looked up, she was holding a dark blue shirt, one of my dad's police uniform shirts. It must have been buried in the bottom of the clothes hamper, from before we left, before he was shot.

Mom just stood there for a second looking at the shirt, then she held it to her face. Nobody said anything for the longest time, then she opened the cellar door that led to the washer in the basement and threw the shirt down the stairs. I could see that she was crying. Then she starting yelling. "Damn it, damn it, I can't do this anymore! I'm done!" She went to go down the cellar stairs but ended up sitting on the top step, sobbing. I didn't know what to do, so I just stood there, holding the bag of granola. Eric and Shawn walked into the kitchen from the living room, where they had been watching TV. "What's wrong?" Shawn asked. He looked nervous.

Don went over to Mom and knelt beside her. "It's okay, it's gonna be okay, it's already okay. He's coming home. It's all going to be fine," I heard him telling her.

"What's the matter with Mom?" Eric whispered to Kelly.

"Nothing, just go back into the other room," Kelly said, getting up. She tried to scoot us down the hallway.

"Look, you're scaring the children," I heard Don say quietly.

"Oh, mustn't scare the children!" Mom said. She started laughing in a very fake way, sounding like a crazy lady. "My God, someone only tried to kill their father, and probably wants to kill them. You're telling *me* not to scare them?" she screamed. "Look at you!" She pointed at Don's shoulder holster. "How many guns are in this house right now? In our yard? Don't you tell *me* not to scare them!" She was angrier than I had ever seen her before. She stood and started picking up the clothes she had been sorting and threw them down the stairs in big armfuls.

"Mommy's fine." She looked over at me and said in a singsong voice, "Just hate to do laundry, that's all." I could see tears on her face. She picked up another pile of the clothes she had carefully sorted and hurled them through the cellar doorway. When she had emptied the hamper, she turned and went down the stairs too, slamming the basement door behind her. After a few seconds of silence, Don opened the door and followed her.

"Come on, you guys," Kelly said, motioning us out of the kitchen and into the living room. "Your mom was at school all day, she just needs a break. Give her a minute and she's going to be fine."

And Kelly was right. We went into the other room and I sat with Tigger on my lap and petted her soft, floppy ears while my brothers watched TV. After a while, Mom called us into the kitchen for dinner. She had heated up the turkey and the house smelled like Thanksgiving. Kelly was sitting next to Stoney at the table, blushing. Don and Stoney had pulled out the table extension to make it large enough for all of us to sit and have this feast, and they'd brought in the extra chairs from the den. Mom seemed okay again; you couldn't even tell she had been crying. She fixed some plates of food for the cops who were on duty in the yard; she was smiling and looking like the picture of a perfect mom. No one would have guessed that she had had a meltdown just an hour before.

The next morning, we got ready for school and Kelly made us breakfast. Everything was starting to settle into a pretty regular routine. We were walked to the bus stop by an officer. Two cops followed us to school in a cruiser. An armed officer guarded each of us at school. Then the procedure was reversed on the way home.

One afternoon, Eric went to hang out with the kids at the Zylinskis' house after school. I don't know how he managed to get out of our house and cross the yard without one of the guards seeing him, but he did. When we noticed that he was missing, everyone started to freak out.

"When did you last see your brother?" a cop asked me. I couldn't remember; I'd been watching *Little House on the Prairie.*

"I think he was going over to the Zylinskis'," Shawn finally said, and the cop took off running down our street, holding his gun at his hip with one hand as he ran. A few minutes later, he was back with Eric, who looked like he'd been crying.

"You can't just go off without telling anyone!" Mom yelled at him. I knew Eric had no idea that what he'd done was wrong—none of us really did. Later, when everyone had calmed down, Eric told us how the cop had run into the Zylinskis' yard and grabbed him and yelled, "You must always remain in my eyesight!" We kind of laughed it off, like the guy was a little crazy. No harm done; it was forgotten. Until that night when I was lying in bed, trying to fall asleep. I could hear Mom and Kelly out in the living room, talking to a couple of cops who were visiting. They were discussing how the security would have to change when Dad came home. More guys on duty. A sniper on the roof with a long-range rifle, that kind of thing. I hadn't really thought too much about when all of this would end. Somehow, I had convinced myself that once Dad was able to come home, things would be normal again.

We had all been so caught up in the urgency of Dad's injuries and his "accident" that I almost hadn't thought about the reason behind all of this security. But in the dark, alone, Richie's words that day in the lunchroom came back to haunt me: "Maybe they'll come to school and shoot you, too." Dad's shooting hadn't been an accident. Someone had wanted to *kill* him. I was just starting to understand this. Someone *hated* him. The thought made my chest ache. I just couldn't imagine someone hating my dad that much, wanting to hurt him this way. And now I was starting to see that they hated me, too, and my brothers. They wanted to kill all of us—really kill us. We couldn't go anywhere without the police. To the grocery store, to a friend's house, to school. There was no safe place. *You must always remain in my eyesight.* I wanted to imagine a time when this would be over and we could go back to living the way we used to, but the more I thought about that, the more scared I got. There would be no going back to normal for us. There were only two choices now: live like this, or don't live at all.

chapter 18

JOHN

DON Price, two guards, and Polly and I made the trip back to the Cape with all my new equipment. I was due for checkups every three days in Boston, so although it would be a lot of traveling, it would be worth it just to get home.

Don was cheerful on the trip, talking about how my security detail was the best job going, and everyone in the department wanted to sign up for it. "No traffic or pissed-off tourists to deal with. Time-and-a-half payscale." I had a small pad with me and wrote, "Sounds like my shooting will fatten the wallets of a lot of cops/friends." Polly read it off to him and they both laughed.

I looked out the window, watching the tranquil cranberry bogs pass by. As happy as I was to be going home, I could feel anger welling up inside me as we crossed the Bourne Bridge. I was returning a different man. I couldn't escape it; there were too many reminders. The fact that I couldn't talk. The tube sticking out of my stomach, the hole in my throat. I didn't want to see my face. *Look what they did to me*—that was all I could think when I saw my reflection. *I can't wait to get those bastards.*

The kids were thrilled that I was home, though it meant tighter security for them. A sniper was added to the security detail, and he took up position on top of the house, right over the boys' room. "No way," Polly said. "Tell that guy to get down. If his gun goes off by mistake or something . . ."

I wanted to point out that the chances of him misfiring, of a shot going through the roof and somehow finding one of our sons was pretty slim, but she had been through a lot and it was the least I could do. We asked him to move to the other side of the roof.

Don was right about the guard detail—most of the guys watching the house were friends of mine, and those first few days it probably felt more like a party than a job. Everybody came by to visit and pay respects. One guy, I think it was Paul Carreiro, pointed out that while some cops on the force had been retired early due to physical ailments and injuries—bad backs and the like—no one had ever been shot like I was. "You'll be the first Falmouth cop to retire with a gunshot wound," he told me. The comment hit me hard. I hadn't really thought too much about the future, but now it had become obvious that I couldn't be a cop anymore. Somewhere in the back of my mind, I must have assumed that I would work again. Thirty-six seemed young to retire, for that part of my life to be over, but it was.

Friends kept things light; no one mentioned the investigation when I first got home. I didn't realize how careful everyone was being around me until somebody slipped up and mentioned that Chief Ferreira had filed for early retirement due to some heart condition (news to me). He'd put in his paperwork the week after my shooting and would be gone by the end of the year. Clearly he wanted out, and pronto.

"Polly sure ripped him a new one when he came by here," Rick Smith said, and several fellow officers clinked beer cans in agreement. "Good riddance," someone said.

I wrote Rick a note: "He was here?"

"Polly didn't tell you?" he asked. "He was here all right, and he probably won't ever be back. I don't know what she said to him, but we could hear her yelling all the way out the driveway."

"John, he came out of your house so red, he didn't say another word. Just got in his cruiser and took off," Paul Carreiro added.

I would excuse myself every couple of hours to go into our back bedroom and use the suction machine, with Polly's help. The machine was a little loud, but so far the kids hadn't really noticed it. We kept it covered with a towel on the floor on the other side of the bed, out of sight. That afternoon, when Polly was helping me use the suction, I wrote her a note, asking her about the chief's visit. "Chief F. came by? When? What happened?"

"I didn't want to tell you when you were in the hospital," Polly started, "but yeah, he came by one afternoon, after I brought the kids home. Came in here telling me that he knew just how I felt, because he'd had a car go up in flames in his driveway years ago, and he knew it was Meyer who did it." Polly stopped for a second and focused on the gauze and tape she was putting back over my trachea hole. "I told him that if he had the balls to suggest that having a car burn in your driveway is anything like having your husband get his face shot off, that he better goddamn rethink things," she said.

I could tell she was getting mad. "And I told him what I thought of how he's running that police department, and your investigation. I don't remember what else I said." She looked like she was going to cry. "I'm sorry, but that man just made me so mad! How dare he come by here with that sob story, with you still in the hospital. I mean, who does he think he is? What a bastard."

If I could have smiled, I would have. I was so proud of her for standing up to him. We'd all been cowards for so long, doing what we were told, not writing tickets to certain connected people, backing down to Meyer and his city contracts, his connections, his threats. I was glad to see my wife fight back. Maybe I wasn't so alone in this after all.

The local papers and even the Boston papers had been having a heyday with my story; a week didn't go by without an update. An article had run in the local paper when Polly and the kids got home, announcing a twenty-thousand-dollar reward for any information about my shooting. So far a sixteen-man investigation unit made up of state and local cops hadn't turned up any leads—no one wanted to talk, and without any ballistic evidence, they had nothing legal to go on except for my word that Meyer wanted me dead.

The two detectives assigned to my case stopped by the house shortly after I got back from the hospital. Detective Sergeant Curt Reaves and Detective Charles Dimatto. I knew both of these guys, though not that well. They had no luck tracking down Meyer's missing wife, Brenda. Also didn't have a lot of luck finding the guy who shot Jeff Flanagan with a shotgun then dumped his body in the bogs across from the Meyer compound. So I wasn't expecting too much.

"We've been questioning owners of registered white VWs; so far nothing," Reaves told me. The night I was shot, I'd seen a white VW turning into Pinecrest Beach Drive. The white VW must have been a little bit ahead of me on the road that night, and my theory is that the shooters thought that VW Bug was mine. They had probably planned to pull out into the road in front of me, block my car, and then shoot me good while my car was blocked and I couldn't get away. So when this car comes down the road at just about the right time, looking like mine, they almost pull out in front of that one. But the guy in the white VW goes to turn on Pinecrest Beach instead—they realize it's the wrong car, so they back down. Then here I come down the street, but my car is now green, thanks to Polly's and the kids' paint job that afternoon. They let me drive by—mistaken identity number two—then realize it's me and follow. They have to pull up alongside me to shoot, and their aim isn't as good. By this time, the guy in the white VW is probably long gone, down Pinecrest and on his way to wherever.

The detectives want to talk to this guy in the white VW and see if he remembers anything about the blue car, the people in it. I want to talk to this guy because I want to shake his hand. If they did mistake his car for mine and it bought me some time, then I owed him my life.

The detectives keep asking me over and over again what I remember about the blue car, but my memory of the night is full of holes. "How would you feel about undergoing hypnosis?" Dimatto asks me. "Might help you to remember something—a plate number or something distinctive about the car." I'm a cop, so I'm pretty good at eyeing someone's plates and remembering the numbers. If they get the plate numbers out of me under hypnosis, then we've got a lead. I'm game, though I figure the whole hypnosis thing is just treading water—to help them look like they're doing something on my case when really they're just wasting time. I'm pretty sure I know who wanted me dead, but these two guys aren't about to go there.

From what I'm told, Meyer's lawyered up and won't talk to anybody, and without a motive, the detectives feel like they can't question him. I was about to go to court to testify against his brother, James Meyer, on a pretty serious charge. Guess that's not a direct enough motive for them. "But we're interviewing everyone you've arrested in the past few months," Reaves tells me.

"There are a lot," Dimatto adds with a grin. "You were a pretty busy guy, Busby."

I think, *Just doing my job.* But these guys wouldn't get that. They're too busy covering their own asses to actually get shit done in this town. When they leave, I'm so angry I start pacing the house. It's time for the kids to come home from school, and I should be thrilled to see them, but these bastards have got me so worked up I can't see straight.

Polly tried to calm me down. "Just sit for a minute. It's time to do a feeding, so let's get that done before the kids get off the bus." She knew me and knew just what I was thinking. I knew I was going to have to take care of this myself, but seeing the sorry state of this noninvestigation just pissed me off. While she helped me draw the fluid out through my GI tube, she tried to talk some sense into me. "You just got home, you're with your family now, please, please, please don't do anything stupid. Let's just get you better; that's your focus right now."

But watching her mix the formula for my next meal made me seethe. *Look what they've done to me. Just look at what they've done to me.*

chapter 19

CYLIN

EVEN though I knew I wasn't supposed to talk to my friends about Dad coming home, I couldn't help myself. "My dad got home yesterday," I told Amelia the next morning on the bus.

"I know," Amelia said. "My mom read it in the newspaper."

We were both quiet for a second, then Amelia added, "My mom said that it's really sad that they shot him in the face because he used to be so handsome."

I didn't know what to say to that. "What does he look like now?" Amelia asked. When I didn't say anything back, she quickly added, "I mean, the principal said we're not supposed to talk to you about your dad at school, but we're on the bus, so maybe we can talk about it here?" Amelia's blue eyes were all sparkly and narrow the way they got when she was doing something bad. But I liked her reasoning, and I was happy to have a friend to talk to about what was going on.

"He looks the same. We can't see his face because the bottom part is mostly covered in bandages. And he already has a beard on the part you can see, so you can't really tell much," I explained.

"But he can't talk, right?" she asked.

I shook my head. "He writes everything down. But he's going to have an operation to fix that, right after Christmas. Then he's going to be fine." I knew this wasn't exactly true, but I hoped that Amelia would go home and tell her mom so maybe she would still think he was handsome.

As if reading my thoughts, Amelia whispered, "I won't tell anybody that we talked about your dad, okay?" She slipped her hand into mine and we rode the rest of the way to school holding hands. I was worried that someone on the bus might see us and make fun, but Amelia never really cared about stuff like that anyhow.

Later that day, I saw Meg in line at lunch. She used to always sit with me and Amelia on the bus last year, but now I almost never see her. I grabbed a tray and stood behind her in the long lunch line even though I was just getting a juice and could have cut to the front. I hadn't talked to her since we'd gotten back from Boston. "Hey, how come you never ride the bus anymore?" I asked her.

"Because you're on it," she said. "So my mom drives me now."

That didn't make any sense. Meg couldn't be mad at me; I hadn't seen her in months. "What do you mean, because I'm on it?" I asked her. She turned to face me and jutted out one hip, the way she liked to when she was feeling cocky. I thought she was about to remind me, yet again, that she was six months older than me—she liked to do that when she was mad at me and wanted me to feel babyish. "Look, I'm not allowed to talk to you. My mom said."

"Why aren't you allowed to talk to me?" I could hear my voice going up high like I was about to cry.

"You know why," she leaned in and said in a mean whisper. Then she turned and went to the cash register, skipping in front of a couple of kids in front of us.

Had I done something over the summer to make her mad? There was a time last year, in third grade, when Amelia and I had a playdate and didn't invite her and then she cried about it. But that was a long time ago, and I didn't remember doing anything like that since then. Did it have something to do with Dad's shooting? I couldn't think of why her mom would tell her not to talk to me because of my dad, though.

After school, when my brothers and I got home, Dad was there with a bunch of his cop buddies all sitting at the kitchen table. Everyone was drinking beer except for Dad. Mom was at nursing school, and Kelly was out somewhere. I looked at Dad sitting with his friends. He was thin, really thin. His face was still swollen and distorted but mostly covered; each cheek had a large square of white gauze taped down over it. A couple of months ago, if I had come home and found Dad hanging out with his friends, I probably would have climbed up into his lap for a minute, just long enough to tell him about my day at school. But now that he had that tube sticking out of his stomach, I didn't think I could sit on his lap even if I wanted to. I didn't like getting too close to Dad anymore. But not because of the stomach tube or even how his face looked. It was the hole in his throat that really bothered me. He kept it covered with a big bandage, but you could still tell it was there, and when he had to cough up stuff, it sounded disgusting.

"Here are the Busby men!" Don Price said, and clapped Eric hard on the back. Eric gave him a shy smile, but I could tell he was glad to be called a man. "We're going to take you boys out and teach you how to shoot, how does that sound?" he asked Eric and Shawn. "Get you some gun training."

I didn't wait to hear their response; instead I went to the other side of the house to peek in my parents' room. I wanted to check out all the medical stuff they had brought home for Dad. The room was dark; they kept the shutters closed all day so that when Dad needed to use his medical equipment, his friends and the guards out in the yard wouldn't be able to see in. I turned on a light next to the bed and it cast a warm glow over the room. Dad had been sleeping in a special hospital bed that was set up next to their regular bed. It could be moved up and down with a little remote control that was attached with a wire. I sat on the bed and used the little remote to make it move up and down a few times. Maybe when Dad doesn't need this bed anymore, I can have it, I thought. But I'd have to put in dibs before my brothers. I made a mental note to tell my mom when she got home that I wanted the bed. Then I noticed a brown stain on the white sheets next to where I was sitting. I scratched at it with my nail, but it stayed. It didn't look like blood; it was really dark and brown. Then I noticed some other stains on the bed and I jumped up quick. What were they? Maybe I didn't want the bed after all.

Over on the floor by Mom's side of the bed was something under an old blue beach towel. It was a red metal box with what looked like a gas gauge on the front. A plastic tube ran out of one side of it, and another tube ran out of the other side. I couldn't figure out how to turn it on, so I left it alone.

On the bedside table were lots of big syringes and more long rubber tubes. I knew that Dad was using these to eat with, but I didn't quite understand how. There was a can of something sitting there too. I smelled it, but it was empty and just smelled like wheat bread or something floury. Beside that on the bed stand was a picture of my parents when they got married. My mom looked so young, her dark hair brushed up in a fancy style, her petite figure draped in a fashionable white mini-dress, and a tiny hat perched on her head. Dad was wearing a suit and looked the same way that Shawn looked when he got really nervous—wide-eyed and serious. He was still handsome though, you could tell. I picked up a white plastic bracelet that was sitting on the table. It said "BUSBY, JOHN" and "O+" in black letters. I slipped it over my wrist, but it was so big I could push it all the way up to my shoulder.

"There you are, honey," Mom said, coming into the room.

"Hey," I said quietly. I wondered if she was going to be mad at me for looking at Dad's stuff.

"Want to help me make a salad for dinner? A bunch of the guys are going to stay."

"Sure." I took off my dad's wristband and put it back down where I had found it. "Mom?"

She carefully took off the small leather pouch that she wore as a holster for her gun. "What?" she said, changing out of her school outfit and into more casual jeans.

"Meg doesn't ride the bus to school anymore."

"Well, who do you sit with?" Mom asked, pulling a T-shirt over her head.

"Amelia."

"That's good, I always liked her," Mom said. I could tell she wasn't really listening. She picked up a brush and quickly ran it through her hair, looking in the mirror behind the door.

"Mom, Meg says that she's not allowed to ride the bus because I'm on it. And she's not allowed to talk to me, either. Her mom said so."

Mom stopped what she was doing and put the brush down. "What?"

"That's what she said. She can't ride the bus with me or talk to me. Is it because of Dad?"

"Her mother said that?" Mom sounded angry.

She opened the bedroom door to go back out, then closed it

again. "Guess what? You're not allowed to talk to Meg anymore, and you can tell her that I said that next time you see her."

"Okay," I said. But I knew I wasn't about to tell Meg anything ever again.

"Come on, let's go make the salad," Mom said.

I walked around the bed and came over to where she was, and she put her arms around me. "I would fix this if I could, you know that, right?" she said, holding me tightly. "I'm so sorry."

I looked up at her and felt my throat tighten. I didn't want to cry, especially with Dad's friends over. "Don't tell your dad what Meg's mom said, okay?" she told me.

"I won't," I promised her. As we left the bedroom, I was careful to close the door tightly behind me.

chapter 20

JOHN

THE kids were becoming targets at school—Eric and Shawn were getting harassed for special treatment, or what the other kids perceived as special treatment. This, at least, is what the principal explained to us when he called us in for a conference. Shawn had gotten into a fight with one kid in his class. Seems that I'd arrested this kid's father at some point for something, most likely DUI. When the guy was reading about my shooting in the paper, his kid overheard him saying that I had gotten what I deserved. The kid passed this tidbit on to Shawn at school, and next thing he knew, Shawn jumped his sorry ass and started beating the shit out of him. Probably would have killed the kid if they both hadn't fallen to the floor, Shawn catching his head on a desk as he went down.

"The other students see that Eric and Shawn are treated differently by the teachers and the staff," the principal explained.

Since when is having a cop take you to school to keep someone from killing you "special treatment"? I didn't understand that, and wrote him a note telling him so. On the way home, I got an earful from Polly—the cops who were guarding me that day and sitting in the front seat were probably very uncomfortable with the one-sided conversation.

"I know you're angry, but you have to get it under control. You think the kids can't tell that you're mad all the time? Look at them, look at what is happening to our family." I wished I could make her feel better, but the truth was that I was angry and planned to stay angry until I got back at the bastards who did this to me. I just didn't see any way around it. But it killed me to know that my boys were feeding on my hatred and taking it out on kids at school and vice versa.

After a couple of weeks at home, I got more relaxed about my physical state and didn't run off to the bedroom to put food in my GI tube. When the kids were at school I'd sometimes do it right at the kitchen table, like a regular meal, with the guys sitting there.

"What the hell is in this stuff?" Rick asked at one point, picking up a can of my meal replacement formula and checking its ingredients. He smelled it. "Man, how do you eat that?" he joked.

"Easy," I wrote on my pad. "I just open the can and pour it in my tube like this." This was a reference to an incident involving Don Price, a gruesome vehicle fatality, and a doughnut—it was a story we still liked to tease Don about. I knew Rick would get the joke, and he did. "Very funny, Buzz." He grinned as he passed the note over to Don.

The incident in question happened one night when Rick Smith was still a RAC, summer special, and he had asked to ride with me on the night duty after his shift ended. Most of the summer specials either wanted to be full-time cops or at least wanted to see some of the action that we full-timers got. So I said yes, and that night we rode in Oscar 8 in East Falmouth, working backup. We were over in Hatchville on a report of a prowler when a call came in about a motor vehicle accident. I was the EMT officer on duty that night, so the accident took precedence over the prowler. We headed over to the scene, a narrow two-lane road called Wild Harbor Road that ran straight for over a quarter mile, then took a quick, hard curve to the left. Right at the corner of the curve was a utility pole, and that's where we found a Corvette. The car was completely demolished—the passenger side crushed into the pole like an accordion.

I stopped thirty feet away because I could see power lines on the road. I put on both spots and headlights, flashing and blues too. I told Rick to start spreading flares along the road near the lines. I radioed in what I'd observed and grabbed my EMT case. I approached the vehicle, shined my flashlight in, and saw nobody. Then I saw two stumps of legs in the crumpled passenger compartment. They'd been torn off just below the knees. So whoever they belonged to should've been down the road a bit—ejected through the windshield and in need of major medical attention.

As Rick set the flares out, I proceeded slowly through the light brush alongside the road, looking for our accident victim. I found a young male facedown, forty or fifty feet from the wreck. I felt at his neck for a pulse and noticed there was a huge puddle of blood where his face should have been. No pulse. I reached down his chest to feel for a heartbeat and my hand went right inside him. No heartbeat. This guy was dead three ways from Tuesday—legs torn off, face smashed, chest wide open.

I returned to the cruiser to radio for sergeant's response to a 10-34 fatality. As I'm walking back to the victim, I noticed something sparking about a foot off the ground and just to the side of him. It was a high voltage power line and I'd somehow crossed it twice without touching it. I got some flares to mark its location and noticed it was moving in an arching dance, winding slowly down and back. Maybe I didn't cross it, maybe I did. Turns out that it has four thousand volts running through it, a near miss on my part.

About this time another cruiser showed up, driven by one of our auxiliary cops, a guy named Bobby. I left Rick at the scene and went with Bobby to find the rest of the car scattered down Wild Harbor Road. We found the gas tank and a seat and another young man over two hundred feet from the pole. He had lots of cuts and scrapes but no major damage visible, not even a broken bone. He was stunned and incoherent, probably from head trauma. I had Bobby call for the ambulance and power company and managed to keep the driver calm until the ambulance could get through to take him to the ER.

We found the engine of the Corvette about three hundred and eighty feet from the pole—an accident scene over a football field in length. Meanwhile this four-thousand-volt line had settled on the dead young man. It's snapping and crackling and we're waiting for the power company to turn it off. The sergeant sent for coffee and doughnuts, which arrived long before the power company. We radioed in again and were told they had had to rouse their emergency guy to come out, and they said he was on his way. So Rick, Bobby, Sarge, and I passed the time just standing across the road, making sure the flares were up and keeping any passing cars from coming too close to the scene. We were having our coffee, trying not to notice as the air filled with the smell of a body that's on fire, because by now the kid's clothes were in flames and there was nothing we could do about it until the power company got there. A car coming from the other direction slowed down to look at the scene, then pulled over to us. A woman got out, and we could tell she was mad as hell. "How can you do that?" she asked Don.

"How can I do what?" Don asked her.

"How can you stand there and eat doughnuts while that person is on fire over there!" she yelled at him.

"Well, I just open my mouth and take a bite like this, ma'am," he said, and took a big bite of doughnut followed by a long swallow of coffee. She marched back to her car, no doubt full of contempt for these coldhearted, disrespectful, bastard policemen. There really wasn't anything we could do until the power was cut. By the time it was, the guy's backside had been turned into charred ashes, his pants were burned, and a large portion of his rump was cooked. Talk about overkill—it was definitely this young man's time to die.

We got information from the driver about who the victim was and where he'd been staying, not too much farther up Wild Harbor Road. The victim was Catholic, so we got a priest from St. Patrick's up, gave him some coffee and doughnuts, and had him accompany us to the victim's residence. The families of both boys, from New York, were staying on the Cape for vacation. The sergeant handled the ceremonies of introducing the good father, who broke the news. One family so crushed, one so elated, over the outcome of the same accident.

After I investigated the scene thoroughly, I charged the driver with speeding and reckless driving. Don't know exactly how fast he was going, but from the looks of things, and how far he was thrown from the wreck, it was way too fast. In court on the stand, the kid testified that he'd since purchased another Corvette because he "liked" them. The judge found him guilty, took his license, and fined him. I don't know if the two families are still on friendly terms, but for a couple of feet the story could have been reversed, with the driver torn to pieces and the passenger sliding to a stop down the road with just bumps and bruises.

Ever since then, we'd hassle Don when we got the chance about the irate citizen and his matter-of-fact doughnut-eating answer. I guess the joking was probably our way of dealing—of processing what we had seen and had to clean up that night. But jokes aside, this was one fatality that haunted me for a long time. One of the firemen who came to clear the scene that night asked me if I was going to early Mass the next morning to thank God. "You walked over that wire," he pointed out. "That's four thousand volts. You should be dead right now." I told him if the sarge would let me off early, I'd be there when the doors opened. I tried not to think too much about it—fate, karma, whatever was at work that night. It was his time to die, my time to live. I put it out of my mind, stopped by the church on my way home, and called it a night. Amen.

chapter 21

CYLIN

AS that fall slowly became winter, it was clear that school this year would be very different for all of us. Eric got a black eye from fighting some guys in gym class. "I'll kill that dick if he ever comes near me again," he told Shawn after school. And Shawn said he would help. "I'll hold him down and we'll beat the shit out of him."

Shawn had a concussion two weeks earlier from a fight he had been in at school and had to go to the emergency room. I'd started to hear rumors in the elementary school about my brothers: They got into fights all the time. They were bad. Shawn was crazy. Eric was about to be moved into the "special" class. I didn't understand how they could have gone from being really good students and good kids to being bad practically overnight, but it had happened. Now they liked to swear all the time and go shooting with Dad's cop friends. They had been to the firing range with Dad and Don Price and had learned how to use guns. Shawn told me that it was really loud, but Eric didn't say anything about it. "Eric's a pretty good shot," Shawn told me after one of their practice sessions. "But I flinch too much." He must have heard that from one of the cops, because the way he said it, it didn't even sound like him talking.

. . .

One Monday morning at school, everyone in my class was talking about Cathy's slumber party. I knew Cathy pretty well, and I would have said we were friends, so I was surprised that she had a slumber party over the weekend and hadn't invited me, especially when it sounded like every other girl in our class had been there.

At recess, I sat by her on the swings. I could tell she was as uncomfortable as I was about things. "Was it your birthday over the weekend?" I finally asked.

"Yes," she said, and looked down at her sneakers. She dragged her heels back and forth through the sandy dirt. "Look, I wanted to invite you, but my mom said that you couldn't come anyhow, so I didn't."

"That's okay," I told her. "But I could have come, just so you know."

"You could have?" Cathy looked over at me, surprised. "My mom said she didn't want a police car sitting in our driveway all night. And then Dad said the other girls' parents wouldn't let them come if we had you over, so . . ."

"Oh, right," I said. "Yeah, don't worry about it."

"It wasn't anything special anyway," Cathy said, then added in a whisper, "and don't worry, I didn't let anyone talk about you."

• • •

After recess, I sat at my desk and took out my hairbrush to pull my hair back into a ponytail. The brush was grabbed out of my hands by someone standing behind me, and when I spun around, I saw that it was my teacher, Ms. Williams.

"No hair brushing in my class," she snapped at me, then she marched up to her desk and slammed the brush into a drawer. "I just want to remind all of you that you are not allowed to have any personal objects in this classroom. I told you the rules of my class when school started."

Cathy raised her hand, then said, "But Cylin wasn't here when school started, so she didn't know."

"The fact that she wasn't here is her fault. No one gets any special treatment in my class."

After school was over for the day, I went up to Ms. Williams's desk. "Can I have my brush back now?"

"No, you cannot." She didn't even look up from the papers she was grading.

"When can I get it back?" I asked her.

"You don't get it back," Ms. Williams mocked me, talking in a high, singsong voice.

The brush was a special one that Mom had given me. It was a travel brush that folded up on itself. I really wanted it back. I sat on the bus trying hard not to cry, but when I finally got home, I ran into my room and burst into tears. Kelly asked me what was wrong. When I told her, she said it wasn't a big deal. "Isn't she that teacher Shawn had a few years ago? Didn't he say she was really mean?" She handed me a tissue. "You just can't let her get to you. In fact, if you act like you don't care, that will really bother her."

I didn't mention being left out of the slumber party. Kelly wouldn't have understood, and I didn't want to make Mom mad at another one of my friends.

By the time Mom got home, I was feeling better. But I heard Kelly tell her the story about Ms. Williams as they were fixing dinner for everyone. "What?" Mom yelled. "That bitch, she's not getting away with it this time. She made Shawn's life hell when he was in her class."

The next morning, Mom drove me to school with a police cruiser following closely behind us. We were a little bit late when we got there, and I thought she was going to take me straight to Ms. Williams's classroom, but instead we went to the principal's office. "You wait out here," Mom told me, and I sat in the outer office by the school secretary. I could hear my mom talking to the principal, and when she came out, she still looked mad. The principal came with her.

"Let's go," Mom said, and took my hand and held it hard. We followed the principal upstairs to Ms. Williams's classroom. He knocked on the door, and when Ms. Williams came out, he said,

"I need a quick word with you." Then he turned to me. "Cylin, go clean out your desk."

I went into the classroom and everyone stared at me. I opened my desk and there, on top of all my books, was my red plastic hairbrush. She had put it back for me, even folded it up the way it was supposed to be. I grabbed my stuff and walked out without talking to anyone. When I came out to the hallway, Ms. Williams went back into the room and closed the door behind her, and the principal led Mom and me down the hall. "You'll be in Ms. Campbell's classroom now. It's an open classroom, with grades two through four. Everyone learns at their own pace. It's sort of an experiment; we think you'll like it."

When we reached the new classroom, I took a peek inside. There were no desks. Instead, kids were sitting in small groups on the floor. Some were reading, others were doing math flash cards or art.

"Hi," a lady with crazy curly hair said as she came over to the door. She was small, like my mom, and wore a printed hippy shirt and jeans. None of the other teachers at school wore jeans. "I'm Joyce." She shook Mom's hand.

Mom gave her a weak smile. "This is Cylin," she said, putting her hands on my shoulders.

"Well, come on in, Cylin!" she said to me cheerfully. "She's going to be fine here; you don't have anything to worry about," I heard her say to Mom.

I didn't know where to put my stuff, since there weren't any desks. But Ms. Campbell showed me my "cubby," which was like a wooden locker, and had me put my stuff in there. I didn't know most of the kids there; I hardly knew that this class even existed. But I did know that by lunchtime everyone at school was going to be talking about how my mom had come and pulled me out of Ms. Williams's classroom.

My family had been trying so hard to pretend that everything was normal, that we were all fine. But now there was no hiding the fact that things were not normal, even at school. My brothers were failing out of their classes, swearing and punching kids every day, and I was suddenly in a special class with no desks and weird kids. I didn't want to be special, but maybe I needed to be. I joined the circle of kids reading on a colored rug, and a pretty redheaded girl shared her book with me.

"You're going to have a really good time in my class, I promise," Ms. Campbell said as she sat down beside me. Why was she being so nice to me? She didn't even know me. Suddenly, tears filled my eyes, and before I could stop myself, I was sobbing. "It's okay to be sad; you can be sad here whenever you want. You don't have to be brave." Ms. Campbell wrapped her arms around me and told the other kids to go on reading. "You're going to be okay, Cylin." She put her hands on my shoulders and gave me a real smile. "You're going to be okay." I hadn't realized how much I needed someone to tell me that until she said it.

chapter 22

JOHN

ONCE my trachea hole started to heal up, I found that I could put my fingers over the gauze on my throat, keep the air in, and actually try to talk a little bit. "Talk" is a strong word—I could make some noises that no one understood as language. Portions of my tongue had been pretty badly damaged in the shooting—it was almost severed—but the surgeons were able to remove the damaged part (about an inch) and reattach it. This had healed up, but since my jaw was wired shut, I was still on written correspondence.

Another big development was that a couple of months after I got home, my doctors decided that I could have the GI tube removed and start feeding myself through my throat. This would require a liquid diet that would be injected down my throat using a large-capacity syringe with a six-inch-long rubber tube attached. I would suck up the food in the syringe, then insert the long rubber tube into my wired-shut mouth and push it far back to where my throat started (trying hard not to gag myself), push slowly on the plunger, and inject the food that way. The process was long, tedious, and a real pain in the ass, but I was ready to have the tube removed from my stomach, and I knew that I could eventually move myself up to real blended foods and not just meal-replacement drinks. Hovering at about twenty to thirty pounds under my usual weight, I was ready to eat something real again, even if I couldn't taste it.

I went into Mass General to have the procedure done, and it was no big deal. GI tube out, some minor stomach cramping, and a couple of stitches, and I was all closed up. So now I had no trachea hole, no stomach hole. That was starting to feel pretty good; I was seeing some progress.

The first day on blended food, I whipped myself up a milkshake with the works: ice cream, banana, and chocolate syrup— all in the blender. The process of using the syringe took forever, and I actually found myself missing the convenience of a GI tube that you could just empty stuff into. Another problem was that I had lost the ability to tell when I was full, so I managed to get a whole milkshake in and then started to feel seriously ill.

When your face is wired shut, throwing up is not only uncomfortable, it's impossible—and somewhat life threatening. But I was trying to do it, very unsuccessfully. I had to keep swallowing down the stuff that was coming up my throat, and I knew I couldn't do it for long, so Polly took me to the hospital. I got a shot of Compazine—an antinausea drug that worked fast. I felt better in minutes, great after half an hour, and they let us go home. When we reached the house, I noticed that the guards outside had changed shifts. There was a guy with dark hair who I didn't recognize. He introduced himself to me, told me he was a summer special, now full time. The name still didn't ring a bell. Neither did the face.

We went inside and I was feeling full of energy. Usually I'd be exhausted by a trip to the hospital, but I was twitching all over. I tried to tell myself it was from having real food for a change. Too much energy, first real chow in months. Dave Cusolito heard about my trip to the hospital and stopped by to see how I was doing and if I wanted to play some chess; I didn't. He asked if he could come over later to watch the Bruins game. Sure, sure, I told him. But right now, I just couldn't sit still.

I looked out the window at the guys in the yard. There was something about that dark-haired cop I didn't like. He gave me a bad feeling. What was it about this guy? I didn't know him. He was a new cop. That's what it was. My mind was racing, like I'd had too much caffeine. I watched the guy through the window, and I started to have a bad feeling, a very bad feeling. What if Meyer hired him to infiltrate the police department, then get on duty guarding my house? He could kill Polly, the kids, and me. Make it look like an accident.

I was wearing my shoulder holster, so I took my gun out and checked to see that it was loaded. I cocked the hammer. *I'm ready for you bastards,* I thought. I started pacing the carpet in the living room. *Come on in, just try it.* I could feel the sweat running down my face. What was wrong with me? I had to try to keep it together. I felt like I was losing my mind.

I looked out at him again and he was sitting in the car, talking with the other guard. Maybe I was wrong; he looked like a good guy. But then I started pacing again. He's probably just checking out the house today, and he'll set it on fire when we're asleep tonight. Or he's waiting for my next trip to Boston so he can kill my family. Insane thoughts were racing around in my head.

"What are you doing?" Polly asked me, and I spun around, my gun pointed at her. "John, what's wrong?" She looked terrified.

I wrote her a scrambled note: "I don't know, feel funny. I don't trust new guy outside."

"He's okay, Don would never have let him on this detail if he didn't check out. You know that," she tried to reassure me. "Put your gun back, no one is threatening you."

I gently uncocked the hammer and laid the gun down on a table by the couch. "We need to do your suction; you can hardly breathe," Polly pointed out.

When she left the room, I picked up my gun again and resumed pacing. She came back in with the syringe and asked me to sit down.

"Can't sit, I have to get out of here," I wrote to her. I felt like something was crawling under my skin.

"Oh God," she said, looking scared. "You're having an anxiety attack—a bad reaction to the antinausea medication they gave you. We have to get you back to the hospital." Then she went to the door and motioned to the guys outside. "I need a guard to drive us back to the hospital. He's having a really bad reaction to the Compazine."

So I was loaded back into the car and had to be convinced that it was going to be okay, that I could put my gun away. "Trust me," Polly said. "It's the medication they gave you; you're going to be fine." But the whole drive to the hospital, I couldn't stop my legs from twitching, my hands from shaking. I was looking for that blue car, just knew I was going to see it. Thinking, *He's coming to finish me off.* When we got to the hospital, they quickly gave me a shot of something to calm me down.

"This happens to a lot of folks," the doctor explained as soon as the drugs took effect. "There's something in Compazine that causes extreme anxiety in some patients." Everything around me was slowing down again to a normal speed, and my heart stopped racing. The doctor got very close to my face and spoke loudly. "John, remember the name of this drug so that if anyone gives it to you again, they can also administer some Benedryl to help keep your anxiety down, okay?" I wanted to write him a note to tell him that just because I couldn't talk didn't mean I couldn't hear. Then I realized he was probably talking loud because, suddenly, I was completely out of it. I could hardly keep my eyes open on the ride home. Whatever they gave me to calm me down sure did the trick. I think I slept for the rest of the day. So much for the first day back on real food.

I hadn't talked to the detectives who had been assigned to my case in a while, but I heard from my buddies that they were slowly working their way through interviewing everyone I'd arrested over the past twelve months, looking for a motive. So they said, anyhow. If that was true, if they were doing their jobs, I knew they'd eventually get to the night I arrested Paul Cena—Meyer's illegitimate son—and that should raise some red flags. And the charges I filed against Raymond's brother, James Meyer—assault and battery against a police officer with a deadly weapon. Our court date had been set for about two weeks after the day I'd been shot and had to be postponed while I was in the hospital. It would have been very convenient for James Meyer if I hadn't survived—his case, and it was a serious one, probably would have been dismissed due to lack of evidence. Looked like a motive to me. But I still wasn't holding my breath waiting for the detectives. I was becoming more convinced that my family would be safe only after I took matters into my own hands.

Meanwhile, the town had been spending a fortune protecting my family and me around the clock. Until the police could lock someone up for my attempted murder, they needed to protect us from this person or persons. It had been a new part of our police contract with the town, and we had just recently accepted it. I actually laughed at this clause when I read it, thinking, *I don't need anyone to protect me. If someone fucks with me, I will blow his ass away.* Turns out that I was the first cop on the force to need the new protection clause—and I wasn't laughing anymore.

There had been some rumblings in the department from the top guys and town officials. With my multiple surgeries, lengthy hospital stays, and twenty-four-hour security detail, I was turning into the real-life "Six Million Dollar Man," without Steve Austin's special abilities. You would think this would light a fire under the detectives to get the case solved a little faster. But instead it led them to another avenue altogether.

One day, a detective came by to talk to Polly. He had some delicate questions to ask. Before my shooting, had she been having an affair? Was there anyone else in her life, anyone that she was romantically involved with? Polly tried to keep most of this interview from me, but she was so irate afterward that some of it came out. Basically the insinuation was that perhaps she had hired someone to pop me. Or that her jealous lover tried to kill me, something like that. I could see where they were going with this. If it's personal, and not related to police business, then the police department doesn't need to pick up the tab, right? But they couldn't be more wrong—I knew it and Polly knew it. Everybody on the force knew it too, especially the detectives. My shooting was work related, and that was the bottom line.

We had a lot of other folks asking us questions too, more pressing questions—these came from the reporters at the local and Boston papers, and the local TV news guys. There was one reporter who wouldn't let the story go, who came by on a regular basis to talk to me. It was equal parts horrifying and amazing to her that people were seemingly allowed to get away with murder and attempted murder right in a beautiful little town like Falmouth. She asked me once how I felt—really felt—about the case. I didn't want to give her any information that would come back to haunt me, or that Meyer and his cronies could read and laugh about. But the answer was that I felt pissed off, and this was pretty much all the time. I probably should have been feeling happy to be alive, blessed to still be with my family, glad that I didn't have brain damage, all of the above. Instead, I was just angry. I couldn't wait to get back at the people who had caused me so much pain and misery. I didn't realize until I got home from the hospital how poorly the investigation was going. I knew it was going to be mishandled, but this was just plain embarrassing. I also quickly realized that the guys protecting me from Meyer were also protecting Meyer from me. I wasn't able to acquire any new weapons; even if I wanted to use my police-issued guns to avenge myself, I wasn't able to sneak out. I was, in effect, under house arrest. Confined and accompanied wherever I went.

The only way out of this mess that I could see was leaving town. I would have to move my family somewhere safe first, to get away from all this surveillance and the guards. By then I would be healthy and strong and able to arm myself with an untraceable weapon. I had walked the trails through the woods to the dump entrance and knew right where I could shoot from and leave without being seen. I would learn Meyer's schedule, just like he had learned mine, and then I would be there at just the right time. Every night, when I closed my eyes, I would walk that trail in my mind. I knew every inch of it. Where I would be, the gun I needed, how I would wait for just the right shot. I would do this when I knew my family was safe, out of Falmouth, somewhere else. When I didn't have guards on my back all day and night. I just had to wait until the time was right. When he least expected it, when he thought we were gone for good. That would be the day for payback. And it was coming soon.

chapter 23

CYLIN

MONTHS after Dad got home, reporters would still sometimes come by the house, mostly to talk to Dad and to take pictures. One afternoon, a photographer came by after school and
wanted us all to stand together out in the yard, so they got Mom
and Dad lawn chairs and we stood behind them while they took
some pictures. I was excited to see a picture of myself in the
paper, but when it came out that weekend, it was a picture of
Mom and Dad in the chairs, not one with us in it. "They decided
it wasn't a good idea to show you guys in the paper," Mom
explained, but I was still a little disappointed, especially since I
had told Amelia and a couple of other girls at school that I was
going to be in the newspaper.

One afternoon, the phone rang while Mom was at school
and my brothers were watching TV, so I picked it up. "Is this
where John Busby lives?" a man asked.

"Yes," I told him.

"How's he doing?"

"He's doing good," I said, thinking that the caller was one of Dad's friends.

"Can he talk yet?"

"No, he can't, but if you want to talk to him, he can write things down," I explained.

"Do they know who did it yet?" the man asked.

"Did what?"

"Who did it, who shot him? Did they find the guy yet?"

"I don't know," I told him. I didn't know what else to say.

"Do they have any idea who it might be?"

Suddenly I felt scared; who was this guy? Why was he asking so many questions? "Kelly!" I yelled to my cousin. She came in from the kitchen and took the phone from me. She could tell from my face that something had happened.

"Who's this?" she demanded.

I couldn't hear what the guy said, but Kelly looked angry. "Uh-huh, well let me tell you something, don't ever call here again. You had a little kid on the phone; that was totally inappropriate. Don't you think she's been through enough? Don't call here anymore. Leave us alone!" She slammed the phone down. "No more answering the phone," she told me. Then she went in and told Eric and Shawn the same thing. "If the phone rings, let your mom or me answer it, got it?"

Then she went outside and called over the guards on duty. I

pushed back the curtains in the living room and watched her. She was pretty mad. One of the cops came into the house and picked up the phone. He called someone at the phone company and then radioed into the station. By that night, we had a black box and a tape recorder attached to our hallway phone with a bunch of wires. "It's really important that you kids don't pick up the phone anymore," Mom explained to us at dinner. "If someone calls and says something about Dad, we need to record it. Kelly and I know how to use the tape recorder, so leave it for us."

"What if nobody else is home?" Eric asked.

"Somebody will always be here with you guys; you're not ever going to be alone in the house again, so don't worry about that."

That was true, we were never alone anymore. Before Dad was shot, we could play out in the yard or with the neighbors with no problem. We could walk down to the Zylinskis' house. And when Mom had to go and run an errand or do something after school, Eric was in charge. He was thirteen and could run things pretty well. But since we'd come back from Boston, all of that had changed. We didn't play outside. I couldn't ride my bike anywhere; the cops outside wouldn't let me. We weren't allowed to have anyone over to play, and no one invited us to their house, either. Sometimes Eric and Shawn would play touch football or baseball with Dad's cop friends when they were over on the weekends, but it was always in our small yard and under the watchful eye of at least two armed officers.

So the next time I heard that Eric and Shawn were going

shooting with Dad and his friends, I begged to come along. At first, Dad said no. But I knew if I whined a little, I could get what I wanted. "Please, I never get to go anywhere fun. It's not fair!"

Mom was still in class, so Dad thought about it for a second. He wrote a note to Rick: "Maybe she can handle a .22?"

"As long as you think Polly would be okay with it," Rick said. He looked over at me, and I could tell he would rather I just stayed at home.

"Okay, Cee," Dad wrote in his small notebook. He motioned to everyone: *Let's go.*

"This might turn out to be a good idea," Dad's friend Roger Gonsalves said as we all went out to the cars. "You've got a lot of guns in the house; she should understand how to use them, for her own safety."

Dad nodded.

We drove out to an area just off the town dump. It was a chilly late-fall day, so the garbage didn't smell, plus most of it had been recently plowed under. Dad and his friends poked around in the trash nearby for bottles and cans to shoot, and Eric and Shawn helped. I just looked around for anything good, broken toys and that kind of thing, but found nothing.

When they had found a few bottles, they lined them up on the ground and had Eric and Shawn and I stand back about twenty feet away. Dad took out his revolver and handed it to Shawn. He wrote something in the small spiral notebook that he always carried and showed it to Shawn and Eric. "I remember," Shawn said, nodding. The revolver looked gigantic in his hands. He opened the chamber and spun it to look at the bullets inside, then clicked it shut. Eric held a gun that Don had handed him, and he did the same thing.

"Locked and loaded," Don said. He had another gun, which he aimed at the bottles. He took a shot and the bottle in front of him, a green 7UP bottle, shattered instantly. The gunshot was loud, and I could still hear it after the bottle was broken on the ground, echoing in my ears. Shawn went next, holding the gun straight out in one hand and supporting his wrist with the other hand. When his gun went off, he missed the bottle and he also jumped back a little bit. His hands shook, not like Don's, which didn't move at all. Then it was Eric's turn. He aimed the same way Shawn had but squinted down the barrel of the gun for a second. His gun went off, and the bottle in front of him broke in two. "That's it!" Don boomed in his deep voice.

Dad came over and put a small gun into my hands. He showed me, without talking, a tiny button on the side of the handle. "That's the safety," Roger leaned over and said. "The gun won't work unless you press that button in, like this." He pressed it for me. Then Dad held my arms out like Eric and Shawn had held theirs, and put my finger on the trigger. With his hands on my arms, he nodded to me and I knew he meant that I should pull back on the trigger. I pulled my finger back, but it wouldn't budge. I tried harder, but I still couldn't move the trigger. Rick just laughed and watched us while Dad put his index finger over mine and pushed down. I felt the trigger snap back quickly and the gun went off, but we missed the bottle. "Ow!" I cried out. Something on the top of the gun had kicked back and pinched the top of my hand. I had a red mark that looked like a little blood blister forming.

"That .22 has a bite," Don explained. "Got to keep your hand down here." He showed me with his big hands how to hold the gun the right way. The gun looked like a toy when he held it. "That there is the same kind of gun that your mom has," he pointed out, "and she had the same problem with it at first."

When Don said that, I suddenly remembered one afternoon, shortly after Dad got out of the hospital, when Mom and Dad went gun shopping with some friends. Dad had a couple of police-issued firearms, but Mom didn't have a gun and it had been recommended that she get one. She picked out a pretty gun, small with a pearl handle. She had a license to carry it, and the picture on the license was kind of silly because it had been taken while she was wearing her nursing uniform. She looked like some kind of superhero—the nurse lady with a gun. She even had a little leather holster for it that she wore to school or whenever she left the house.

"I think Polly got the semiautomatic, didn't she?" Rick said, taking aim. He shot at a bottle and shattered it.

"Oh yeah, maybe you're right," Don agreed.

"Ready?" Dave said to Shawn, who nodded nervously. He took aim again, doing a little better this time. He actually hit the top of the bottle, but it just fell over, broken on the top. Eric took a turn and hit a can with a loud ping.

It was my turn again, but when Dad went to put the gun into my hand, I just shook my head. "I don't want to," I said.

"Let me see your hand there," Don said, looking at where the gun had pinched me. I had a tiny blood blister in the web between my thumb and index finger. It hurt, but not too much. "Don't you want to try one more time?" Don asked quietly, and I shook my head and turned away. I wandered off, poking through the garbage with a stick, listening to the sounds of my brothers shooting. I could hear some of the things the cops were telling them. "If you need to shoot repeatedly, you cock the gun like this," Don told Shawn. "No, no, you don't bring it down and look at it. Hold it up like this, pull it back, and just fire again. If someone is coming at you, you don't want to give him a second chance, right?"

"You want to aim here, not just at the head, because most people aim too high and miss," I heard Rick explain to Eric. "The body is bigger, so look for the chest first. Second shot, go for the head."

I dug around in the garbage pretending that maybe I would find a piece of jewelry—a necklace or a ring that someone had lost. I wondered if Eric and Shawn would ever really need to shoot someone in the chest first, then in the head second—an actual person. I looked over at Dad. Whoever shot him didn't take Rick's advice; they just went for the head. They probably didn't know much about guns. I already knew more than they did about guns and I was only nine.

I watched Dad take a shot. He looked good with the gun in his hands—strong and powerful. I hadn't seen him look that way for a long time. His shoulders looked broad from the back when he held the gun out in front of him. He fired the revolver, hitting a bottle, then shot again, and again. *Bang, bang, bang.* All the bottles in a row cracked and shattered, one by one. No one said anything as Dad shook a box of ammo out of his pocket and quickly reloaded. His eyes were blank as he slid the bullets into the chamber and snapped it back. He stood for a moment, the gun in his palm, looking off into the distance, at the hills just beyond the town dump.

"Dad, can I have another turn?" Shawn asked, breaking his trance. Dad looked over at him as if he had forgotten who Shawn was.

I picked up some bottles I'd found and brought them over to the guys so they could break them. I searched around the rest of the dump and brought over cans and other stuff for them to shoot at too. It started to get pretty cold, and I was wearing just my light fall jacket, so I sat on the ground behind the guys and pulled my knees up to my chest, tucking them under my jacket, until it was time to go home.

"Look," Shawn said in the car on the way back, "my hand is still shaking." He held out his right hand and I touched it. I could feel a little shiver running through him, like he was cold or scared. "That's from shooting," he said.

I looked down at my own hand, running my finger over the tiny red blister. *That's from shooting too*, I thought. I never wanted to hold a gun ever again.

chapter 24

JOHN

THE days got colder, shorter, and before we knew it, winter had arrived on the Cape. The cold made my face hurt so badly it was almost impossible to go outside. The pain was mind-blowing, like an intense ice cream headache that didn't go away, so cold days were to be avoided whenever possible.

Sometime in November, I became aware that I wasn't dreaming at night, or at least I wasn't remembering any dreams. I also started having a hard time remembering people's names, something that had never been a problem before.

"Everyone dreams," Polly told me. She had learned in her nursing psych classes that people who don't have dreams have something wrong with their brains—psychotic folks, schizoid. "Maybe you just don't remember your dreams, but you must be dreaming. Right?" She looked a little worried. Next visit to Mass General, I mentioned this to Dr. Keith.

"You lost a great deal of blood after your shooting," he pointed out. "There is a chance that your blood oxygen levels got so low, a part of your brain was damaged or affected." I might make an interesting case study, he added, to see if there is a small portion of the brain that controls dream memory and is also linked to remembering names and faces. Overall, he didn't seem concerned about it, so I wasn't either.

Around this time I was also taken in for hypnosis, something the detectives had recommended. "We have some information that we believe is related to the car you described in your shooting," Dimatto told me one day. "We have a witness who saw a similar car in that area, with Florida plates. It could be that the car was a rental."

"Maybe these guys were hired out of Florida, and if that's the case, we're going to have a hard time tracking them down, or that car," Reaves added.

I don't know how much of what they were telling me was legitimate, but I went along with the hypnosis to see what I could come up with. They wanted me to try and remember the plate numbers, or if the plates were from out of state. Maybe I was wrong about Meyer pulling the trigger. If he was the one who wanted me dead, maybe he did hire someone to whack me. It would have been a smart move, considering that if I'd died he would have murdered a police officer, a serious offense, even for him. And Meyer, with his previous criminal experience, would know this.

So I was taken in to meet the doctor who was going to hypnotize me, and the two detectives came along, and a couple of guards. The doctor asked me to sit in a comfortable chair and then close my eyes and put my hands out in front of me. "Imagine that in your left hand, you are holding a dictionary. It's a large dictionary, very large, like the kind you see on a wooden pedestal at the library," the doctor said. "And in your other hand, you are holding the string to a balloon." Then he started talking in a very soft voice about how heavy the dictionary was and how light the balloon was. My left hand started sinking down and down, and I was leaning over toward the left, trying to hold up the dictionary, while my right hand floated upward into the air. Then, suddenly, the objects were gone and I heard the doctor say, "Go back to when you were driving down Sandwich Road on the night you were shot. The moment you hear the gun go off, you will feel no pain, just the situation as it happened and what you saw and did."

Under hypnosis, I tried to talk, answering the doctor's prompts, but no one could understand me in my guttural voice, jaw wired shut. But once I was awake, I remembered everything I'd seen and wrote it all down for them. The doctor had me go through it two times, to be sure I was truly hypnotized and that I had gotten all the information possible.

I could see the car, but no plates. After I'm shot and the car pulls in front of me, there is a moment where I can see three silhouettes inside. Two are men. One is smaller, but I can't tell— the hair went down and then curled out, so it's hard to say, could have been male or female. No faces. That's all I could remember, which was of little help to the investigation.

I had told myself in advance not to put too much hope in the hypnosis, but I guess a part of me still thought that maybe I would remember something that would point to Meyer, something undeniable, something even the detectives couldn't ignore. But my subconscious only contained a few bits and pieces of the night, and I ended up, after all was said and done, feeling that little was gained.

I was still getting a lot of visitors at this point, one of them an old friend and local attorney, Winny Woods. She had just been starting as a lawyer when I was still new on the force, and I would often see her in court. Don Price and I had helped her through her initial phase as a prosecutor in the district court, since most of our cases were open-and-shut textbook law. I didn't arrest someone for a crime if I didn't really think, or know, they had committed it, so most of the cases I went to trial on were pretty easy for a lawyer to wrap up. After a few years of meeting in court, Winny became a friend. Polly and the kids thought as much of her as I did, and we all tried to get together on a regular basis.

After my shooting, Winny came by one afternoon for a visit. We got to talking about the case, the "noninvestigation" as I liked to call it, and I noticed that Winny got quiet for a minute.

"You know, John," she finally said, "I'm really concerned with your anger level."

"Join the club," I wrote to her in my notebook.

"Seriously," she said, meeting my eyes. "I can't believe that the police department hasn't recommended that you talk to someone. I think you need to, before you do something that you're going to regret."

I had to agree with her. I had been spending too many hours a day plotting my revenge against a man whom I suspected of trying to kill me. What if I did whack him and it turned out to be someone else who had wanted me dead? What if those bullets were meant for someone else—mistaken identity? The detectives on the case couldn't seem to find any links to Meyer, so maybe I really was just crazy and paranoid.

I promised Winny that I'd see someone but dragged my feet about it until she pushed me to actually make an appointment with a shrink she knew and thought was pretty good. My first visit to this doctor took about two hours, in part because I had to write down everything I wanted to say, and he also needed the whole backstory. But eventually we got around to the point at hand: I was angry and couldn't seem to get unangry. I wanted to blow someone away and felt that I would never rest until I did.

"I agree with you," the doctor told me. "I agree with your attitude. You have been dealt a great injustice, and I think anyone would understand how you feel."

For a moment, it sounded like he was giving me license to go out and murder Meyer, but then he went on to argue against taking any action. "We need to work on getting you over your anger another way." We talked about ways that we could do that, focusing on my family and how I had conducted myself at other times in my life. But obviously it was going to take more than a few sessions with this guy to resolve my problems.

Before I left, he told me an interesting story. "I have to tell you that I've seen you before, before we met today," he said. I thought he meant that he'd read about me in the papers, seen me on the news, knew my case. But that wasn't it. "I live in Hatchville, and for years I used to see you running by our house almost every day. You always looked so serene, confident. I guess it's what they call the 'runner's high'," he went on. "Because of you, I decided to start running, and it's taken me a while to build up to it, but I just ran my first marathon recently. And I have you to thank, so thank you for introducing me to running," he said, and shook my hand. I didn't know what to say. I'd never run more than ten miles a day, but I'd somehow gotten this guy running marathons. It was a strange twist of fate—of all the doctors in town, I ended up seeing this one.

As I rode home from the appointment, I thought about what he had said. Not just about Meyer, but about the coincidence with the running. Call it fate, call it synchronicity: you never know what your actions are going to lead to, or the possibilities they can cause. There is a ripple effect to every action you take, intended or not. I walked out of his office feeling better than I had in months.

The feeling lasted until I got home and a couple of my cop

buddies came by the house. One of them ended up telling me that Meyer had stopped by the police station. Since Meyer had the city contract to haul trash, he seemed to feel like he could come by whenever he wanted, and most of the guys at the station were too scared to say "boo" to him. As Don had told me years before, some hornets' nests are better left undisturbed. So on this day, he came by and actually put his feet up on the chief's desk and said something like, "So, do you have anything that you want to ask me?" This guy had no fear whatsoever of getting caught for anything, and that really burned me.

One of my friends from the force, a former cop, Mickey Mangum, couldn't stand the way Meyer was known to march into the station whenever someone he knew was given a ticket or citation and make sure it was cleared up fast. If Mickey ever saw him there, he would actually stop and say, "Raymond, what business do you have in here?" There was no love lost between him and Meyer.

There had been an incident a few years back between the two of them involving hauling garbage for the town. The cops had set up a detail to block off some roads for the Barnstable County Fair, and Meyer tried to drive through that Friday night. He got pissed off when the cops told him the road was closed— it was like the regular rules weren't supposed to apply to him. A few days later, when he was scheduled to do the trash pickup along the same route, he refused. Obviously, it didn't take a lot to light his fuse. So the trash along that route went without pickup for over a week—long after the fair was over and the roadblocks were down. Mickey had to call up Meyer a couple of times and tell him to go pick up the trash, but he refused. Said he was there to do his job last week and got turned away. Fuck them, and fuck you too. Hung up. Mickey finally had to go and pick up the trash himself in a police station wagon.

Next day, I saw Meyer in the station, who knows what he was doing there. Visiting one of his cronies—Monty, Mustafa, any of the guys on the force that he was related to or friends with. Didn't matter to me; he was invisible as far as I was concerned. He was small-time, or so I thought then. But Mickey saw him and they had some words. Later, when Mickey went to his locker, he found a plain white envelope—it contained two burned matches. He knew what that meant.

After my shooting, I learned that Mickey had the same attitude about Meyer that I did: you couldn't back down, you had to face him with the same level of intimidation that he gave out. And that's what Mickey did. He knew that Meyer hung out at Jake's Tap every afternoon, so he went and found Meyer at the bar. Before saying anything, he put a bullet down in front of him, sharp side up. "That's for your mother," he told Meyer. "If anything happens to me or to my family, I know a guy down south who will come up here and take care of your mom for me. How would you like that?" He didn't wait for Meyer to say anything, just turned and left the bar.

It seemed to do the trick. But a couple of weeks later, a

teenage confidant of Meyer's told his high-school girlfriend that Mickey's house was going to burn that night. The girl was terrified of Meyer but also knew that Mickey had little kids, so she couldn't live with herself if she didn't tell somebody. The information reached Mickey, who got a sleeping bag and his 12-gauge shotgun and stayed outside all night, waiting. Sure enough, around two in the morning Meyer drove by slowly in his truck. Mickey shone the flashlight at him and he kept on going.

A few nights later, when Mickey came into the station after dinner, he saw Meyer sitting in the dispatcher's room, just hanging out. The small-town police politics had worn thin by this time, and Mickey couldn't take it anymore. "Get out of here, Raymond," he told him. "And I don't ever want to see you in here again unless you have some official police business."

But Meyer didn't move, just sat there and smiled. So Mickey pulled his police-issue .357 and pointed it at him. "I should just shoot you right now," he said. It was a tense moment. Meyer got up and left without a word, but it was clear that these two had unfinished business.

By the time I had my major run-ins with Meyer and his family in 1979, Mickey had already resigned from our police department and taken on a teaching job at the community college. Meyer wasn't his problem anymore. When Mickey came to see me in the hospital after I was shot, I could tell that he was thinking it could just as easily have been him in that hospital bed. It could have been any of the cops on the force who had ever stood up to Meyer. I was starting to get the feeling that my shooting was only half motivated by the upcoming trial that I was going to testify in, and half motivated by pure intimidation tactics. Meyer wanted to send a message to the cops, to everyone: "Don't mess with me, I'm not just threatening. I will kill you." And from the look on Mickey's face the day he saw me after the shooting, I could tell the message had been received, loud and clear.

chapter 25

CYLIN

ONE night, just before school closed for Christmas break, Mom asked us all to sit down in the living room for a family meeting. "Your dad is going back into the hospital after Christmas for more surgery," she explained. "Before he goes, the police are going to build a fence around our house with an alarm system."

Dad wrote something in his notebook and showed it to her. "Tell them about the dog."

"Oh, and we're getting another dog. This is not going to be a family dog, like Tigger, it's a trained dog to help keep us safe."

"What kind of dog?" Eric asked.

"We haven't picked one out yet, but it will be an attack dog, so it's not going to be our pet."

"What do you mean, an *attack* dog?" Shawn asked.

"It's a dog that's trained to keep you safe. If anyone is bothering us, the dog will . . ." Mom stopped herself.

"Can it come in the house?" I asked.

"No, it's not that kind of dog." Mom sounded exasperated with us. "It's going to have a doghouse outside, and it will be trained to be your father's dog. We're going to get the dog when Dad comes home from the hospital."

"We won't have to have so many guards all the time," Dad wrote.

"When are you coming home?" I asked him.

"Maybe one week?" he wrote, and looked over at Mom.

"A week or two, that's it, then he'll be back," she said.

The next morning, a truck packed with lumber and workmen showed up in our yard. They were already putting the posts up for the fence by the time we left for school. The weather was so cold that the ground was frozen, and they were using a special tool to dig deep round holes for the posts. One of the guys showed me how they would put the post in, then pour concrete around it to hold it in place. "Nothing's gonna move this sucker," he told me, and patted me on the head.

When we got home from school that day, all the posts were in the ground with concrete slopped around them. There was sawdust and blobs of concrete all over our yard. I touched one of the concrete blobs and it was icy cold but not yet solid. It felt like gritty Play-Doh. "You shouldn't be playing with that," one of the cops on duty told me.

I scowled at him. "It's my yard, I can do what I want," I told him, and marched into the house and slammed the door. I was so tired of these guys always being around, telling us what to do and where we could go. I hated them all, even my dad's friends. I went into my room and noticed that there was a big pole planted in the ground right outside my window. The fence was going to run straight through the bamboo patch that separated our house from the church next door. It was going to ruin our tree house, as we called it. Not that we had played out there in months, but it still made me sad. Kelly came into the room behind me with some laundry that she started to put away. "What's up, buttercup?" she asked me.

"Nothing," I sulked. I climbed up the ladder to my top bunk and laid on my stomach, looking out the window.

"What's on your mind?" Kelly asked, looking at me. "Are you thinking about that guy you saw in the ski mask?"

"No," I said. But once she mentioned it, I remembered that night and felt sick to my stomach. "Why would I be thinking about that?"

"Because it was awful, and I'm sure you must think about it sometimes." She hung a shirt up in the closet. "You know, that's why they're putting up the fence, so that things like that don't happen ever again." She put some pants into my drawers, then turned to leave the room. "If you ever want to talk to me about anything, I'm around," she said.

I didn't say anything and just waited for her to leave.

"Did you hear what I said?"

"I don't want to talk about anything!" I yelled. She walked out and closed the door behind her.

There was a night, a couple of weeks after we had gotten back from Boston, when I saw something outside my window. My dad was still in the hospital, Mom was at a night class, and we were at home with Kelly. Whenever we were alone with Kelly at night, it made me think of the night Dad was shot, and how we had hidden in the attic. I could hear her watching TV while I lay in bed, trying to sleep. I rolled over on my stomach and looked out my window, watching the occasional car go down Sandwich Road, the headlights crawling across the ceiling and walls of my room.

Then I heard something outside, like a branch breaking or something snapping, and I tensed up. I breathed very quietly for a few minutes, my ears straining to hear something else, but all I heard was the TV. I climbed down the ladder of my bunk bed and crossed the dark room over to the window. The shutters that covered the bottom half of the window were closed and I wasn't tall enough to see over them, so I carefully opened one side just enough to look out. I saw nothing but darkness and leaves and was about to get back into bed when a car came around the corner on Sandwich Road and lit up our yard, just for an instant, like a flash of lightning. I saw a man standing in my yard. He was wearing a black ski mask. He was looking right at my window, standing very still. He wasn't wearing a police uniform. Suddenly the light was gone, and it was dark again.

I slammed the shutters closed and ran into the living room. "Kelly, Kelly!" I whispered frantically. "There's a man, there's a man in the yard!"

"What?" Kelly jumped up from the couch. "Slow down, what are you talking about?"

When I told her what I had seen, she went to the back door and flashed the outside porch light twice. In a second, one of the cops on duty—Dad's friend, Terry Hinds—was at the door. "What's wrong?"

"Cylin thinks she saw someone outside her window," Kelly told him. I could tell by the way she said it that she didn't really believe me.

Terry asked where I had seen the guy, and I explained. "You two just sit tight. When I blink my headlights once, you throw the switch to the floodlight on that side of the house, okay?" he told Kelly. She nodded.

We stood by the back door, Kelly's hand on the light switch, and watched the undercover cop car for what seemed like forever until finally Terry flashed his headlights. Kelly hit the switch for the floodlight on the other side of the house, and suddenly lights came on from everywhere, through almost every window of the house. The cops had called in for backup cruisers that were now parked at the church and on the street in front of our house, all shining their floodlights on our windows.

"What's going on?" Shawn said. I hadn't even noticed that he'd woken up and come downstairs.

"What are all the lights for?" Eric asked, coming in behind him.

Kelly opened the door to see what was going on. "Oh my God," she said. She turned to me and I saw, just for a second, a man in handcuffs being pushed into the back of a police car in our driveway.

"Who's that?" Shawn said nervously, looking out the window. The guy's ski mask had been rolled up on his head like a hat and I saw his face, just for a second. He looked like a regular person. Was that the guy who shot my dad?

"Well, I'll be damned," Kelly said. "You really did see someone in the yard!"

One of the officers—another friend of Dad's, named Craig Clarkson—came to the door a few minutes later to make sure we were okay. "We're just going to do one more search around the property," Craig explained.

"Who is he?" Kelly asked. "What was he doing here?"

"Don't know. He doesn't have any weapons on him. We're going to take him in and book him," Craig said. "You'll have a bunch of guards outside until we figure out what's going on, so you have nothing to worry about. You can all go back to sleep."

It was almost time for Mom to get home, so we sat in the living room and waited for her. When her car pulled into the driveway, I saw Craig get out of his cruiser and talk to her. She ran into the house and found us all watching TV with Kelly. "Everyone okay?" she asked. She sat beside me and brushed my hair back from my face.

As we started to tell her the story, two of Dad's friends, Terry Hinds and Rick Smith, knocked at the door.

"Well, you're not going to believe this guy's story," Terry said, shaking his head. "He said he noticed the big bamboo patch that you have on the other side of the house. He's a horticulturist and wanted to grab a sample, but he didn't want to bother you guys, so he thought he'd just come by at night and get it."

"You've got to be kidding," Kelly said.

"Nope, and his story checks out," Rick added. "He really is a horticulturist. He's got an alibi for the night of the shooting. Only thing we've got him on is trespassing."

"And destruction of personal property," Terry pointed out. "He dug up some bamboo."

"Why was he wearing a ski mask?" Mom asked.

Terry shrugged. "Beats me. The guy is obviously a wacko, but he's no big-time criminal."

Mom just shook her head. "This is insane," she said. "Kids, you all need to head back to bed; you have school tomorrow."

I went to the bathroom and looked at myself in the mirror. I had big purple half moons under my eyes from being so tired, but I liked it; the dark circles made me look older. I was so proud that I had seen that guy and the cops caught him. I could hardly wait until Dad heard the story. I could hear Mom and Kelly still talking to Dad's friends. They were laughing and that made me feel better. Everything must be okay if they were able to joke about it.

I finally fell asleep and dreamed about a scary clown that I had seen at the county fair a few years back. In the dream, he was at my window, looking in at me, tapping on the glass. He had a big red smile drawn around his mouth, but it was raining, so the paint was running down his cheeks, dripping off his face like blood. "Cylin, Cylin, I can see you." He was whispering, but I could hear him clearly, even through the glass. *Tap, tap, tap.* "I can *seeeeee* you."

I woke up screaming, and Kelly jumped out of the lower bunk. It was still night, and dark in our room.

"What's wrong, what's wrong?" Kelly asked. "Did you see something else?" She ran to the window and opened the shutters.

I jerked up in the bed. "Keep the shutters closed!" I yelled at her. I realized that I could hardly move my head. "Something's wrong with my neck."

Mom came in and turned on the light. "What's wrong?" she asked. "Did you have a nightmare?"

"Mom, I can't move my head," I told her.

"Oh," she said, climbing up the ladder. She took a look at my neck and had me try to turn my head. "You must have pulled something. Come on, I'll get you the heating pad."

I carefully climbed down the ladder, but I could barely lift my arms because my neck hurt so badly. Mom set me up on the couch with the heating pad. It was really early in the morning, still dark out, but she put on the TV for me and let me watch cartoons while she sat with me. Kelly went back to bed. *Sesame*

Street was the only show on this early, and I was way too old for it, but we sat there together and watched it for an hour, until the sun started to rise and my brothers came downstairs. They didn't ask what we were doing or why I had the heating pad on my neck; they just got ready for school and I didn't.

I spent the rest of the day on the couch with the heating pad and a new library book. I napped in the afternoon until my brothers came home, then they wanted to watch a show on TV I didn't like, so I grabbed my blankets and went into my room.

In my pile of stuffed animals, I had a long-legged clown doll that someone had given me. I picked it up and looked at its smiling face. It had these long skinny arms and legs made of red and white striped fabric and a white plastic face. I took a black Magic Marker from my art supplies and started rubbing it all over the clown's big white teeth. Then I covered its eyes with black too. But it looked even scarier like that, so I decided to just color its whole face black. Then I took a shoe box out of my closet and stuffed the clown inside, facedown. It didn't really fit, so I had to get some tape to keep the lid down. I ran the tape around and around the box, until the roll was almost gone. When the box was done, I took one long piece of tape and stuck it on the shutters over my windows. Then I taped the other side shut. I used piece after piece of tape until the roll was empty.

I shoved the shoe box far under my bed and stuffed the empty tape roll under there too, so Mom wouldn't find out that I had used it all and get mad.

chapter 26

JOHN

THE day after Christmas, I checked into Mass General to have my second major surgery. This time they wanted to remove the pellet from the sinus cavity under my eye—something that had been lodged there since I was shot but was too difficult to remove earlier. They would also insert a thin steel rod to replace my jawbone and transplant bone cells from my hip—called osteoblasts—into the space where the bone was missing.

The surgeons basically drilled a hole into the area of my pelvis called the iliac crest, removed a section of marrow, and transferred it up into my face, where it would hopefully grow and replace the missing pieces of bone. I was prepared for the surgery to be extremely painful, but the marrow extraction from my pelvis hurt almost more than being shot did.

When I woke up after the surgery, my right hip hurt like hell and an area on my right thigh—over a foot long and at least half a foot wide—had gone numb. I called it the Dead Zone. Collateral damage of the surgery and couldn't be helped, I guess. My head also started hurting—not just my jaw where they had gone in with the steel bars and the marrow, but my whole skull. All in all, I was in for a good three days of unreal pain. The medication they were giving me usually wore off about an hour before I was due for more, making for miserable in-between time.

I ended up on a different floor of the hospital this visit, and for some reason—maybe because of the holidays—the place was overbooked and understaffed. Overnight, there was just one RN and two LPNs for fourteen patients. I was in a four-bed ward with my guards standing outside the door—Jack Coughlin, Charlie Day, Mitch Morgan, Paul Stone, and Jim Fagan; one guard at a time around the clock from December 26 to January 4.

Mitch Morgan was on guard duty on New Year's Eve, and we watched the Boston fireworks go off from the roof of the hospital. Ironically, it was the best seat I'd ever had for those fireworks, and I saw the city of Boston in a whole new light. That night, I got some pain meds around 1:00 a.m. and went to sleep. I was awake when the meds wore off around 4:00 a.m., waiting for that long hour to pass until I'd get my next dose of happy juice and go back to la-la land. During that hour, I got to thinking about Job in the Bible and all the things that God put him through. Job went through a living hell, but no one ever shot him, so by my reasoning he got off pretty easy.

Right around the time I woke up, the nurses brought in an

old man. He was a dermatology patient, but the hospital didn't have any rooms left on that floor, so we got blessed with him. He had a skin rash, and no matter what the nurses tried he was uncomfortable. He was moaning and groaning that everything hurt. "No, no, I can't lie on my side. No, not on my back. Oh no, my stomach hurts too much. I can't sit in the chair, my ass is killing me. Oh, now my elbows hurt, the bottoms of my feet, my legs, my legs." After about forty-five minutes of hearing this guy complain, I waved over one of the LPNs and wrote her a note: "Please bring a sleeping pill." When she got back with the pill, I wrote: "Please shove it down his throat—NOW" and pointed at the rash man. Around 5:00 a.m. they took him off somewhere, right around the time I got my next dose of painkillers. I was in la-la land already and couldn't care less. Good-bye rash man, good-bye pain . . . for now.

. . .

Before the surgery, I had graduated to blender living and feeding myself with my syringe and a big bowl full of whatever. It wasn't a pretty sight and one I didn't particularly want to do in front of the kids or company. It was Polly who convinced me that since this was the way I'd be eating for the next few years, I should treat it as my normal life and get on with it. So I started sitting at the kitchen table at mealtimes with my blender full of whatever the others were having and tried to get over the awkwardness. My favorite meal was lunch, when everyone was out. I'd whip up a milkshake with lots of ice cream, eggs, and fruit. I'd consume the forty or so ounces and feel quite satiated. I wasn't gaining anything, but at least I wasn't losing—I was still about twenty-five pounds underweight. In the hospital, I wanted to stay on a blended diet to avoid having the feeding tube reinserted, but they kept bringing me soft foods that they thought I could eat with the syringe. I kept trying to tell them that I just wanted them to take a meal, throw it into the blender, and bring me what was left— that's what I ate at home. But the nurses didn't have a blender, and they didn't seem to think it was a good idea to grind up the Salisbury steak and mashed potatoes that everyone else was eating and bring it to me in liquid form. Instead, I got by on Cream of Wheat and vanilla ice cream dissolved in milk for the week, but I lost about ten pounds that I really couldn't afford to lose.

During this hospital stay I met a young man from Dennis, on the Cape, seventeen years old. He had a severe case of Crohn's disease. He had a TNA (total nutrient admixture) given through a central line into his superior vena cava to keep him fed. He'd heard about what happened to me and had a case of hero worship. Wanted to spend all his time with me and the guys guarding me. A nice youngster. We were both quietly starving—me because they wouldn't give me the right type of foods and him because they couldn't give him enough. I was able to leave Mass General a day early to avoid a predicted snowstorm, and I didn't get a chance to say good-bye to him. I've no idea how he made out. On the way home, thinking about him and hoping that he'd have some kind of a life, it hit me that he was the same age as Jeff

Flanagan—the kid whose body was found in the bogs across from Meyer's house. The one who had been shot execution style with a shotgun. This kid in the hospital seemed so young and naive, not quite a man yet. Christ, seventeen years old—both of them had their whole lives ahead of them. It bothered me to make the connection.

When I got home, it was a brand-new year. Nearly four months had passed since I'd been shot. There was an eight-foot-tall, stockade-style fence up around the house that would be wired with an alarm system. This was for our protection, but it was also to save the town money. Falmouth was going into debt trying to keep me safe; it couldn't afford to have two cops on duty guarding our house around the clock. A fund had been started in my name, and local businesses and residents alike had been sending in money and their well wishes. This money was collected under the guise of "helping" the Busby family, but it would eventually be pooled and used to relocate us from Falmouth to an undisclosed location—a cheaper alternative to the constant protective services.

As soon as I was well enough, Polly and I were taken to a kennel where specialty dogs were trained—police dogs, seeing-eye, search hounds, etc. The first one they showed us was a Rottweiler. As we walked by the cage, the dog charged at us in his pen, and I saw the bar that held his door shut actually start to bend. He was like a bad nightmare. "There is no way that dog is coming anywhere near my children," Polly said.

Then they took us to meet a large-chested German shepherd named Max, who weighed in at about a hundred and twenty pounds. The woman who had trained him put him through his paces to show us what he could do. He could climb a ladder just as nimbly as a cat, walk a beam like a gymnast, then turn and attack a guy in a padded suit like he was going to eat him for lunch. This dog could go from sweet and eager to please to vicious attack dog in about two seconds flat. I liked him right away, and he seemed to like me. Best of all, he had been trained to follow hand signals, not just verbal commands, an important factor since I couldn't talk.

I went to the training center every day for about a week to work with the dog trainer and Max. He would become my dog and listen only to me. The trainer reminded me constantly that he was not a pet; he could not come into my house or play with my children. During one training session, they put a steak down in front of Max, and he never took his eyes off of me. He wouldn't so much as look at it until I signaled him that he could.

After a week of training, we brought Max home to live with us. A couple of fellow officers had built him a big doghouse outside, which Cylin had outfitted with some old blankets and pillows to keep him warm at night.

I continued to work with Max every day. He was an amazing dog—a true friend, smart as hell, and he never once faltered. But as soon as we got him home, it became clear that our family dog, a little old beagle named Tigger, didn't really feel the same love for Max. She was terrified of him and didn't even want to go outside anymore. She started peeing in the house, especially whenever she heard Max barking outside. One day Tig was looking out the back door when Max jumped up on the stairs, startling her. Tig turned to run in the other direction so fast she pulled something in her hip and could barely walk for days, dragging her hind legs. After about a week with both Max and Tigger, it became clear that we were giving our family pet a nervous breakdown. But getting rid of Max just wasn't an option, so I called up my sister, Bernadette, in Maine to see if she could take Tig. Bee and her husband, Dale, were Kelly's parents, and lived up in Belgrade, a beautiful town situated on a series of lakes— our favorite summer vacation spot. Bee was more than happy to take Tigger for us. This was also about the time that Polly and I decided that Kelly should leave us too. She had been a huge help, and it was nice to have her around, but it felt wrong to have my nineteen-year-old niece subjected to the prison we were now living in. An eight-foot fence, a vicious dog, no visitors besides cops, the constant threat that someone might want to do harm to us. Why would anyone want to live like that? We sat her down one night and explained that she needed to get on with her life. Her brother Lucky came to get her and also took Tigger with him. To say the kids were devastated by this double loss would be a great understatement.

While I was in the hospital right after Christmas, Polly had taken our friend Winny's advice and brought the kids in to see the psychiatrist whom I had visited. They went in as a group, and

Polly sat outside. After about an hour, he called Polly in and sent the kids out. What he told her was pretty disturbing. Their answer to every question was that things were "fine" and that everything was "okay." They were not scared; they were not getting into trouble at school. They were not bothered by the police protection, the fence, the dog, the guns. "They've become very adept at deception," the doctor pointed out. "I don't know if they are just trying to deceive me, or if they have actually convinced themselves of this, but the picture they paint of your home life is not accurate; it just can't be. As a rule, we don't like to see children, especially this young, suppressing such strong emotions. Or becoming this good at deception. Either way, it's not good for their mental health."

Polly told him that we were thinking about moving to a safer place, to an undisclosed location where we could all live normally again. We were just waiting to see if there would be a break in the case, give it a few more months. "I would encourage you to relocate sooner rather than later," the doctor said. "I don't know how much more your family can take under these conditions."

Polly was horrified. "Maybe we should just pack up and go, disappear," she told me one night. But she was in the middle of her final year of nursing school, the kids were halfway through with school. Maybe we hadn't given the investigation enough time. I didn't have very high hopes, but it had been just four months. Maybe they would get some sort of lead and be able to arrest someone, make our lives safe again.

"If nothing happens by the time I graduate in May," Polly said, "then we are gone."

I agreed. I was still angry, especially hearing about how my shooting was now affecting the kids. But the urgency of my revenge was fading. There was no rush. If the detectives couldn't do their job, then I would. It was as simple as that. I had no job to go back to, no life waiting for me. I had nothing but years and years of surgery stretching out in front of me. The way I was looking at it, I had nothing but time.

chapter 27

CYLIN

WHILE Dad was in the hospital having his jaw rebuilt, Mom took us to see his psychiatrist. He had a nice house up on Hatchville Road, the road that Dad used to take us on when he went running or when we rode our bikes. His office was in a building attached to his house, like a little studio office.

"Well, hello," he said when we got there, like we were just visiting him at his house. "Come on in." He was very friendly looking, bald on the top of his head, and he wore little round glasses like John Lennon's. Eric, Shawn, and I all sat in his office together. It wasn't like a doctor's office, more like a small living room with a desk in it. We all sat down, right next to each other, facing his desk, and he started talking to us about how things were going at school and at home.

"Now we're going to talk about your dad a little bit, if that's okay," he said finally, changing gears. "I know that your father was injured very seriously a few months ago. Are you ever afraid that someone is going to hurt him again?" he asked us. I knew what the answer should be, so I shook my head. I heard Eric say, "No," as well.

"What about fear of someone hurting someone else in your family—your mother, perhaps, or one of you?"

He looked at us, waiting for us to say something, but we didn't.

"And having the police around all the time, does that bother you? How do you feel about it?"

"It's fine," Shawn said. "They're there to protect us." I could hear Mom's words, almost exactly, in his robotic answer.

"It doesn't bother you?" he pointedly asked Eric.

"It's okay." Eric sort of laughed nervously.

I quickly understood that this was a test of some sort and that we were not supposed to tell this guy anything. Who was he anyhow? What was he writing down on that pad of paper on his desk?

"What about you," he said, looking at me. "Your friends? Your mom says you've been having some problems with them."

"No. Everyone is really nice to me," I heard myself say. It sounded just right. I hoped he wouldn't ask me about Ms. Williams or Cathy's birthday party, and he didn't.

"And trouble at school for you two," he said to Eric and Shawn. "Fights, aggression . . ." He looked down at a piece of paper on his desk for a moment. "Your mom tells me that you're angry a lot. Shawn? Eric?"

"Just regular school stuff," Eric said. He sounded very grown up. "It's seventh grade, you know."

Eric and the doctor stared at each other for a moment. After a few more questions, the doctor said we could go. We stepped out into his little hallway and sat there waiting for Mom, who went into his office right after us.

We said nothing to each other, just sat silently, but I felt really good. My brothers and I knew what we had done, we didn't have to discuss it beforehand to get our stories straight or afterward to congratulate ourselves. We were getting really good at telling adults exactly what they wanted to hear.

. . .

After Dad got home from his surgery, he had to use a cane to walk. The doctors had operated on his hip to move some bone into his face—he said it was really painful. On days when it was cold, his hip seemed to hurt worse. This was the first time I heard Dad complaining about pain, and even though I'm sure it must have hurt him to be shot, for some reason the hip pain was worse. His face was shaved and all bandaged up again, and he was really skinny; it looked like his whole body was shrinking except for his big mummy head.

Before Dad was shot he spent his off hours wrestling with my brothers on the living room floor or running or fixing up his junk cars in our driveway. He loved taking us to the beach in the summer and to the dunes in the winter to fly kites. Every couple of weeks he'd take us all out to the movies—even if the film playing wasn't for kids. And I was his little girl. Everyone liked to tease me about how spoiled I was, but I didn't care. I was the baby of the family, and the only girl, and that made me feel special. "Cylin can't do anything wrong," Shawn hissed at me one night when we had been in a fight about something and Dad had taken my side. I knew I was Dad's favorite, and I loved it.

That changed when Dad came home from the hospital. He wasn't the same Dad we had known before. There weren't any more fun wrestling matches or movies or runs. Instead, there was nothing.

Dad couldn't talk, and he was angry all the time. He didn't seem to notice when we were around or when we weren't. I felt like he didn't even like to look at me anymore. He and Mom both spent most of their time taking care of him and his feeding schedule and other medical needs. When they weren't doing that, they were all sitting at the kitchen table with the cops who were over, smoking cigarettes and drinking beer. I would watch him sometimes and think about how much I missed my old dad. I wondered if maybe after this surgery he would be more like he used to be. But he came home worse—thinner, more angry, hurting.

The doctors said that his jaw would be wired shut for six to eight more months; then he would go back in to see if the surgery had worked. Sometimes he got terrible headaches that would last for days. When this happened, he would go into the bedroom and lie in the dark for a long time. We couldn't watch

TV or do anything but be very, very quiet, or he would start throwing up. Mom had a set of wire cutters that she could use to open his jaw in an emergency, but she said, "God help us if that happens."

A few weeks after Dad got home from the surgery, he picked up our new dog, the one Mom had told us about. Max was at the house when we got home from school one day, along with a new doghouse and a big dog chain. He was a giant dog. If I had wanted to, I could have climbed on his back and ridden him like a horse. But Dad reminded us that he was not a pet, and he was here to watch over us. He would only follow hand signals given by my dad, so we were not allowed to be in the yard unless Dad was holding him or he was chained to his doghouse. Max wouldn't trust anyone except Dad, and would take food only from him. When Dad was with him, Max was the sweetest dog in the world. But the second Dad was out of sight, Max would bark at me and pull at his chain. His eyes were totally different, like he wanted to tear me apart. He was terrifying.

Dad would work with Max out in the yard some afternoons when it wasn't too cold for his hip. One afternoon, I watched Dad give Max the "hit" signal, punching his fist into his open palm. Then he pointed at the fence. Max growled, and in about a second had crossed the yard and hit the fence at full speed, jumping up. He almost cleared the eight-foot fence—I couldn't believe it. Then Dad clapped his hands twice, and Max ran back over to his side like a happy puppy, his tail wagging. Dad gave the "sit" signal, and Max sat right in front of him, watching Dad's face the whole time. Dad then circled his hand and touched his hip and Max came around to sit next to Dad's left hip. He petted Max on top of the head to let him know he did a good job and waved his arm out, which signaled the drill was over and he was free to go. I knew then that one signal could change this easygoing dog into a vicious attack dog. He loved Dad and would do anything for him, even if that meant killing someone at his command.

I didn't really like Max; in fact, I was terrified of him. So was my little dog, Tigger. She knew that Max could eat her in one bite, and she refused to go outside, even to pee. It was really sad to watch her shake and hide every time Max barked in the yard, which was often. So, just a few days after Max moved in, Mom told us that Tig would have to move out. "She is going to be so much happier with Aunt Bee and Uncle Dale up in Maine," Mom explained. "And you want her to be happy, right?" My brothers didn't seem to care that much, but I cried. Kelly was also leaving, going home, and she took Tigger with her when she went.

When they left, the house felt dead and empty inside. Kelly had been sharing my room since the summer, and now I would have to sleep in there alone. I missed her, even though she got on my nerves sometimes, always asking me how I was feeling and wanting me to talk to her about stuff. And now we didn't have Tigger either. I woke up at night sometimes and thought I heard her paws on the kitchen tiles, the way I used to when she would get up in the middle of the night for a drink. I would fall back asleep feeling so happy that Tigger was there again. But in the morning, I would remember that she was gone.

Once the fence was put up, it was so close to my window that it blocked out the sun, and my room stayed dark all day. The wood was new and white and reflected into the windows, making me think, for the first few mornings when I woke up, that it had snowed overnight—all that whiteness outside everywhere. From the inside, we were cut off. We couldn't see the church next door or our other neighbors, and they couldn't see us, the fence was so high. It looked strange from the outside, too, unrecognizable as our house, our yard.

When the construction was done, a security company came and installed an alarm system and an intercom, which Eric and Shawn and I loved. When someone came over, they had to push a button on the outside of the fence, and it would ring inside, like a phone. You could push a button in the house and talk to whoever was outside and decide if you wanted to "buzz" him or her in. This meant pressing a button to undo the lock on the gate outside. We never did buzz anyone in because of Max—if he wasn't chained, Dad would have to hold him before we could let anyone in.

The large gate across the driveway always had to be opened manually, and this was a huge pain, especially in the winter months when it was cold and snow piled against it, making it hard to move. Now anytime we went outside, or anyone else came in, we had a series of steps to go through: turning off the alarm, securing the dog, swinging open the big driveway fence, then closing it and resecuring everything. Even to take the trash out, Dad had to be there, holding the dog, and the alarm system had to be disarmed.

The fence also had a motion detector that would go off if someone tried to climb over it. "If you hear that alarm at night," Mom told me, "you go up into the attic with your brothers and stay there until we tell you that you can come out, okay?" After we were woken up one windy night, terrified that someone was trying to scale the fence, we realized that the motion detector was so sensitive that almost anything—even Max walking near it— could set it off, sending the shrill alarm cutting through the house and notifying the police department immediately. Dad decided to turn off the motion detector and just leave the gates armed.

Our bus driver and the school principal had to be notified right away if we weren't going to school, because if we weren't on the bus or in class, our teachers and the bus driver had been instructed to contact the police immediately. Mom sat us down with Dad and Don Price the night before school started back up after Christmas break. "You cannot be late for class, you cannot miss the bus," Mom explained. "You understand that the police will be looking for you if you are late, even by a few minutes?"

Don told us that when we got home from school, we were to

use a special code to be let into the fence. "You guys might be targets for someone trying to get to your dad," he told us. "If someone comes over to you while you're trying to get into the fence and puts a gun to your head, you're going to have a special code to let us know that."

I had been so happy to lose my police escort that I forgot about the real reason a cop had been following me to school. Suddenly, I wanted Arthur the Bear to walk me to the bus again and stand outside my classroom. The embarrassment of dealing with the other kids at school was better than someone putting a gun to my head.

"This code needs to be easy for you guys to remember," Mom said. "If everything is safe and you want to be let in, you ring the buzzer, then say over the intercom, 'I don't have any homework tonight,' like that. If someone is with you, or something bad is happening, you say, 'I have *a lot* of homework tonight.' Okay? Can you remember that?" She was looking right at me. It made me mad. Just because I was the youngest, she thought I didn't get it.

"I can remember it," I told her. I just didn't want to ever have to use it.

"So the cops won't be at school anymore?" Shawn asked.

"They will sometimes, just not every day, and not right outside your classroom. They'll still swing by to check on you guys a lot," Mom said.

"You'll never know we're there, sweetheart," Don told me. I

think he was trying to make us feel better, like our lives would be more normal, but I was terrified. Having the fence up, the alarm system, this vicious dog, the code words—it just made everything more surreal. Things weren't getting any better. They seemed to be getting worse.

A couple of nights after the security guys put in the alarm system, Eric and Shawn and I were sitting in the living room watching TV after dinner. Mom and Dad were in the kitchen with a couple of Dad's friends from the force, John Ayoub and Craig Clarkson. I was lying on the rug in front of the TV doing my homework when suddenly the TV cut out and the whole house went black.

"Oh Jesus, Johnny," Mom said in a high-pitched voice. She sounded scared.

"What's happening?" I jumped up and screamed. Was someone in the kitchen hurting my mom?

I heard chairs being pushed back from the table and everyone scrambling around and talking at once. "Kids, kids, get in here now," Mom called to us. As we moved through the dark into the kitchen, the control panel for the alarm system starting flashing and letting out a high-pitched warning sound. "That's okay, just means that the system isn't working," Craig said.

Someone grabbed my arm and pulled me over to the attic doorway and shoved me up the stairs. I didn't want to be first to go up into the dark, but I didn't know what else to do, so I climbed the steep ladder without complaint, Eric and Shawn behind me, then Mom. I could hear Dad and the guys talking quietly downstairs. "They're going to get Dad's rifle, don't worry," Mom whispered to us as we sat on the carpet in Eric and Shawn's room. "Each one of these guys has at least one gun on him, so you don't have anything to worry about."

"Mom, do you have your gun?" Shawn asked her.

"Oh damn it, I don't," Mom said. "I took it off." In the dim light I could just see her as she felt along her side where she usually carried her gun. "Wouldn't you just know it?" She sounded like she was trying to make a joke.

I couldn't hear anyone downstairs anymore. Eric moved over to the window. "I see someone," he whispered. I looked out the window too and saw a figure moving along the fence. It was a man holding a long gun that looked like it had a flashlight on top of it. "Who do you think that is?" Eric whispered.

"That's your dad, that's his gun," Mom said. She sounded pretty confident, but what if she was wrong? What if that was someone else?

We watched the person with the gun walk the perimeter of the fence until he rounded the corner and we couldn't see him anymore. I was waiting, tensed up. Somehow, I just knew I was about to hear that gun go off. I was ready for the sound of it, just like when we went shooting. I tried to remember the advice that Rick and Don gave my brothers that day, how to hold the gun, how to shoot it. If I had to get Mom's gun from downstairs, I was pretty sure I could use it. Turn off the safety, I remembered. Aim for the body, not the head. I was nervous that the trigger would be too hard to pull, but maybe Mom's gun was easier than the one I had used that day and I could do it. I just had to pull harder—

We heard a door open, then footsteps downstairs, and we all held our breath. Then John Ayoub called up to us, "It's okay, power's out all over the street."

"Jesus, Jesus, Jesus," Mom said as she hurried down the stairs. When we got to the kitchen, Mom started lighting some candles. I watched Dad slide the small black flashlight off the top of his rifle and put the gun back into a big black suitcase that was open on the kitchen table. The inside of the case was made of black foam that had an imprint of the gun, so it fit perfectly inside. The flashlight had its own little spot too, right above the rifle. As Mom lit more candles, Dad snapped the case shut and took it out of the kitchen. "Bedtime," Mom said to us.

Even though it was still early, my brothers and I went to our rooms without a word. When I lay down to go to sleep, I started thinking about what had happened. I realized that if someone had come for us tonight, I didn't have a weapon anywhere that I could use. I didn't have a gun, and I hardly knew how to use my mom's. My dad's rifle was too big, and his revolver was almost too hard for my brothers. What could I use?

I waited in the dark until I heard the other cops leave, until Mom and Dad went into their room for the night, then I waited until the house was quiet. I crept into the kitchen and opened the silverware drawer. I knew exactly what I wanted: one of Mom's good steak knives, with a wooden handle and serrated edge. Perfect. Back in my room, I hid the knife underneath my mattress, where I could reach it easily but no one else could see it.

The next morning on the bus, Amelia asked me if our power had gone out the night before. "It was so funny, my mom was right in the middle of making us a milkshake and the blender just died," she told me. "She tried to mash it up with a fork, but it didn't work. The bananas weren't even cut up; there were big chunks of ice in it. It was so gross we just had to throw it out!"

I smiled at her story, and opened my mouth to say something. For some reason, Dad's rifle with the mini flashlight came into my mind and I almost told Amelia about it. But then I caught myself.

"Yeah, our power went out too," I told her, and left it at that.

chapter 28

JOHN

WE were living in a fortress, hiding in plain sight. With the eight-foot fence around the house, the guard dog, and the alarm system, it felt more and more like prison every day. I was nearing the end of my rope and wanted this all just to go away.

Some days, the anger overwhelmed me. Why should my family have to live like this when they had done nothing wrong? The police department needed to move their asses and get something done. After the shooting, the focus of my hatred had been Meyer, but now that was morphing into something larger—I was mad at the cops who weren't doing their jobs, the selectmen in town, the detectives, the principal at the boys' school. The list was getting long. It was enough that Meyer had wanted me dead, that was personal. But I worked for these guys, for the town of Falmouth, for ten years, protecting residents and keeping the general population law abiding. And now that I was in need, where were they? Who was protecting me and my family? The investigation into my shooting had gone from a good-natured bumbling attempt to pushing it away like it was something that smelled bad to a flat-out fiasco.

There was one aspect of my shooting that continued to haunt me that I just couldn't shake: the fact that someone on the force—a fellow officer—must have given Meyer my work schedule. There's no other way he could have set up the ambush the way he did—knowing right where to wait for me and at what time. So when I wasn't thinking about ways I was going to off Meyer, I spent my time thinking about which one of my brothers-in-arms had turned rat. There was only one guy who kept coming to mind, and that was Larry Mitchell. He seemed like a pretty decent officer, but I'd heard he was friends with Meyer—though I didn't know how close. That didn't bother me as much as a couple of stories I'd heard about him from other cops, guys I trusted. First, Mitchell was the guy Rick and some other officers had seen the morning after my shooting talking to Meyer in the parking lot of the police station. According to the reports I heard, they were laughing and having a nice little chat, while inside the station everyone else was busy looking into what had happened to me the night before.

On the night I was shot, Mitchell had been assigned to ride in the "party car" with a friend of mine, Rufino "Chuck" Gonsalves. Chuck was a small-built Portuguese guy, with a full black mustache and a great smile with a little space between his front teeth. If things were slow during his shift, Chuck had a habit of swinging by his home, about two miles down from our house on Sandwich Road, to see his wife and take a short coffee break. Whoever was riding with him would usually come along for some fresh coffee and pie. Then they'd go back to work.

About a week before my shooting, Mitchell told Chuck that he knew a guy who had some information for him; it was something important. Mitchell set up a meeting between Chuck and this "informant" at the Dunkin Donuts on Main Street. When Chuck arrived at the appointed time, it was Mitchell's buddy, Raymond Meyer, who was there to meet him. Raymond, playing the good guy, told Chuck that he'd heard something through the grapevine. "The town selectmen are watching your house," Meyer said. "They know that you go home during your shift and spend time with your wife. They're planning to take pictures of your cruiser in the driveway and get you fired." Chuck could hardly believe this. Why would the town selectmen care where he took his break—why would they focus so much energy on him?

"If I were you, I'd stop going home for your coffee break," Mitchell warned his partner.

On the night I was shot, Mitchell called in sick, so Chuck was riding with a temporary partner. He had been thinking about what Meyer said, and it just didn't add up. He chose to ignore the warning—let the town selectmen come after him for drinking coffee at home for fifteen minutes if they wanted to. Good luck.

He went by his house about ten o'clock that night and brought his partner with him. They had coffee and apple pie and hit the road around 10:20, back to the Heights to break up any parties that were getting too loud. But before they had gotten very far, they heard the radio call that an officer had been shot— back on Sandwich Road. The site of my shooting was less than a quarter of a mile from Chuck's house.

The next morning, Chuck started piecing things together: clearly the "warning" from Meyer had been a ruse—he just wanted to make sure that no other cops were in the area that night. But there was only one logical way Meyer could have known that Chuck's routine was to go home in the evenings around that time—and that was through his partner, Mitchell. So Chuck went in and told the investigators what he knew. They questioned Mitchell, and he claimed to be an innocent lamb. Sure he knew Meyer, but he didn't know anything about my shooting, wasn't there, wasn't even working that night. They asked him to take a lie detector test, and he refused. Most unusual.

Word of this got around the department, and the guys who were my friends or were straight cops quickly labeled Mitchell a rat. No one knew, fully, what his involvement was in my shooting, but there was something connecting him with Meyer and the night I was shot—and it smelled bad. Refusing to take the lie detector test didn't add to his credibility either—that could be grounds for dismissal for an officer, so it made me think he must have had good reason to avoid it. So there was one lead that the detectives were letting get cold. When I asked them about it, they told me that they were "working on it," and to let them do their jobs.

I was wondering, too, when they were going to get around to interviewing me about the recent arrests I had made involving members of Meyer's family. But I wasn't holding my breath. During one arrest—the night I brought in his son, Paul Cena—Meyer was there and actually told me he was going to kill me, in front of witnesses, other cops. It should have been of interest to the detectives, but it didn't seem to send up any red flags when I mentioned it.

Paul Cena's arrest had occurred the previous spring, about six months before my shooting. The Bruins were playing their archrivals, the Montréal Canadiens in the playoffs for the Stanley Cup. It was in overtime of Game 7, sudden death, and I had to go to work. I got to the station and found out that Tom DeCosta and I were going to ride overlap.

They had the game on the radio at the department, and right after I arrived for my shift it went into a second overtime. We were standing around listening to the game when the car patrolling the Far East section of Falmouth radioed in, saying they were in pursuit of a vehicle that wouldn't pull over. Not high speed, just wouldn't pull over. The Main Street car joined in, and they both started slowly winding their way around town behind this guy. Then Jean Beliveau scored for Les Habitants and ruined the Bruins' season. It still wasn't quite time for us to go on duty, but there wasn't any point in standing around either—the game was over. I turned to Tom and said, "Let's go catch this bastard," meaning the low-speed perp.

We headed out to Teaticket, on reports that the vehicle had pulled into a yard and stopped. Upon arrival, the three pursuit vehicles and the chase car were parked in a long dirt driveway off Brick Kiln Road. Six cops were milling around with their thumbs up their asses. Turns out the driver had gone to his own house, parked in his own driveway, locked the doors and windows, and wouldn't come out of the car. "He won't cooperate. What should we do?" DeCosta said to me.

The driver had been initially observed speeding but then slowed down and wouldn't stop. Failure to stop for an emergency vehicle or police car is an arrestable offence, so I figured this guy needed to be brought in by the Far East cruiser that originally gave chase. But if he won't come out, how do you arrest him? "I think I can fix this dilemma." I turned to DeCosta and said, "Those windows are glass, aren't they?"

DeCosta caught my drift. "That's Ray Meyer's son in there; I'm not breaking any glass," he told me.

I grabbed my "prosecutor"—a type of nightstick, about twenty inches long, with a six-inch handle at the side—and approached the car. The engine wasn't on, so I knew he could hear me. I yelled, "Open up," to the guy inside. One last warning. He was a mousy dude—small and thin. He wouldn't even look up at me, so I made a quick jab at the glass with the stick, and the driver's-side window shattered. As I reached for the lock button inside, the driver reached forward and started the car, quickly putting it into gear. I wrapped my arm around him, trying to reach over to pull the key out of the ignition, but I couldn't get it. The guy started to accelerate forward in a semicircle, dragging me with him as he swung the car around to exit the driveway. I was holding on and running as fast as I could, but he started doing twenty-five to thirty miles per hour. I couldn't keep up at those speeds and decided to let go—better to drop at this speed than later, on the pavement, if he decided to go any faster. I rolled down the driveway, shaken, bumped, bruised, covered with dirt but not seriously injured. The other cruisers all turned around and commenced the pursuit. By this time, a state trooper, Ted Tessasini, had heard the call on his way home and joined in too.

It took me a minute to get back to my cruiser, and when I got there the dispatcher was reporting that the perp had pulled into another driveway, down the road a bit. I knew that address. It was Raymond Meyer's house. When I arrived, another standoff was in progress, this time with Ray standing out in his yard yelling at the cops. I grabbed my nightstick, got out of my cruiser, and headed straight over to the perp's car. I wasn't giving him any more warnings. A quick, sharp tap took out the passenger-side window. I didn't bother to brush the glass away, just opened the door, climbed in, and grabbed the keys from the ignition. Then I realized that the perp had tied the belt from his pants around the gearshift. It was the first time I'd ever seen somebody do that, but I guess there's a first time for everything. I yanked the belt loose, grabbed him, lifted him up, and threw him out the driver's-side window. He didn't resist, and there was nothing said. I cuffed the perp vigorously, my knee in his back while he was facedown on the ground. "He'd better not be hurt! If there's one mark on him . . . ," Ray started yelling at me, still standing in the yard. I ignored him until he shouted, "I'm gonna get my shotgun!"

I looked over at Meyer and yelled, "Hey, Ray, are you interfering with an arrest? 'Cause if you are, you can come down to the station with us."

Meyer glared at me, turned, and went into his house. Dave Cusolito took out his nightstick and slid over to the door of the house, waiting for Meyer to come back out. The other cops on the scene got into position behind their cruisers, guns out.

Meyer came back out, holding up something. I was relieved to see that it was a baseball bat, not a shotgun. "Your head is gonna be in your lap, Busby!" he hollered at me, waving the bat.

"Drop it, right now!" Ayoub had his gun pointed right at Meyer. "Put that bat down."

Meyer looked over at the guns pointed at him, dropped the bat, and put up his hands. "That's my boy," he said, waving a finger at me. "You better not hurt him."

I lifted the perp off the ground to shove him into the back of the cruiser. "Ray, you're more than welcome to come down to the station and see justice being administered," I yelled over to him. Meyer didn't do anything else, just continued shouting about how I'd better not hurt his boy. "All I have to do is drop a dime, Busby!" he threatened me. "Your head will be in your lap!"

When we got down to the station, I learned that the perp in custody really was Ray's boy: his illegitimate son, Paul Cena. The Far East cops issued a citation for speeding and failure to stop, and then I charged him with assault and battery on a police officer with a deadly weapon (the car). Sonny boy sat there like a wilted flower during the entire process. Before we'd even been at the station a half hour, a lawyer, hired by Meyer, of course, showed up to bail him out. We hadn't even fully booked him, leaving me with hours of paperwork to do on the arrest.

So now I'd bothered one of Ray's nephews in public and arrested his bastard son—on his property, no less. This was on top of issuing citations to other members of his family and friends, instead of looking the other way like I was supposed to. And I was tight with the other guys on the force who couldn't stand him, like Mickey Mangum. I'd not only shown Meyer that I wouldn't back down to his intimidation, but I'd become public enemy number one, a real thorn in his side. I wouldn't say that I went looking for trouble with him, but by nature of doing my job, I'd found trouble with him. And it only got worse from there.

chapter 29

CYLIN

ONE cold, clear Saturday that winter, Mom decided that we should go and do something as a family—with no guards for once. Instead, she and Dad would wear their guns and we would bring Max for protection. "It's time we started acting like a family again," she said.

By this point, my brothers and I had overheard enough conversations to know what was going on. Mom was tired of the constant fear and anger, living in seclusion and under protection. She wanted to move away if there wasn't a break in Dad's case soon. "This is no way to live," she had told Dad. "It's not fair to any of us." The town of Falmouth also wanted us to move; the selectmen had offered to pay to help us relocate, which really got Dad steaming mad. "They'll spend money to send us somewhere else but they won't spend money on the case," he wrote in his notebook. "They want to make us disappear." If we did want to move, the town had collected over fifteen thousand dollars—most of it donations from the townspeople—that would be ours for a down payment on a new house. The police department would sell our house for us after we left, and all tracks would be covered. No one would know where we had gone.

"Let's go down to the pond and go ice-skating," Mom suggested. My brothers and I raced to our rooms to get ready. Ice-skating was something that we used to do all the time before the shooting. My dad used to play hockey, and he was a great skater. Shawn was also pretty good, and fast, but Eric and I were just so-so. Mom had grown up in Houlton, Maine, on the border of Canada, where it gets really cold in the winters, and she had been skating for years.

We all packed into the van with our hats, mittens, skates, and thick socks, and Max. Mom drove while Dad held Max's leash. When we reached the pond, Dad would usually find a big log or something heavy and throw it out onto the ice to make sure that it was solid enough to support us. It had been a cold winter, so testing the ice didn't seem necessary, but Dad found an old tree trunk and went to lift it. He strained under the weight, and Eric and Shawn came over to help him. It was the first time I noticed how weak he had become. He looked emaciated and drawn, his face still covered with bandages and some patchy beard growth. His jeans were several sizes too big, belted to stay up, and his winter coat hung loosely from his thin shoulders. He barely lifted the trunk, then slammed it down onto the ice. It slid out to the middle of the pond and held firm.

"Okay, looks good!" Mom said happily. She didn't seem to notice how tired and weak Dad was, or else she pretended not to. We headed out onto the ice while Mom stayed at the edge of the pond, holding Max. Before Dad came out, he gave the hand command for Max to stay, and Max did, never taking his eyes off of us.

It felt good to be out on the ice, free, skating, moving through the cold and not worrying about anything for once. I tried not to notice how thin Dad looked as he skated around us. He had brought a couple of hockey pucks and sticks and started a game with my brothers while I practiced my figure eights. I felt pretty, my long hair streaming out behind me, my breath floating up in white puffs as I twirled around and around. Our voices echoed off the ice and trees—laughter and loud talking. We were just like any other family.

I tried to do a pirouette and promptly fell on my butt—the ice was rock hard. "Nice!" Mom called over from the shoreline. "What do you call that move?" I looked over at her and grinned. Behind her, I noticed a woman in a red coat and two kids coming down the path; they were carrying skates over their shoulders. I was a little bummed that the ice would no longer be just ours, but the pond was big enough for everyone, so it wasn't really a problem.

Suddenly, Max began to bark. I looked over and saw him lunge at one of the kids while my mom was doing everything she could to hold him back. Max strained against the leash—he weighed at least twenty pounds more than Mom did. He was growling and barking violently, and I knew we were about to see him tear someone to pieces. Dad quickly skated over and used hand signals to command Max to stop and sit, and he took the leash from Mom. But by then, the two kids had already run, crying, into the woods to hide, terrified of Max.

"What are you doing bringing a vicious dog like that down here?" the woman in the red ski coat yelled at my mom. "There are children here!"

"He's our guard dog," Mom started to explain. "We have to have him with us . . ."

"How dare you! That dog is violent and should be put to sleep! I should call the cops on you!" the woman shouted.

"We are the cops!" Mom yelled back, getting in her face. "My husband is a cop, and someone tried to kill him. That's why we have this violent dog, for your information."

Dad motioned to us to come in off the ice. I moved toward the shore, but my brothers both stood like statues. We had never seen Mom talk to someone like that.

We sat on the log by the pond and quickly pulled our skates off as the woman went over to console her kids. As we hurried back up the trail to our van, I heard her say, "Go on and take your horrible dog with you!"

"Bitch," Mom said under her breath. We all got into the van without a word. Dad held Max, who was now happy as a puppy, his tongue out and tail wagging. He was content to be by my dad; his job was to protect us, and that's what he had done. I was glad the woman hadn't noticed that both of my parents were carrying guns. I wonder what she would have thought of us then.

When we got home, Mom took out the typewriter and put it on the kitchen table, got out some nice paper, and started typing. I came into the kitchen and stood behind her. "What are you writing?" I asked her.

"My résumé," she said without looking up. "I'm going to find a nursing job somewhere far away from here, and we are going to move."

I pulled out a chair and sat next to her, watching her fingers move quickly over the keys. "I don't want to move."

"Yes, you do," she said. She stopped typing for a moment and looked at me. "You *do*, sweetie. We can't stay here and live like this. It's dangerous for your dad, and for us, and we can't do it anymore. We have to leave."

"What about my friends at school?" I asked her.

"Oh Cee, you hardly have any friends left. Haven't you noticed that no one is allowed to play with you? No one can have you over at their house? You don't get invited to anyone's birthday parties anymore. The other kids are scared to even ride the bus with you." Mom laughed a little, then stopped herself and looked at me. "I'm sorry, but that's how it is."

"Just Meg can't ride the bus, nobody else ever said that," I pointed out. Suddenly I was sorry I had ever shared that story with her. "Besides, now that the cops aren't at school all the time, I think my old friends are going to like me again."

Mom let out a sad sigh and stopped typing for a second. "Cee, go watch TV with your brothers, okay? I have a lot of work to do."

The next week, I tried to act like everything was great so Mom would change her mind. I was even nice to Erin at school, hoping that maybe she would be the one person who would finally invite me over to her house to play. One afternoon when we got home from school, I rang the buzzer and said the code: "I don't have any homework tonight." When Dad came out to hold Max, I asked if we could play with him in the yard a little bit. You could throw him a ball, and no matter how high or far you tried to throw it, Max would catch it before it hit the ground. He moved so fast, he was like a blur of brown and black. Eric and Shawn came home and we all started playing with Max, while Dad and his friend Craig Clarkson stood by and watched us.

"I'll get it," Eric said, racing over to retrieve the ball that Max had dropped. Max saw Eric reach for the ball and turned to snap at him, lunging so fast it caught us all off guard. Dad moved to restrain him, and Eric tripped over himself running to get away. Dad got Max secured and pulled back on his collar until the dog's front legs came up off the ground. He was almost choking Max. "My ankle hurts," Eric said, standing up and limping. Dad motioned for us to go into the house; playtime was over. I watched from the kitchen window as Dad dragged Max back over to his doghouse and chained him roughly. Then he turned and came in the house, leaving Max whining and heartbroken. The dog knew he had disappointed Dad, and he was visibly crushed.

That night when Mom came home, Eric's ankle had ballooned to three times its normal size. She moved it around while Eric winced in pain. "It's sprained, not broken," she sighed. She got out an ice pack and an Ace bandage and wrapped it tightly. Dad brought up an old pair of crutches from the basement and adjusted them to Eric's height.

"No more playing with that dog," I overheard Mom say to Dad as they were making supper. "We're very lucky it was just a sprain. That dog is trained to kill—don't ever forget that."

I felt horrible. My brother was hurt. Dad was angry at Max. Mom was mad at Dad. And Max was crushed. He lay in his doghouse whining for attention until Dad finally went out that night and petted him and told him he was still a good dog. I had wanted to show everyone that we could be happy, that things were returning to normal, but my plan backfired horribly, only making it more obvious that this could never work.

That night the sounds of the house kept spooking me and I couldn't sleep. Every time the furnace kicked on, I felt under my mattress for the steak knife that I had hidden there and wrapped my hand around the wooden handle. I was tired of always being afraid. Mom and Dad weren't the only ones who had given up; now I had too. If we did move, I was never going to tell anyone about what had happened here in Falmouth. I would make up a whole new story, about a whole new girl, leaving in only the good stuff and pretending that was still me. I fell asleep thinking up new names for myself and stories that I would tell.

chapter 30

JOHN

ON July 4, roughly two months before my shooting, there was a fatal accident on Route 28. The victim was an assistant district attorney. I'd pronounced him dead on the scene and called the sergeant. Because it was a fatality, it had to be investigated before traffic could pass. A tow truck arrived to deal with the wreck, and I diverted traffic east of the area. The first vehicle I stopped was a tractor-trailer. It was taking a while for the tow truck to pick up the car, and the guy in the semi was getting impatient, revving his engine and looking generally pissed off. I looked into the cab at the driver and recognized him as Ray Meyer's brother, James, but didn't think anything of it. I wasn't doing anything to him that I wouldn't do to the general public: there was an accident on the road ahead and no way around it. I couldn't have given anyone preferential treatment, even if I had wanted to make an exception.

Since traffic wasn't going anywhere for a while, I got out my clipboard and starting filling out the shift log. James Meyer was revving his engine, letting me know he wasn't happy, and it was loud and hot as hell standing right next to it. I yelled up through his passenger side window that if he was in a rush he could turn around and take a side street down to the ocean and up Maravista. As I walked back in front of the rig, he dropped it into first and hit the gas—and me. He didn't stop at all. He caught just enough of me to spin me around and knock me down but not actually run me over. I got up, dusted myself off and picked up my clipboard, but before I could approach him, he drove directly through the accident scene and trucked on down the road. Except for some minor abrasions to my hands and arms from the pavement, there was no physical harm done, but I was angry as hell.

As soon as the accident was cleared up, I went straight to James Meyer's home and arrested him. I took him down to the station and charged him with assault and battery on a police officer with a deadly weapon. Our original trial date was set for mid-September. After my shooting, the case against James Meyer was in limbo, under a postponement.

That winter, a couple of weeks after I got home from my second surgery, I read in the paper that James Meyer had been arraigned that Monday in Superior Court. The judge had decided there was not sufficient evidence to hold a trial. I had not been notified of the new date for the arraignment. To say I was irate would be an understatement. This was the case that was set to go to trial two weeks after my shooting. And if I was right about who had shot me, then this case had a lot to do with why someone wanted me dead.

At that time, Sergeant Robert Peres was our brand-new court officer, the guy on the force who was in charge of letting cops know when their court dates were, and he didn't tell me about the Meyer case date. When I asked about it, he was all apologies; he had no idea that I'd want to follow up on any of my old cases. Wasn't I officially retired from police duty? "I wasn't even sure you were out from your surgery yet." The excuses went on.

By this time, Chief Ferreira had officially retired and Captain Martin became the chief of police. Captain Robichaud went from court officer to line captain, and that moved Bob—as we called Peres—up to a captain and into the position of court officer. Once he became court officer, I wasn't informed of any court cases again. Bob knew Meyer and his family; they had been neighbors for years. Back in the late 1960s, before we even lived in Falmouth, there had been a dangerous fire at Bob's junkyard (his second business, the one he ran in addition to being a cop). Meyer for some reason was the first person on the scene. He rushed Bob to the Hyannis hospital and probably saved his life. I wouldn't say they were friends, but Meyer always had that over Bob. So he didn't let me know that I was supposed to turn up to testify against Ray's brother James. Just an oversight, a slipup? Who can say. All I know is that I wasn't informed, the trial happened without me, and the case was dismissed. Just like Meyer wanted it to be.

I'd charged James with assault and battery on a police officer with a deadly weapon—a serious charge, and about the same one I'd given Ray's son, Paul Cena. It was getting to be a habit with this family. Ray was more pissed about the charges against James, though, seeing as how they were partners in their trucking business. A charge like that could mean not only jail time and fines but also a loss of his Class A license, which would be most unfortunate for business. And that was exactly what I had had in mind. Considering that this case against the Meyer clan was probably the proverbial straw that broke the camel's back, maybe I should have just counted myself lucky that I didn't know to show up. Who can say what would have happened if I had testified against James Meyer. I'm sure it wouldn't have been good. But then again, if I look at everything my family and I had to go through because of my shooting, it would have been nice to face this guy in court, even if just to show them I was still around, still unafraid, still ready to make the charges stick and cause them a bit of unhappiness for a change.

I pointed the news item about James Meyer's arraignment to Polly in the paper, and at first she was as pissed as I was. She was horrified at how I was being treated, how our family was being treated. And it was looking more and more like there was nothing we could do about it.

Later on that night, after the kids were in bed, we were sitting on the couch and Polly looked like she was going to cry. I knew something was up. "Remember that kid you guys told me about last year, the one who went missing?"

At first I didn't know what she was talking about. "The kid who was going to testify against Meyer," Polly said, and this jogged my memory. The kid she was talking about was Paul Alwardt, a seventeen-year-old who was in the care of the department of youth services. He was a troubled kid, estranged from his family for some reason, and he'd found his way to Meyer, who had hired him to work at the trucking company.

In 1977, Meyer was charged in another arson case. There had been two mysterious fires on Paola Drive, close to where Meyer lived. After one blaze, a fireman followed footprints from the scene all the way back to Meyer's mother's house on the Meyer compound. Most unusual. The fire chief came into the police department and pulled Meyer's file. And surprise, surprise, somehow Meyer found out about this. He actually had the balls to call the fire department and ask them why they were pulling his file, telling them they had no right, they would be sorry, this and that. But they filed the paperwork for an arson investigation anyhow. This time there was going to be a grand jury looking into the charges because Meyer had already served time for a previous offense. The problem was finding witnesses who would be willing to testify against him to make the charges stick. That's where Paul came in. He had information about

Meyer, had seen and heard things that would most certainly put the guy away. He agreed to tell the grand jury what he knew but asked the police to protect him until trial time. He was terrified of Meyer, and with good reason. So one of our guys, Officer Carreiro—a good guy and excellent cop—escorted the kid to the Martha's Vineyard ferry one evening. Paul wanted to go out to the island to stay with relatives where he'd be safe and no one could find him until the trial date. But he never arrived on the island, and his body was never found. It was like he had vanished into thin air, just days before he was going to testify.

"The detectives, they didn't do anything about it, they never even looked for him," Polly pointed out. "No one cared, because he didn't have any close family. He was a human being, probably murdered, and no one cared." She started to cry. "He was seventeen years old!"

I didn't know what to tell her. The poor kid had joined the others who had crossed Meyer and "disappeared." And now I was a part of that club. The only difference being that I was still alive. "If you're right about who shot you, and I think you are," Polly confided, "this guy is so crazy, I wouldn't put anything past him. And no one seems to be willing or able to stop him."

I nodded. She was right.

"We don't know for sure who he's connected to, and how far those connections reach. I know you're angry, but I don't want you to do anything stupid." She eyed me knowingly. I wasn't out with my guns taking target practice every week because I was bored, and she knew it. "I don't want you to end up like that kid, for any of us to end up like that," Polly said. She sat quietly on the couch, probably thinking the same thing that I was: it was up to us to decide how to play this now. So what were we going to do?

chapter 31

CYLIN

ONE afternoon that spring, I came home with some exciting news. Mom was sitting at the kitchen table, studying for her nursing exam. "Amelia wants to know if I can come over to play one day after school," I told her, and watched her face carefully for any reaction.

She stopped reading and looked up. "Really?" She smiled. "Really? Well, that's great." I could tell she was as happy as I was. Finally, somebody wanted to be friends with me again, *real* friends. And if the other kids at school heard that I was going over to Amelia's, then maybe I'd also get invited to the next slumber party. Or was that too much to hope for? I was so excited I couldn't even eat dinner that night.

"Shut up about it already!" Eric finally said. "God, we know you're going over to Amelia's house already."

"Yeah," Shawn agreed. He had a sour look on his face.

I was done pushing the food around my plate. "Mom, can I be excused?" I wanted to go to my room and pick out the perfect outfit to wear for my playdate at Amelia's.

I heard Mom on the phone later talking to Amelia's mom, and they worked out when I would get off the bus at Amelia's house and stay over there for dinner. There wouldn't be any guards watching me—Amelia's mom said they weren't worried about that.

The next day, Mom walked me out to the bus to let the driver know that I would be getting off the bus at Amelia's house after school. And everything was set. This would be my first playdate in eight months. All day at school I couldn't focus, but around Amelia I tried to play it cool. I sat with her at lunch and casually said, "So what's up for this afternoon?"

When she didn't answer for a second, I was terrified that she had forgotten all about it. "Oh right, you're coming over!" she said. "You haven't ever been to my house, right?"

I shook my head.

"Then my mom has to make you a banana milkshake after school—it's the best!"

When we got off the bus that afternoon at Amelia's, her mom met us at the door. She was tall and pretty and blond, just like Amelia. And their house was big, with lots of extra rooms. "Who would like a snack?" her mom asked us, and took us into the living room, where two small plates were set up on the coffee table. We ate sliced fruit and graham crackers, and I was happier than I had been in weeks. Amelia's mom came in to check on us after a few minutes. "Everything okay in here?" she asked.

I nodded. "We don't get to eat in the living room at home," I told her. I was worried about dropping any crumbs on their couch or carpet.

Amelia laughed. "We don't either!"

"Well, today you do because it's a special day, your best friend is over," Amelia's mom said. I was Amelia's best friend? I felt my throat tighten up.

Amelia and I decided to play dress up and ran around in princess outfits until it was dinnertime. After that, we wore the princess dresses on the swing set outside, pumping our legs to get up high on the swings and make our skirts billow out like airy parachutes. "I'm flying!" I yelled, swinging higher. I looked over at Amelia, in a pink princess gown, her long blond hair tumbling out of her braid. Her cheeks were red from the cold—she looked beautiful. Last year, I would have taken our friendship for granted—it was no big deal to play at someone else's house. But now it meant everything to me. Instead of being in our small house with Dad's friends, their cigarettes and guns, I was outside. Instead of hiding in my room, waiting for the hours to pass until I could go to bed, I was having fun. And I wasn't worried, I wasn't scared, not about anything, for the first time in a very long time.

Amelia's mom came out and took some pictures of us. Before it was time to go home, we made a banana milkshake—Amelia's favorite. I didn't like it, it was too milky, too sweet, and made me think of the blended stuff Dad had to eat, but I pretended it was amazing. I wanted everything to be perfect.

When it was time to go home we got into their car, which was nice and smelled new inside, and drove down the road to my house. The minute our big, stark fence came into view, I got embarrassed. "How will you get in? Where's the best place for me to park?" Amelia's mom asked. I told her to pull up to the gate and that I would ring the buzzer. I didn't want to have to ask Dad to come out and hold the dog so my brothers could open the big driveway gate. "You can just drop me off," I told her.

"No, no, I want to make sure you're inside first," Amelia's mom said, pulling up alongside the gate. I got out and rang the buzzer. "It's me," I said. There was silence on the other end. "I don't have any homework," I added quietly so that Amelia and her mom wouldn't overhear.

"Coming," Eric mumbled over the intercom.

I turned back to Amelia's mom in the car. "They're coming," I told her.

"That's okay. We're not in a hurry, are we, Amelia?" Amelia just shook her head. She looked scared. I could tell my house, the big fence, creeped her out. Suddenly I wasn't just her best friend Cylin, as I had been all afternoon. Now I was back to being that girl whose father was shot, the girl everyone was afraid of. Finally my brother came and opened the gate. Through the open gate, in the dusk, I could see Dad holding Max by the back stairs.

"Hurry up, I don't have shoes on," Eric sighed as I leaned into the car to give Amelia a hug.

"Thanks so much," I told her. "I had the best time."

"You tell your mom to call me and set up another day. You can come over anytime you want." Amelia's mom gave me a big smile as I turned to go inside.

"God," Eric said under his breath as we walked back into the house. He was acting like I was annoying him and taking too long, but really I think he was just mad that I had a friend and a playdate while he had been stuck at home.

It was getting dark out, and the inside of the house smelled like whatever Mom had made for dinner. "How was it?" Mom asked me from the kitchen. I went over to where she was standing in front of the sink doing dishes.

"Their house is *so* nice!" I told her. "And we got to eat in the living room, but Amelia's mom said they never get to do that. It was special just because I was there."

"Sounds nice," Mom said, but I could tell she was only half listening.

"We dressed up like princesses and then made a banana milkshake."

"Uh-huh," Mom murmured. I watched as she used the special pipe-cleaner brush by the sink to scrub the inside of one of Dad's syringes, forcing the soapy water out of the rubber tube to make sure it was really clean. Then she scrubbed the plunger part of the syringe and put it in the drying rack beside a couple of other syringes and the glass container from the blender. The drying rack was full of Dad's stuff—his syringes and rubber tubes, plungers, the sharp paring knives he used to cut up his food before blending it, the parts of the blender.

"What else happened?" Mom said, turning to me. She was holding another soapy syringe in her hands. She looked really tired.

"Nothing," I said, and walked away. I hated the way we lived now. The fence, the dog, the guns, the cops, the alarm system, the tape recorder on the phone, the constant fear that someone was going to hurt Dad or one of us. I hated the gross syringes and the blender. I hated the horrible sounds Dad made when he sat at the table with us, almost choking every night with the tube down his throat, trying to eat. I would never be able to have Amelia or anyone else over to my house ever again.

A few weeks later, Mom graduated from nursing school. She had sent out résumés to a few hospitals in states that were far away from Falmouth—jobs she'd seen listed in a nursing magazine. She had been offered a couple of interviews, but we had to make sure each location was a good match, a safe choice, before she traveled anywhere.

"You can't be too close to any family, that's a dead giveaway," Rick Smith pointed out. He and Don Price came over one night after dinner to talk to my parents about our relocation.

"Not in the same town, but what about the same state?" Mom asked.

"I don't think so," Don said. They were looking at a big map of the United States that Dad had spread out on the kitchen table.

"I sent my résumé to a place here," Mom said, pointing to North Carolina. "They're interested in me, called me yesterday."

Don shook his head. "Your sister lives in North Carolina, that's easy to figure out. Even if you moved to another town in the same state, it's one of the first places they'd look."

"Right, I didn't think about that," Mom said quietly.

I looked over Dad's shoulder at the map. There were a few places I'd like to move to. "How about Florida?" I asked. That's where Disney World was.

Mom looked over at Dad. He wrote in his notebook: "Too humid."

"You also shouldn't pick a place that's on the water—another dead giveaway. Anyone looking for you will figure that you'd want to go to a place that feels like home, a beach town," Don said.

"Okay, no ocean, no relatives, so what are we left with?" Mom asked.

There were three towns. One in Virginia, one in South Carolina, and one in Tennessee.

"Well, let's see what they each have to offer, how safe the town feels, what housing is like," Rick started to say.

Mom laughed. "Let's draw the names from a hat!"

Dad shrugged.

"Really, one town is the same as the next, right?"

Don and Rick didn't disagree. They all kept talking about different ways that we could stay safe after we moved, how our mail would be forwarded, and our phone calls could still be traced and recorded. After the guys left, Mom got the map back out and put it on the table.

She went to the stairs and yelled up to Eric and Shawn. "Hey, one of you bring me a hat."

Shawn came down in his pajamas with his woolen winter toque. "What's up?" he asked, seeing the map on the table.

"We're figuring out where we're going to be living for the next five years," Mom said.

She wrote down the names of the three places on little pieces of paper and put them into the hat, then shook them around. "Go ahead," she said to Shawn. "Pull one out." He looked scared as he reached into the hat. "Tennessee?" he read off the piece of paper.

"Grand Ole Opry!" Mom said loudly. "What do you think of that, John?"

Dad just shrugged and shook his head. "Sounds good," he wrote down.

"We'll be sort of close to Jackie," Mom said, mentioning her sister. "And you'll have all the country music you can take." She smiled at Dad.

Dad looked at the map for a second, tracing a line between

the town in Tennessee and North Carolina. "About a six-hour drive to Jackie's," he wrote down.

"Still, that's a lot closer than we are now," Mom said. She looked pretty happy. My parents were acting like this was the best place ever. Maybe they knew something I didn't know.

chapter 32

JOHN

SHAWN picked the state of Tennessee out of the hat. We knew where we were going now, a small town called Cookeville. Didn't know the population, but it was small, about halfway between Nashville and Knoxville. The town's claim to fame was that it was basically the perfect stopping point off the highway for a break if you were driving between those two cities. The money from the Busby fund would help us to relocate—it was enough for a down payment on a farm with some left over to rent a moving van.

The town of Falmouth offered to sell our house after we were gone—a hard sell; it was the infamous Busby house now and had an enormous fence around it. Not the most attractive piece of property on the Cape. Our phone number would be transferred over to Rick Smith's house, and he would keep the recorder on it, on a separate line, to screen any unusual activity.

Our identities would not be changed, but we would have to cover our tracks pretty thoroughly. Polly had to tell the personnel department at the hospital in Cookeville that if they wanted to hire her, they could not reveal that she worked there unless they ran the inquiry by her first. She told them the whole story of what had happened to us in the past year, and they were most understanding.

Our mail would be forwarded first to the police department, then, in large bundles, to Polly's sister in North Carolina, who would in turn send it to us. I wished we could have told a few guys on the force where we were going, but for everyone's safety it was best to keep it a secret, even from our closest friends. I knew there were a handful of fellow cops that I could trust with my life, but even they had to be kept in the dark. No slipups, no turncoats. Once the information was out, you couldn't know where it was going to end up.

Polly graduated at the top of her nursing class, with honors. How she did it, I'll never understand. She had only been halfway through the two-year program when I was shot. She missed a lot of school and study time, but she still managed to ace her tests and outsmart everyone else in the program. She graduated summa cum laude and was awarded a scholarship that she could use toward tuition at Northeastern University for two more years of nursing school and a BSN, but she had to turn it down because we were leaving for God knows where. Her instructors told her to stay in touch, and that if she ever wanted to continue medical school, they would all write references for her. That's probably why, when Eric and Shawn brought home their not-so-stellar report cards at the end of the year, Polly wasn't having it.

"Don't try to use what happened to your dad as an excuse," she said to Shawn, shaking the report card in his face. "If I managed to get all A's on my tests, you guys should be able to do just as well. You have to apply yourself, no matter what else is going on in our lives. School comes first."

Cylin was too young to have a real report card yet, but from what we were hearing, she also wasn't doing that well in school. She loved to read but was way behind in math—the second and third graders in her open classroom were doing better than her. The teacher told us it was something to keep an eye on.

The day of Polly's graduation, we packed the whole family into the van. It was probably the second time we'd been out of the house together as a family in almost a year. I went armed with my shoulder holster, and so did my friend and fellow officer, Dave Cusolito. His wife, Ethel, was a graduate in the same class. Fortunately, the ceremony went off without any problems.

By now, I had a pretty good beard growth over most of my lower face and no bandages. To the unknowing eye, I looked almost normal, but inside I was still tightly wired shut and had steel rods in my face. I had been back in to Mass General in March for another round of the osteoblast transplants, this time to the other side of my face, but they went into the same site on my pelvis to harvest them, which was extremely painful. For the hospital stay and recovery time, I bought an electronic chess game, ordered from the back of a chess magazine. It had the dubious name of "the Chess Challenger," but it sometimes took eight minutes to make a move—not too challenging. I could beat it even during my worst pain days. A newspaper reporter who came to see me in the hospital after this round of surgery had an unusual question for me.

"I see that your constant companion is this chess computer," he pointed out. "You don't have to talk to it, is that why?" He looked at me very sympathetically. I could tell he wanted to pull some heartstrings with his story in the paper, make it a little melodramatic. Readers loved a sob story.

"What did you name it?" he asked me, looking at the computer.

I'd never thought to give it any special name other than what it was called by the game makers. But I understood what the reporter was getting at: I was unfit for company, unable to talk and constantly under protection, I had become so isolated that this machine was my only friend. The only one I could really trust. Maybe that's how he saw it, but I didn't. I still had a life; a different life, but I still had friends, my family. The chess computer was just something to take my mind off of everything else: the pain, the present, and the future. And that's all it was.

As soon as the kids were out of school, we put Max into a kennel for a month and headed up to Maine and my sister Bee's cabin on the Belgrade lakes. Polly still had to pass her national nursing boards, so we weren't going anywhere until that was done—then she would officially be a nurse and could take the new job in Cookeville. But we didn't want to sit in our fortress on the Cape for a month, unable to go to the beach—or anywhere for that matter. Better to spend the time in a cabin in the woods where no one knew us, and no one in Falmouth knew where we were. I told the detectives and my friends on the force that if they needed to reach us, they could contact my sister and she'd get the message to me. The cabin had no TV and no contact with the outside world. It was a wonderful escape.

Polly was able to study in peace, I played a lot of chess and swam in the lake when the temperature got over seventy (which wasn't that often this early in the summer), and the kids got tan and bug-bitten. It was great to see them outdoors and playing with other kids—kids who didn't know anything about us, or have a reason to be scared of us. Polly had warned the kids on the ride up not to say anything to anyone about us, and I could tell by the way they were making fast friends that they had taken her advice.

In the evenings we'd all make dinner together, then wash up and tackle a giant puzzle on the big kitchen table, or play cards—long games of Bastard Bridge and "thirty-one" with my sister Bee and her husband, Dale, on nights when they joined us. Their house was only about a twenty-minute drive away, so they spent a lot of time with us. I could tell by the way I sometimes caught Bee staring at me that she could hardly believe what had happened to my face, but she never said anything about how I looked, and I was happy to avoid it. I didn't need comments from someone I had grown up with about how different my appearance was, or how handsome I used to be. This was how I looked now, and everyone just needed to get used to it.

At night, after the kids had gone to bed, I usually sat out on the screened-in porch and listened to the loons on the lake, their sad, haunting calls ringing out over the water. It should have been a serene way to pass the evening, but not for me. I'd sit with my pistol in my hand, just waiting for someone to approach. All those years of working the midnight shift, all I wanted to do was sleep. Instead I sat up every night with a paranoid insomnia I couldn't shake. If a drunk had stumbled by, walking on the shore path, lost his way, I would probably have shot him first and asked questions later.

Polly came out late one night to see why I was still awake. I heard the screen door open behind me but didn't have time to put the gun away, so she saw it on my lap. "No one even knows we're here," she whispered to me, leaning over to give me a hug. "You have to stop now, okay? Please come to bed."

She went back in the cabin and left me out on the porch with my demons. I knew she was right, but for some reason I just couldn't turn off that part of my brain. No matter where we were,

I wasn't able to feel safe. And I was beginning to wonder if blowing Meyer away was really the answer. Even if I did manage to kill him—and I knew that I could—there was still his brother, his sons, his other "partners." Who knows how far his reach extended. I had heard rumors that he was connected to a big crime family in Boston. I didn't know if any of that was true, but Meyer certainly hadn't done anything to dispel the rumors. True or not, that was a whole different can of worms, and one I didn't especially want to open.

I had been so angry about what had happened to me for so long, I hadn't thought about my exit strategy. I wanted to kill Meyer, but then what? I would go to jail, my family would be left God knows where without me to protect them. That wouldn't work. So I told myself I wouldn't get caught. Even then, we would have to live in hiding for the rest of our lives, all of us. It would start a revenge game, tit for tat. Did I really want to play that game? The only other option was to scuttle away, hide out somewhere, and keep quiet forever. Leave our old life behind. Stop fighting and give up. That would mean that Meyer had won. Or would it?

I went into the cabin and checked on Polly. She was sound asleep in the queen-sized bed downstairs, still a young woman—just thirty-six years old, the fate of our family's financial future on her shoulders. I crept up the spiral staircase to the loft and looked at the kids in their beds. All asleep, tired from the day of swimming and playing with their new friends. I watched them for a few minutes, listened to their quiet breathing, then went back to my watch on the porch. I would do whatever I needed to do to keep them safe. That had to be my priority now—not revenge, not my personal anger, no matter how much it would kill me every day to let Meyer live.

chapter 33

CYLIN

MY mom was graduating from nursing school, and we all got to attend the graduation ceremony. I was so excited to go—finally a chance to wear the silk Chinese dress that my cousin had given me ages ago. But when I went to try it on, I couldn't get the shoulder snaps done. It was suddenly too tight—and too short. "MOM!" I yelled from my room.

"What's wrong?" she said, opening the door. "Oh." She looked at the dress. "Well, that didn't take long."

"I never even got to wear it!" I cried. "Now I don't have a dress to wear to your graduation!"

"You're growing," Mom pointed out. "Actually, I noticed that your pants looked a little too short too," she said. "It might be time for a shopping trip." I hadn't really noticed, but now that Mom had mentioned it, most of my clothes were too small. I hadn't gotten anything new since we went shopping for back-to-school clothes before the shooting.

"Let's take a trip to the mall," Mom said. "Without your brothers or your dad. For your birthday."

"No guards?" I asked.

Mom shook her head. "Just us girls."

So that Saturday we went to the mall. It was the first time Mom and I had done something, just the two of us, since Dad was shot. We tried on a bunch of stuff—I got some new shorts for the summer, a new bathing suit for our trip to Maine, some sandals that actually fit, and, of course, a dress for Mom's graduation. It was knee length and beige, with a print of tiny blue flowers, a lacy trim, and a little white belt that came with it. "You look very grown up!" Mom said when I came out of the dressing room. "Look how tall you're getting." She stood behind me in the mirror. "You're going to be taller than me pretty soon." She sighed.

We went and had some pizza at our favorite restaurant, Papa Gino's, and I got to have a soda too. It was nice to eat out somewhere, with just Mom. I was thinking about what a great day it was when someone approached our table. "Hello, girls, having a nice shopping trip?"

It was Don Price. Even though he wasn't in uniform, I could tell that he had a gun under his jacket. Now I remembered seeing him in one of the stores, too, where we were trying on clothes.

He had looked familiar, but I was having so much fun, I hadn't really registered it.

"Oh hi," Mom said, looking up like she was totally surprised to see him. "How are you?"

Mom looked over at me and I scowled at her.

"That pizza sure looks good," Don said.

"Sit with us," Mom said. "There's plenty."

I moved over to make room, and he scooted into the booth beside me. "You should see the new dress we just got for Cee, it's beautiful," Mom said, lifting up the bag next to her on the seat. "Want to show him?"

I put my pizza down on my plate and shook my head. They talked for a couple of minutes, while I sat there silently seething. I couldn't believe that Mom would have a cop follow us around the mall in secret, and then just "show up" at the pizza place. I was so angry with her. It was supposed to be our day. Now it was ruined.

When we got into the car to go home, I stayed silent. "Is something wrong?" Mom asked me.

"No," I said, looking out the window. I hated this town and I just couldn't wait to leave.

. . .

On the day of Mom's graduation, Dad wore his old suit, the one he used to always wear to court, and I wore my new dress. Eric and Shawn wore their old Easter suits from last year—Shawn's wrists sticking out a few inches too many where he had outgrown the jacket, Eric barely able to button his.

Dad, on the other hand, looked like a skeleton in his suit and tie. The neck of the shirt didn't even fit right, a few inches bigger than it should have been. And under the jacket, he had both his shoulder holster and a gun in his belt. Another cop was coming with us to the graduation, and he also had a couple of guns on him. Dad had been growing a beard to cover his face since his last surgery, and it looked all right. It was spotty in patches, and you could still see that his face didn't look totally normal, but the beard was a lot better than the bandages. He fluffed it out so that it filled in the spaces where his bones were still missing.

Right after the graduation, we went back to our house and packed up our summer clothes, then got into the van and headed up to Aunt Bee's cabin in Maine. "You guys can do whatever you want all day, go wherever you want, and there won't be any cops around," Mom told us on the ride up. "We want you to have fun, but you have to remember: don't tell anyone anything about us."

"What if someone asks what's wrong with Dad?" Eric asked. "Like why he can't talk?"

Mom was driving, so she didn't turn around to look at us. "Just say that he was in an accident," she said quickly. "That's not a lie."

"It wasn't an accident," I heard Shawn say quietly, looking out the window from the backseat of the van.

"What'd you say?" I asked him loudly. I wanted to see if he would repeat it for my parents to hear.

"Nothing," Shawn glared at me.

"I heard you," I told him. I gave him a cocky smile. "I'm telling."

"I hate you," he said under his breath.

"I hate you back," I said.

"Kids!" Mom yelled from the front. "Knock it off right now or we aren't going to Aunt Bee's at all."

The weeks spent at the cabin that year were the best ever. We got to see Tigger again, and she had missed us so much she jumped all over us, then peed all over the floor, she was so excited. We met some neighbor kids, a few cabins down from ours, and hung out with them every day. We could swim in the lake, canoe to Little Island, fish off the dock, go wherever we wanted to. We just had to be back by 5:00 p.m. for dinner. That was the only rule. It felt great to be free—no fence, no dog, no cops. We could almost forget that anything was wrong, that we were different, at least until dinnertime. That's when Dad would get out his blender and whip up whatever we were having into a liquid that he could eat. Usually, the mixture would turn out a light shade of brown, and he would sit at the dinner table with us and draw it out of the blender with his syringe. He would some-times write goofy notes to us while at the table. "Liquid hamburger—yum! Delicious, want to try some?" I was happy that he could joke around about it, but the stuff he had to eat was truly disgusting. No wonder he couldn't keep any weight on.

When the month was up and Mom was ready to take her big test in Boston, we drove back down the coast and went straight to Uncle Joe's house. It was the first time we had been there in almost a year. Lauren was taller, and she'd had her hair cut in the feathered style that was really popular that year. Cassie was growing up too. They were both pretty, and I felt little and boyish next to them, with my old clothes and my same boring hair.

"Here, I just got this and it's already too small," Lauren said, handing me a bright blue and red bathing suit. "You want it?" I tried on the suit in her room and it fit me perfectly.

"I'm getting breasts," Lauren said, standing next to me in the mirror. "I have to wear a bathing suit with a built-in bra now, see?" She pulled another bathing suit out of her drawer, a beautiful black and cobalt blue one. She turned the top inside out so that I could see the white shelf bra inside. "You'll probably have to get one of these next year," she told me, looking at my flat chest. I looked at myself in her full-length mirror and turned sideways. Then I turned the other way.

Nothing.

It would be great to start at my new school in the fall wearing a bra with something to put in it, but so far things didn't look too promising. At least I would be going to a school where no one knew anything about us. That was almost better than having boobs anyhow.

chapter 34

JOHN

WE headed back to the Cape once Polly was done with her boards, but our days at home were numbered. We would stay just long enough to pack up. The kids didn't really grasp the situation—they knew that we were moving and had seen the Polaroids of the farm, but they didn't really get it. Didn't understand that we wouldn't be at the beach all summer or living in a pretty resort town anymore. We would be out in the middle of nowhere, on a country road where neighbors were sometimes a mile apart. Where it would take them an hour on the bus to get to school, and another hour to get back home. Where the school year was dictated by the seasonal harvesting of tobacco crops and not by the calendar.

As a last good-bye, we decided one night to go out to the dunes—the miles of rolling sand protected by the National Seashore Park. The kids loved it out there and so did Polly and I.

You could take off your shoes and walk forever; all you'd see was sand and more sand and then, finally, the ocean. It was an amazing place.

I was packing as always, my .357 security blanket, and Polly also had her gun, but we didn't bring anyone else. It was just us. She and I sat in the sand and watched the kids run around with a kite, the sun going down behind the dunes.

"I never thought we'd live anywhere but here," Polly said sadly, looking out over the sand and, in the distance, at the big rollers coming in with the tide. Neither did I.

When I'd first applied to be a cop in Massachusetts, I could specify where I preferred to live, and Polly and I had agreed that we wanted to live on the Cape and Islands. After the application process, which included being interviewed by two cops, filling out various forms, and lots of fingerprints, I had to pass a strength and agility test. While I was still working at Hamilton Standard I was notified that the test was going to be held one weekend in Boston at some armory. So we packed up the boys and went to stay in Natick with Joe and Kate, who at that time had just one daughter, Lauren. Joe took me into the city and dropped me off at the designated place, where I had to fill out still more forms and be fingerprinted yet again. This was so no one else could come in and take the physical part of the test for me—something I guess a few guys had tried to get away with, and I would soon see why.

About fifty guys dressed in gym shorts, T-shirts, and sneakers were all patiently standing around to take the test. There were a couple of guys from the Lowell and Lawrence area with Greek names who were built like Greek gods, and a huge guy from Roxbury who looked like he could lift the whole building, not just the weights they'd put out. They walked us through the first round—getting over a four-foot-high barrier without making body contact. A guy from Sandwich had three tries at it and kept getting his legs or ass or belly on it. Everyone else did fine. We did a standing broad jump, with a minimum distance to make. Sandwich guy failed again. Then it was the rope climb. Sandwich guy couldn't make it, and he was out. If you failed three events, you were out of the running. After he left, we all agreed that the guy was a loser—all you had to do was listen to the explanation of how to do the event and anyone who was halfway fit could do it. I'd prepared for the test by running sprints and miles and lots of pull-ups in the pit at Hamilton Standard, using the stainless steel water lines running to the space simulator for chinning.

After the rope climb, we had to lift weights and run a quarter mile. My sprints came in handy for the run: I had the best time of the day. Running scared can do that for you. I was pushing for all I could at each task in case I failed any, which fortunately I didn't.

Everyone made it to the last event—the fifty-yard swim. Twenty-five yards out; twenty-five yards back in. This was called the "easy" test—there was no time limit, no particular stroke, just show them you can do it, down the pool and back. But this one was the third rail; fail it and you were automatically disqualified. Eight guys went in the pool at a time, and I was in the third group. First group did okay. But in the second group, the guy from Roxbury jumped and went straight to the bottom and stayed there. The lifeguards had to go in and haul him out. Turned out he'd never swum in his life, but he wanted to be a cop so badly he thought it was worth attempting. He was out, even though he'd passed everything else and put up more weight than the rest of us combined. I was in the next group and swam easily; it was over in a few minutes. Then more fingerprints and forms and we were on our way.

After a couple of months, a notice came in the mail about a job opening with the Chatham Police Force. We didn't want to live down Cape, it seemed so far away then, so I ignored that one. Then I got a notice of an opening in Edgartown on Martha's Vineyard. We'd never been to the Vineyard before and had heard it was really nice. We set out from Connecticut to Woods Hole one Saturday, only to discover that a ferry trip over and back for the four of us would be twenty-six dollars. But with no credit cards and less than twenty dollars between us, we thought maybe I should just head over alone and check it out; Polly could stay in the car with the boys and keep warm while I was gone. But it was February, and we'd heard on the radio that a blizzard was coming. Polly was pregnant, due in a few months, and with snow on the way, I didn't want to take a chance.

The next month, there was a notice that Falmouth had a job

opening, so I went to interview with Captain Martin. "The pay is one hundred and twenty-five dollars a week, overtime in the summer. When can you start?" That was about all he said to me.

I explained that Polly was due to have a baby any day and I didn't want to change my insurance until then. He handed me some police shirts and told me to call him when I was ready to start. Cylin was born May 1, and I went to work right after that, looking for housing while Polly stayed up in Connecticut with the boys and new baby. I found our little red house on Sandwich Road, the only one we could afford a down payment on, and we moved in that summer. Strangers in a strange land.

I couldn't help but wonder what might have been if we'd had the money for the Martha's Vineyard ferry that day, or if the weather had been different that weekend. Maybe we would have been living in Edgartown—maybe we would still be there. Somehow I felt that Falmouth was the place we were meant to be—what happened had happened; there was nothing we could do about it now. Looking out at the dunes, at our kids playing, it was hard to believe that we were meant to live in some tiny farming town in the middle of nowhere Tennessee, but that's right where we were headed.

chapter 35

CYLIN

WHEN we got back to Falmouth from the cabin in Maine, the sight of our house was depressing. We would be here just long enough to pack up our things; then we would be on our way. The phone rang the next morning while we were helping Mom pack some boxes in the kitchen.

I heard Mom talking to someone; then she came into the room. "It's for you," she said, and I grabbed the phone.

"Hi!" It was Amelia. "My mom thought you might want to come over one last time before you guys leave. Want to? We can come and pick you up. And we'll go in the sprinkler!"

I looked over at Mom, sweating in her shorts and tank top, an old bandanna tied over her hair. "Mom . . . ," I started to say.

"It's okay," Mom said, standing up and wiping her hands on a rag. "You can go over. Be home for dinner."

An hour later, Amelia's mom picked me up outside our gate.

Amelia and I were wearing almost the exact same outfits: shorts, sandals, and string halter tops. I was glad to see that Amelia hadn't gotten any boobs while I was gone. "Did you bring your bathing suit?" she asked me. I nodded. I brought the new one that Lauren had given me. I felt a little bad going over to Amelia's nice house while my mom and brothers were stuck at home packing boxes, but once we got there and starting running around in the sprinkler, I forgot.

"When you girls are done out there, I have some pictures to show you," Amelia's mom called outside. We came in, still dripping wet. "Let's go put your things into the dryer," her mom said, bringing us into the laundry room. As our suits dried, we stood in our towels while Amelia's mom showed me the pictures.

"Remember that day?" she asked. I looked at the photo she was holding up—it was Amelia and me on the swings in the backyard, in our princess dresses. We looked beautiful and happy. There was another one of us with lip gloss on, posing in front of a mirror with princess crowns on our heads.

"You can have these, since you're moving," Amelia said.

"We'll never forget you; you've been one of Amelia's best friends," her mom said.

"Thanks," I said, holding the pictures. I was glad that I would have these to show the kids at my new school. The pictures made it look like I had a normal life, with friends and everything. Maybe I would tell people that the backyard in the picture was really my backyard and not Amelia's.

"You know, Cylin," Amelia's mom said, "you can tell us where you're moving; we would never tell anyone, would we, Amelia?"

I looked over at Amelia and saw her nod. I didn't say anything for a minute. It was quiet in the laundry room; all I could hear was the sound of our bathing suits flopping around in the dryer. Then I looked right at Amelia's mom. "We don't know where we're moving yet," I lied.

"I thought you were packing up; that's what your mom said . . ." Amelia's mom looked skeptical.

"We're going to stay with friends. They live really far away. Then we'll move later," I told her.

"Oh, I see." Amelia's mom nodded. I could tell from her face she believed me. "Well, when you do know—," she started to say.

"I'll write to Amelia right away!" I said. I gave them a big fake smile. I felt just like I had when we went to see Dad's psychiatrist. I was lying, and knew I was lying, but I didn't feel bad about it at all.

Both Amelia and her mom smiled back. They believed everything I was saying.

"Oh gosh, I better get home and help my mom," I said, looking at the clock.

"Really, so soon?" Amelia's mom looked sad. "You're such a good girl to want to help your mom pack."

I didn't really want to help Mom; I just wanted to get out of there before she could ask me any more questions. They drove me back to my house, and I hugged Amelia for a long time. "You'll write to me as soon as you know where you're going to live, right?" she asked me.

She looked so sad, I almost wished I could tell her the truth. "Sure, you know it," I told her. I pushed the button on the gate and waited for someone to open it. Then I waved like crazy at Amelia as she drove away.

"You're back early," Mom said, looking up at me from the kitchen floor as I walked in. She was wrapping our plates and glasses in newspaper and sticking them in a box. "Do you want to help me or go pack your room?"

I looked at her hands, black with newsprint. "I'll pack my room."

"Good." She stood up and handed me a box. "This should do. Just pack the stuff you really need; we don't have room for everything."

I looked at the box she handed me. "All my stuff is supposed to fit in here?" I asked her.

"No, just your toys—I already packed your clothes. You need to decide what you want to bring and what you don't. You've outgrown most of those toys anyhow—and we just don't have room in the truck." She sat back down and started wrapping more plates.

I went into my room and started sorting through my toys. There was a big wagon full of stuffed animals at the foot of my bed. I knew I hadn't played with them in years, but the thought of leaving them behind was still hard. I picked up my Sally doll from the pile—a blond dolly with a red and white pinafore that I'd had since I was a baby. I smoothed back her hair, then put her in the box. Then I got the steak knife from under my mattress and put that in too. I opened my closet and saw that Mom had taken all the clothes out already. There were just a couple of empty hangers left. In the bottom of the closet were some old toys. A Fisher Price radio that hadn't really worked since some batteries had leaked inside it. I pushed it off to the side. A Monopoly game. That went into the box. I found an old box of sort-of melted crayons and looked at it for a long time. Crayons weren't that special; I could always get more in Tennessee. But what if I wanted to do some coloring after we moved in and it was a while before we could get to a store? I put the crayons aside and went through the rest of the stuff. Pretty soon I had a pile of things that I would leave behind, and the box was getting full. I sat on the floor of my closet thinking about the stuff I was leaving behind, and I picked up the box of crayons again. I noticed that it was starting to get dark outside, but I didn't bother to get up and turn on the light, just watched the early-evening shadows creeping across the walls of my room.

Then I took out a red crayon and wrote very small at the back of my closet: "help me." I wondered who would move into my house after I was gone, and how long it would take them to find my note. Then I wrote it again, right under the first line: "help me."

"Time for dinner!" Mom yelled. I shoved the red crayon back into the box, then stuffed the crayons deep into the pile of the things I didn't want anymore. They were melted anyhow.

chapter 36

JOHN

WE rented a twenty-foot U-Haul truck, and with help from Dave, Tony, Craig, Rick, Don, and their wives, we started packing it up. Then it was on to the van, which we packed with as much as it could hold and still have room for the kids, and we were ready to roll. We had a last good-bye with everyone and hit the road for central Tennessee—have blender, will travel.

Max, our killer dog, was sold back to the training center where we got him, and the town of Falmouth was kind enough to let us keep the money from his resale. About five hundred bucks, and we would need every cent of it. The town also ordered a police escort for us as far as the Bourne Bridge: good-bye and good riddance. We weren't their problem anymore. I assumed the so-called "investigation" into my shooting would end as soon as we cleared the bridge that morning—and I was right.

I drove the truck and Polly drove the van. We spent the first night in a hotel in Connecticut, a small place with a pool where the kids could swim. The next day, driving through the Adirondacks, we pulled over into a rest area, and when the kids piled out to use the bathroom, Shawn ran into an old friend of his whom he had been close to in elementary school. They were on a vacation, and the kid's dad asked where we were headed, but of course we couldn't tell them.

It was early July, and the farther south we went, the hotter it got. The boys rode in the truck with me, and Cylin rode in the van with Polly and our cat, Pyewacket. Neither vehicle had air-conditioning. The sun coming through the windshield was unmerciful, and when we arrived in Cookeville, it was 104 degrees in the shade. The rental truck died in the driveway of the hotel.

There was some sort of paperwork screwup with the new house, so we had three days in limbo. We rented a room at the Howard Johnson's in town; they had a pool, and we spent most of our time in it. There were no pets allowed, so we had to leave Pye out in the van, but we let him out of his traveler, parked in the shade, and put all the windows down. I had planned to sneak him in under a towel or something when it got dark, but that didn't end up happening. Instead, Pye took it upon himself to jump out one of the open windows and waited at the front door of the hotel until someone let him in—so much for no pets! We found him wandering the hallway, meowing for us. He was practically at the door to our room; he had tracked us down, huffing and puffing and none too pleased. He was a Maine Coon cat, and his long, heavy fur was all matted and wet, and his tongue was hanging out; he could not handle the heat. Rules be damned, he curled up on Cylin's cot in the air-conditioned comfort and recovered nicely.

Each morning, looking east was like staring into a blast furnace. I'd spent over half a year in Texas in the Air Force but had managed to miss the summer months. This heat was something none of us had ever experienced. It was over 90 degrees by 7:00 a.m. and the humidity was over 90 percent. Unbelievable. My body weight was still way down, but sweat ran off of me anytime I was out of the air-conditioning. We were used to the beach, ocean breezes, and summer temps in the seventies and eighties. Cookeville was a whole new place, and we were indeed strangers in a strange land.

Move-in day, it was 107 degrees at 3:00 p.m., so we delayed until the evening, when it was only 104 degrees. We did amazingly well getting everything in and the beds set up by 10:00 p.m. We all slept on the living room carpet since it was the only room with air-conditioning—a small unit designed for a much smaller area than it was servicing. Opening windows was futile; we just had to crank this little machine up to max and let time do the trick. The next day, we bought a monster A/C unit running on 220 volts. It weighed a couple hundred pounds and had to be professionally installed, but it kept the house cool even on the hottest days.

The house was a good size bigger than our home in Falmouth, ranch style, and redbrick, just like all the other houses in town. Bricks were plentiful here, the red dirt everywhere was proof of that. The house had three bedrooms and two bathrooms, one just off the master bedroom, the other in the hallway for the kids. Eric and Shawn would share a room, and Cylin would have the small room at the front of the house. Eventually I planned to convert the full basement into a den and family room, a game room, and a large bedroom for the boys to have some privacy.

In back of the squat redbrick house was a circular driveway that ran down to the garage on one side. You could pull into one side of the drive and circle around behind the house and come out the other side, or go straight back to the barn. Directly behind the house was a white fence and beyond that, a big red barn with four good-sized animal stalls, a small tack room, and a loft. The barns were built to air and dry tobacco crops, so the ground floor was open inside, with plenty of space, and the loft ran along either side but was open in the middle. When we bought the house, we inherited a couple of resident barn cats— an old gray female called Mitzi and her sister, Diamond, also gray but with a perfect white diamond-shaped mark on her forehead. We had no idea at the time that Mitzi would go on to have several litters of kittens every summer, starting in the early spring and continuing until the late fall. We were constantly giving away kittens to anyone who would take them. Diamond was either fixed or just couldn't reproduce, but she would usually try to take one of her sister's babies and keep it for herself—we had to watch her to make sure she didn't hide them somewhere and not give them back.

Pyewacket was not a country cat and didn't care for the weather. He went outside occasionally but mostly opted to stay inside. One night he didn't come home, but we weren't too worried about him—he didn't like it outside enough to run away. But the next morning he showed up with his eye socket torn open, wounds all over his body, drooling from what looked like a broken jaw, and an ear almost ripped off. He'd been in a fight with another tomcat in the neighborhood, and it looked like he'd lost. I held him wrapped up in a towel while Polly tended to his wounds with hydrogen peroxide and Neosporin. It took him about a week or two to feel better. I was surprised to see him at the door one morning, ready to go out—I couldn't believe he wanted more of the same. He was tougher than I thought. But this time when I let him out, he didn't come back. We wondered what happened to him, and it was especially hard on the kids to deal with the loss of yet another pet.

Months later, when the weather finally cooled down and I was feeling better, I took up running again, along the empty country roads. I'd never do the distances I used to do, but it was a start, and I'd missed the runner's high. Early one evening, I was trucking down the road, listening to a clicking that I heard in my head now—something that wasn't there before I was shot. About a mile and a half down the road from our farm, I saw a Maine Coon crossing the long front lawn at a neighbor's house.

He came all the way out to the road to see me, meowing that old familiar meow. It was Pye, and he knew me, even seemed happy to see me. He looked good—fat and sassy; he'd been living well. I looked at the farmhouse. It was a nice place where I think an older couple lived, no kids. After some petting and a scratch behind the ears, Pye turned and went back to the house behind the white fence. It was his house now, I could tell by the way he walked up on the front porch and curled up in a little basket that had been set there just for him. I picked up my run, marveling at the little guy.

Sure, he'd had his ass kicked by some tomcat who let him know he wasn't welcome. But Pye was no fool; he nursed his wounds, packed his bags, and moved on down the road. Found a place where he would be welcome and didn't have to look over his shoulder all the time. Sometimes, it's not the worst thing in the world to give up, pack up, and move on.

chapter 37

CYLIN

TENNESSEE was hot, hotter than anything I had ever felt in my life. Once we got all moved in to our new house, even our cat couldn't take the heat and just laid on the floor in front of the air conditioner. The house was bigger and nicer than our house back home, with wall-to-wall carpet and two new bathrooms, but we hardly had neighbors and we were miles from the nearest store. The first morning we woke up in the new house, we were on the floor in the living room in our sleeping bags. Mom had gotten us a few things at the grocery store, so we had cereal out of the mugs that had been unpacked and used plastic spoons. While Mom and Dad tried to organize the house, Eric, Shawn, and I went out to see if there were any other kids around. On our right side was a big open pasture owned by someone way down the road—there wasn't a house or a barn or anything, just acres of open field. To the left lived an older couple who didn't seem to have any kids. Directly across the street was another farm, but their house was set back far from the road down a long dirt drive, closed off with a white fence. You couldn't see enough of their yard to tell if they had a swing set or any other signs that kids lived there.

About midmorning, a guy in a white pickup truck pulled into our driveway and asked to speak to our parents. He had a strong Southern accent, like everyone else in town, and we could hardly understand him. He called me a "young'un."

"Young'un, your ma and pa around?" At first I thought he was talking about grandparents; then I got what he meant and got my parents from the house. When they came out, the guy introduced himself as Mr. Carter and welcomed us to the neighborhood. Then he asked if we'd like to lease our pasture. "Cattle's done chewed ours down to the nub," he explained. He took off his hat when he met my mom, and I saw that he had really thick black hair, combed back with something greasy in it. His face was tanned a dark brown and had a lot of deep wrinkles. He looked like a piece of beef jerky—all brown and dried out.

Mom looked over at Dad. "What do you think? Want to lease the pasture?" Dad nodded his approval. Mr. Carter didn't seem to notice that Mom did all the talking, or at least he didn't ask about it.

In a few hours, Mr. Carter was back with a huge truck full of black and white cows and a couple of younger guys to help him. Dad also helped to back the truck up alongside the barn. One guy went up into the truck and started yelling at the cows and swatting them to get them to move out, which they did slowly, walking down the big metal ramp at the back of the truck. They wandered around in the field and started eating the grass at their feet.

There were two old bathtubs half buried in the dirt alongside the barn, and we used a hose to fill them up for the cows to drink from. The farmer also brought along a big white square that was about the size of a shoe box that he put down on the ground between the bathtubs. When I asked him what it was, he told me it was a salt lick for the cows. "If you don't care to keep these tubs full for those cows," he said, "I'll pay you five dollars when I come back." I couldn't really follow his Southern way of talking—if I didn't "care" to? But I understood that he was asking me to keep the tubs full, and I told him that I would.

"Do you have any kids?" Shawn asked Mr. Carter as he walked back to his truck.

"Naw, they're all grown," he said. He was chewing a big wad of tobacco and had a rusty can with him that he kept spitting brown liquid into.

"Are there any other kids on this street?" I asked.

"Well, let's see," he said. "There used to be a little girl over here at this place." He pointed to the house next door to us on the left. "But that was a long time ago. Prettiest girl you ever saw; she went to New York City to be a model and got the depression. Killed herself. Her ma hasn't come out of the house since."

I looked over at the white house next door. The curtains were all drawn; there was no car in the driveway. "Why did she kill herself?" I asked.

Mr. Carter shrugged and spit into his can. "Who can say? It's the damnedest thing." He shook his head. "Sure was a pretty girl."

"Any other kids around?" Eric asked.

"There's the Simmons twins down the road a few miles," he said. "Ya'll just head on down to the holler and you'll meet 'em." He spat in his can again. "I'll be back in a couple days for them cows," he said, then climbed into his truck and drove off.

After he was gone, I stood in the shade of the barn and watched the cows. There were about fifty of them, all black and white, and all eating the grass in the pasture very slowly. I watched them for a while, and they didn't do very much, just stood and chewed grass. None of them came over to drink from the bathtub or lick the salt block. When it got too hot, I went inside. Dad said he would take us to the mall for a little while just to stay out of the heat and to get something to eat. Maybe we could meet some other kids there.

We hung out at the video arcade while my parents shopped for new towels and sheets at JCPenney. Eric and Shawn ended up talking to a couple of guys playing a race-car game who looked about their age, but there weren't a lot of girls in the arcade. I decided to head over to the bookstore next door to see if I could meet anyone and to look for a new book. I passed a group of girls on the way over who didn't seem much bigger than me, but they had lots of makeup on, fancy skirts, and feathered hair, so I assumed they were older. It didn't matter, since they didn't even look at me.

The next day I got up and checked the tubs up by the barn first thing. It was already about 90 degrees out, and the tubs were only half-full. I got out the hose and filled them up again, then watched the cows for a little bit. They had eaten the long grass down in some spots to where you could see the red dirt below it. Then they would just move on to a new spot and keep eating. I went into the barn and looked up in the loft for the two cats that lived there, and I found Mitzi. I sat and petted her for a while, and she started to purr and fall asleep. The loft of the barn was so hot, you couldn't really move around in there. It was okay if you just sat still, but even then the sweat would run down my back under my T-shirt and along the sides of my face.

I thought about the girls I'd seen at the mall yesterday. What if all the girls around here looked like that? No one was going to want to be my friend, with my skinny body, no makeup, and my long straight hair. I wished that the pretty girl Mr. Carter had told us about still lived next door. Maybe she could give me a makeover, like in the magazines. She had been a model after all. I wished that she hadn't killed herself; maybe we could have been friends.

That night I started writing a letter to Amelia. Mom said that when we had a few letters that we wanted to mail back home she would put them all into a big envelope and send them to

Aunt Jackie in North Carolina. Then Aunt Jackie would put them all into a new envelope and send them to the police department in Falmouth. Then Dad's friends on the force would mail the letters from there. "It might take a while for your friends to get your letters, and for you to get their letters back, but you will get them, okay?" Mom explained. Mom also said that she wanted to look over the letters before we mailed them, just to double check that we didn't say anything that we weren't supposed to by accident. "Can I tell Amelia that it's really hot here?" I asked her.

Mom thought about it for a moment. "Better not."

"What about the barn, can I tell her that we have a barn?"

"I don't know," Mom said. "John, what do you think?" We both looked over at Dad. He shook his head no.

I stared down at the blank page. I couldn't tell Amelia anything. Then I decided to write about the beautiful girl who used to live next door. That would probably be okay, and it was a really good story.

I had to use a few pieces of my new stationery to get the story just right and not include any information that I wasn't allowed to, so by the time I was done with my letter, it was almost bedtime. I took the letter into the living room where my parents were trying to set up the TV and the stereo with Eric and Shawn.

As I walked into the room, car lights flashed across the wall and a car pulled into the driveway. Dad looked out the bay windows at the front of the house—we didn't have any curtains up yet.

"Who's that?" Mom said. She sounded scared. Dad stood still, watching the car for a moment, but it didn't move. The engine was still running. "Maybe they're just looking at the 'For Sale' sign?" Mom asked. We hadn't taken down the sign in front of the house yet.

Dad turned and moved quickly down the hallway, into their bedroom, and came out about two seconds later with his .357 and a box of ammo. He was trying to say something, but I couldn't understand him through his wired-shut jaw. He motioned to the cellar door frantically and pulled Mom by the arm.

"Okay," Mom said, pushing us to the cellar door. "Dad thinks we should go downstairs." I saw Dad turn off the light in the living room and crouch by the base of the window, cocking his gun as we went down the stairs.

We stood on the staircase and Mom used the deadbolt inside the door to lock us in. "Do you think it's them?" Shawn asked Eric.

Eric shook his head, but he looked scared.

There was silence for a few minutes; we just listened to our breathing and waited. Then someone turned the cellar doorknob and pulled the door, but the lock caught it. "Who's that?" Mom yelled.

We could hear Dad's muffled voice on the other side of the door, but we had no idea what he was trying to say. "Stay here," Mom told us, and she opened the door. But it was just Dad standing there, so we all came up the stairs.

Dad went over to the kitchen table and grabbed my stationery. He wrote Mom a note with my purple pen. "Someone lost, was looking at a map in car, false alarm."

"Okay." Mom sighed. "It's late anyhow, time for you guys to be in bed." Dad had set his gun down on the kitchen table and started to pace the room, back and forth. He was sweating under his arms and down his face even though the air conditioner was on. I went to the front window and looked out. Our street was dark; there weren't any streetlights this far out in the country. The only light came from the farmhouse across the way, and that was far. There was no car in the driveway anymore.

"Bed," Mom said again, coming up behind me to look out the window. "It's late, let's go."

I brushed my teeth and got into bed, thinking about my letter to Amelia. I had to remember to show it to Mom in the morning so we could get it sent off soon. As I lay in the dark, in my new room with its bare walls and boxes piled in one corner, I started to think about the pretty girl who used to live next door. I wondered if she had killed herself in her house or when she was in New York—Mr. Carter didn't say. It was creepy to think that we lived next door to a house where someone might have killed herself. When I got to thinking about it, I couldn't sleep. After a long time, I got up to get some water. When I crossed the living room, I saw a figure sitting in front of the window and stopped. Then I realized that it was Dad. He had moved one of the kitchen chairs into the living room and was sitting right in front of the window; his gun was in his right hand, balanced on his knee. He looked over at me for a second and then looked away.

I went into the kitchen and got a drink, standing over the sink. I looked out the kitchen window at the house across the way, the house where a pretty girl had once lived and maybe died. The street was pitch black now; it was so late, even the neighbor's porch light had been turned out. I thought about our old house on the Cape, our little red house, and the new girl who might move in there, who would have my room. Maybe someday someone would tell her a story about me.

chapter 38

JOHN

ONE of the few people who had to know where we were moving was my doctor in Boston, Dr. David Keith. The town I moved to wasn't important, just the state, so he could set me up with some doctors there for an occasional checkup. The team in Boston would still do my major surgeries, but I needed someone closer for the in-between progress checks. Once they knew where we were headed, the team in Boston set up a meeting with the maxillofacial doctors at Vanderbilt University Hospital. Shortly after we were all settled in, we drove to Nashville and did some sightseeing on the day of my appointment. We went to the replica of the Parthenon and to some country music historical sights.

The doctors at Vandy were pretty happy to see me; I was an interesting case, to be sure. But they quickly discovered that the latest round of bone marrow transplants hadn't taken—nothing was growing on the right side of my face, even after all these months. They talked to me about another option. They wanted to start repairing my face by surgically removing the transplanted bone and going with a metal-and-plastic prosthesis instead. This would also involve attaching a ring to my skull, a halo held to my head with screws, which would have to stay in place for months. No thank you. I got in touch with the doctors in Boston to fill them in, and they set me up with another round of marrow transplants for December.

Come December, I grabbed my blender and hit the road for Massachusetts. After my surgery, I planned to be at Joe and Kate's house to recover, then drive back down and hopefully be home for Christmas. Polly was working at Cookeville General Hospital by now, and the kids were in school. The first day on the road, I drove from 6:00 a.m. until 11:00 p.m. and stopped at a hotel on the Pennsylvania/New York border. The place was cold. I'd already forgotten what the northern winters could do to my head, and I woke with one of my mind-blowing headaches. I blended up a milkshake and hit the road again. In the car, I turned the radio on to NPR and heard the top story—John Lennon had been killed the night before. His last words were, "I'm shot." I knew exactly how he felt. I was sure I was dying too. They say you don't hear the one that kills you, but people who say that haven't been shot and lived. You know quite suddenly every minute detail. Time dilates. You've been shot. *I'm going to have to see a dentist.* You're dying. *Please turn the lights off in my car so the battery doesn't die.* I wondered what Lennon's last thoughts were. "Rest in peace, partner," I said to myself as they played an old Lennon song on the radio. "You deserved so much more life."

When I got to the hospital, Dr. Keith told me that they'd take the cells from my other hip this time. Yippee. I'd have symmetrical scars and two dead zones. But in recovery the next day, I found that they'd actually gone into the same pelvic crest and my right thumb was totally numb.

"How are we doing today?" asked the doctor who came in to check on me. "Any numbness in your leg?"

I wrote him a note: "It's been numb there since the first surgery."

He explained that they probably nicked a nerve, but the chances were slim that the numb area would expand any more with this latest surgery. That's why it was better to go back in where the damage was already done.

I wrote him a note about my thumb, which was now turning red and really starting to hurt. He looked it over and was baffled. So were the other doctors. The pain meds they were giving me for the pain helped my face but didn't do much for the thumb, it hurt that bad. Then, after three days, it was like a switch was thrown and the pain stopped. By then, my thumb was a normal color again, but the skin had started to peel off it in big chunks. Finally, one doctor on the team had an explanation. "You were lying on your thumb during surgery, and because you were unconscious, your body didn't tell you to roll off of it. So it lost circulation for a few hours," he told me. "It should return to normal in a few more days. We would probably know already if you were going to lose it."

So I had a numb leg and a thumb that almost needed to be amputated. Their attitude was, "No big deal, it's the face that counts." It had been almost sixteen months since the shooting, and I'd been wired shut the whole time. I was still facing several more months this way. They had said it would take a few years to rebuild my face, and they weren't kidding.

There were no guards this time; I was keeping a low profile. There was no point in even letting the police department know that I was back in the state. This also meant that I couldn't visit old friends, but those days were behind us anyhow. There wouldn't be any more visits. The hospital staff were under orders not to release any information about me to anyone, and hospital security was watching my room for any problems, but there weren't any. No one knew where I was, and by the time Falmouth got the bill, I was long gone.

After a week I was temporarily released, but I needed to come back in and get the okay to go home. As planned, I went to Joe and Kate's place, where Kate checked me every few hours with her nurse's eye for any counterindicative signs and doled out the pain pills. She seemed to think things were okay after a few days, so I decided to use the time to visit some family—knowing that it could be a long while before we would get the chance to do that again. I went to see my uncle John, my mom's youngest brother, who lived with his family in Bellingham. He was only ten years older than me, and we'd always been close. He took after that side of the family and weighed about three hundred pounds—the curse of the big bones.

Uncle John was the family genius, with a photographic memory and a great mind for jokes and stories. He never forgot anything and was always happy to startle you with his total recall of events, names, faces, and places. He was an electrician by trade and could build up or take apart just about anything that ran on electricity. He'd read about electric chairs being used to kill prisoners when he was a kid and actually built one—talked a friend of his into sitting in it and was about to throw the switch when my mother—his older sister—stopped him and made him take it apart. A brilliant guy with a bit of a mean streak.

After we visited for a little bit, he said, "Come with me into the cellar, I've got a project I want you to take a look at." It was a .22 bolt-action rifle equipped with a silencer and a device to catch shell casings as they ejected, leaving no evidence. The serial numbers had been ground off, so attempts to trace the gun would be futile. It shot .22 longs, good penetration; we're talking head shots here.

My uncle demonstrated a few shots into a sandbag bunker he had set up. "Sounds like someone coughing," he said, taking a shot with the silencer on. "Not too bad, huh?" I could tell he was proud of himself, and he should have been. The gun was perfect.

"The accuracy might not be the best since the silencer isn't grooved the same as the barrel is," Uncle John pointed out. "But it's got a scope and you ought to be able to put it within six inches of center at one hundred yards."

As he spoke, I could see myself setting up the rifle in the woods by the town dump, waiting to blow Meyer away. I knew all the trails between there and Hatchville Road. I'd run them for years. I'd just park under power lines in Hatchville, take this gun and hoof it to the dump, do the deed and hoof back. I'd been jogging again, although I'd probably have to walk since I just got out of the hospital and all. But still, it was doable.

The question was: did I want to do it?

It wouldn't be hard to find out that I'd been in Boston; the hospital would have to release that information if there was a murder investigation. But how hard would the cops—any cops—try to convict me under the circumstances? Who knows. It was getting harder and harder for me to picture myself pulling the trigger.

I was still mad as hell, but the anger had changed and morphed into something else. I hated to see my face. I hated the three-day-long headaches. I hated not being able to eat. But the hatred of these things was no longer focused on Meyer. Maybe I just wasn't the hard, coldhearted, revenge-generating psycho that I thought I was. In reality, I was just a man who got somebody mad—mad enough to want to kill him—and survived it. Maybe it should end there.

I looked at the gun my uncle John had put together for me. This was my chance. I wrote a few words in my notebook and

showed it to him. "Thank you for all the effort. I won't need it."
He looked at the note quietly, then patted me on the shoulder. I
couldn't tell if he was proud of me or disappointed.

"The gun is our secret, nephew," he told me quietly. "No one
else knows it's here. If the need arises . . ." He didn't say more. He
didn't need to.

I went back into the hospital the next day for a follow-up and
was cleared by Mass General to head home, so I packed up and
started the drive back down south. I'd be back in six to eight
months for another look at this transplant, to see if the marrow
had taken this time, if bone was growing in my face. When I
stopped at a hotel to spend the night, the look on the clerk's face
said it all. I was bandaged, swollen, couldn't speak. I looked like
someone who'd been in a terrible accident. I wrote him a note
telling him that I needed a room for the night, and he filled out
all the forms and took my money without ever taking his eyes off
my face. It was clear that he was horrified but couldn't look away.
He was kind enough not to ask any questions.

In the room, I used my blender to make dinner, looking at
my face in the mirror over the dresser. It was getting hard for me
to see how I must appear to others; I'd already grown so used to
this as my life.

When I arrived back in Tennessee, I was glad for the seclusion of our farm to rest and recuperate. Maybe the marrow in my
jaw would do its trick and start making me whole again. The
kids were happy to see me, as bandaged and strange as I must

have looked. They had grown used to this life too. And Polly had a surprise for me. She led me out to the barn to show me something—in the few weeks while I was gone, she'd bought a horse. A big chestnut with a white line down her nose, a Tennessee Walker. Polly had always loved horses and learned how to ride when she was young—she was an excellent horsewoman.

"I thought since we have a farm, why not, right?" she explained. A coworker at the hospital was selling her, and Polly jumped at the chance. "What do you think? She's beautiful, huh?"

I nodded my approval. This was our life now. A barn, and a horse to go in it. There would be no going back. For a moment, the image of that gun in my uncle's basement flashed into my mind—the .22 longs in their box, sitting there, waiting for me. "If the need arises, nephew . . ." His hand on my back.

"Here, pet her," Polly said, guiding my hand. I ran it along the horse's side, feeling her strong muscles ripple beneath. "I figure I'll teach the kids to ride." Polly smiled as she looked at her new horse. I watched her face. She looked happy, really happy. It was the first time I'd seen her look like that in a long, long time. And I was glad to be home.

epilogue

IN TENNESSEE, WE LIVED IN THE open, never hiding, and we did not change our rather unique last name, although we had been advised it might be a good idea. My dad was confident that the Meyer family would be satisfied with the mere fact that we were out of town, out of the way. Their purpose had been served: my dad's injuries had prevented him from testifying in the case against James Meyer, Ray Meyer's brother.

Although Dad was not afraid, we were—my brothers, my mom, and I. Dad was the only man who had stood up to this crime family and managed to stay alive. Would they be back to finish the job? Now that we were no longer under round-the-clock police protection, would they find us and burn down our house? Murder us all? When my dad traveled back up to Boston for his surgeries he was gone for weeks at a time. They could find him there in the hospital and pull the plug on him, put a pillow over his face, like I had seen in the movies.

As a family, we never spoke of these fears; my mom and dad did not mention the Meyer name. Dad had been in an "accident." It was our secret, it was understood. And when a car pulled in too close behind him when he was driving, or went to pass him on the country roads where we now lived, I would always hold my breath, but I never saw him flinch.

Mom worked, my brothers and I went to school, Dad ran the farm, when he was able. The other kids at school said we talked funny with our New England accents, and that our clothes weren't cool. It didn't help that our schools back home had been a bit ahead of those in the South, and now we were called out for being smart. My mom bought Eric and Shawn the jeans that everyone else was wearing that year so they could blend in. I started wearing lip gloss like the other ten-year-old girls at school. I hid my glasses in my desk, cut my long hair, and affected a Southern accent. We became very good at our disguises, we made friends, and slowly, Dad started to heal, to become whole again. We pretended this was how it was all supposed to be, that we belonged here. Then something would happen to bring it all back. The phone would ring and no one would be there. A bank teller would be a little too curious, asking questions about the retirement checks from Massachusetts. A few years after the shooting, a reporter for the *Cape Cod Times* wondered about the family that had suddenly, one day, just disappeared. Through a connection on the police force, he was able to secure an interview with Dad. When my brothers and I heard about this plan, we weren't so sure. Was this really a reporter, or someone pretending to be a reporter? We were terrified. No one was supposed to know where we were; no one was to be trusted.

But he was a reporter. He spent a couple of days interviewing Dad, then began to write a huge front-page profile about the case, tying Dad's shooting to the Meyer family. Before the article was even published the reporter started getting strange phone calls. Not threatening, just ominous. "We know you've been talking to Busby," one caller said, then hung up. The calls came to his office at the newspaper and at his home. The reporter took his wife and infant child and quickly left town until the story, and speculation, blew over. Once the article was published and everyone knew what the reporter knew the calls stopped just as mysteriously as they had begun.

As these events happened less often, the day-to-day fears of our family turned into waiting. And after months and then years of nothing, the waiting gradually faded too. All that was left was anger. Dad didn't talk about how he felt, but he was constantly on the verge of destroying things. The hammer that missed a nail and hit his finger was thrown into the neighbor's field, a stream of expletives from his wired-shut jaw following its trajectory. A fence gate that wouldn't close after the winter rains was slammed and kicked into submission one morning while my brothers and I stood and watched from the kitchen window. When we got home from school, the gate had been hacked apart with a chain-saw and strewn across the barnyard; the wood would later be burned. When he was healthy, Dad would spend hours a day chopping wood for our small stove—much more than we would ever need for the average Southern winter. To this day, the sound of someone cutting logs with an ax makes my pulse quicken. Something bad is about to happen, someone is angry. The cut wood sat outside in huge piles—looming, stacked, and waiting to burn—a testament to Dad's temper.

And Dad wasn't alone in his anger; I felt it too, especially late at night as I lay in bed unable to sleep. I would think about all my old friends, the ones I wasn't allowed to write to, the ones I didn't even get to say good-bye to. I thought about our old house, my room with the multicolored carpeting mom had put in, the bunk bed with the Holly Hobbie blanket. I missed our days at the beach, I missed my school, my fourth-grade teacher, I even missed my long straight hair—everything I used to love, that I had always counted on, now gone. I would lie there seething, listening to the occasional car on our rural street. If the engine even slowed outside, I was ready. My hand would go to the place between my mattress and box spring, the place where I now hid my stolen steak knife, and I would hold the handle until the car passed.

. . .

In Tennessee, if you lived on a working farm or ranch, you could acquire what was called a "hardship" driver's license when you were fifteen years old. The point of a hardship license was to allow teens who lived—and worked—on their family's farm to operate farming equipment and also drive vehicles when needed. The license would also allow you to drive on the public roads, though that's not what it was really intended for.

We lived on a rural route with kids who needed the license. These were the kids, like the boys across the street, who missed a month of school in the early fall to harvest and hang tobacco. Or the twins down by Hidden Hollow who needed to drive their dad's pickup into town on a regular basis to pick up feed and seed from the farm-supply store. Since Dad did most of the work on our farm—and we had almost nothing by way of actual farming equipment—my brothers and I did not need a hardship license for any legitimate reason. Our farm was small, and not our main source of income. But my parents allowed us to get our license early because we could, because everyone else was doing it, and because our bus ride to and from the county school took almost an hour each way. Cutting down on a two-hour commute would mean more time for schoolwork—and more time at home doing chores on the farm too. So I guess it was a hardship license in some ways, especially during the seasons when there was a lot of work on the farm and when it got dark early.

My brothers learned how to drive pretty soon after we moved down to the farm from Cape Cod, and both had their licenses by age fifteen. When I was fourteen, my dad started in on the process with me. The spring before my fifteenth birthday, he took me down to the end of our road—past the farms and the holler, out to where the street pretty much turned into packed dirt, and let me have a try behind the wheel. My coordination was never very good, and it was clear I wasn't going to be able to pick up how a clutch worked in time to take my driver's test.

One day when I got off the school bus, there was a new car parked in our cul-de-sac driveway—by "new" I mean new to us, but it was clearly old—maybe even older than me. It was a beat-up, faded orange VW bug, not quite as ugly as the one my dad had owned on the Cape, but pretty near. When I went into the house, I expected to see the driver of the car there, but it was just my dad in the kitchen playing chess against his computer.

"Whose car is that?" I asked him.

"Yours," he said, not even looking up. "Saw an ad for it in the paper. It's an automatic."

"Dad! We can't get a new car!"

"Five hundred dollars," he said. "I figure you guys can all drive it."

I didn't know what to say. I had my first car and I wasn't even fifteen. I didn't care that it was ugly as sin or that I would have to share it with my brothers. Dad and I got in, and he drove us down to the end of the street where I could practice. The car was pretty crappy and stalled out if you didn't apply the gas just right—mastering this was almost as tricky as the delicate balance of a clutch. But I learned it. We went out to the grocery store parking lot and Dad taught me how to parallel park and make a three-point turn. He drilled me on the driver's manual—emphasizing certain points that he, as a former cop, thought were of extreme importance. Rolling stops, left-hand turns, right of way. By the time I turned fifteen, I was more than ready for the test.

We went down to the DMV, and I walked out of there with my driver's license and drove Dad and myself home. When we got back to the house, I parked the car and raced inside to call my best friend, Eve. "Where are you going?" Dad asked me. "Don't you want to take her out by yourself?"

I jumped back into the driver's seat and waved as I (very carefully) pulled out of the driveway. I intended to just drive down to the holler and back, just to see how it felt. It was pretty strange being in the car by myself—no one there telling me what to do every second. I could hear my dad's voice in my head. "Check your mirrors. Watch your speed here. That stop sign was for you. Both hands on the wheel . . ."

When I was about a half mile from the farm, I was no longer alone on the road—there was another car coming up behind me. It was blue. I hated blue cars, and every time I saw a blue four-door car, I would compulsively check for Florida plates. This was because of the last news we had heard—years earlier—about the investigation into Dad's shooting. They could find no trace of the car Dad had described under hypnosis, but one resident on Sandwich Road had come forward to say that he had seen a blue car with Florida plates racing down the street minutes after my dad was shot. The detectives said they suspected the shooters had been hired killers from Florida. This had been burned into my head: hired killers, blue car, Florida.

As the car closed in on me, I checked my rearview mirror for plates. But this car didn't have plates on the front. Suddenly, I felt scared. What if they had been waiting for me? Watching the house. Waiting for just this moment, waiting to get me alone in the car on this lonely stretch of road. My speed—which was already a few miles below the limit—decreased more, and I felt my hands clench the wheel.

The car honked, twice, and flashed its headlights. I slowed more, unsure of what to do, powerless to stop the attack that I knew was coming. Then I heard the car behind me rev its engine and pull out into the opposite lane. And I forgot to breathe. I squeezed my eyes shut and yanked the wheel to the right— forcing the VW onto the dirt shoulder at an angle. I slammed on the brakes and pulled my head down low, by the passenger seat, as the other car roared by.

"Asshole!" I heard someone yell. I lifted my head just in time to see the other car race off down the road. I sat in my car by the side of the road until I calmed down enough to hold the wheel without shaking. I looked at my face in the mirror and wiped away the tear streaks. Then I sat there a few minutes more for good measure. I heard another car come up over the rise and down the hill behind me, but I wasn't worried. I could see in the rearview that it was just the Jacksons' mint green Ford pickup.

They lived a few miles down the road from us, and I knew their two boys from school.

The truck slowed as it neared me, and I saw Jimmy, who was seventeen, inside. He leaned over to talk to me through the open passenger-side window. "This that new car your brothers were talking about?" he asked. He wasn't wearing a shirt and looked like he had been doing some work outside.

I nodded. "What do you think?"

"I didn't figure it would be so small!" Jimmy laughed. "That car's just right for you, though."

"I guess." I shrugged, looking at his pickup truck. People around here didn't drive foreign.

"Well," he paused awkwardly, "reckon I'll see you at school, huh?"

"Sure," I told him.

He gave me a nod, then put the truck back into gear and drove off. I didn't realize until after I watched his truck disappear over the next rise that he hadn't bothered to ask me what I was doing pulled over on the side of the road. But that was pretty typical of our neighbors—they all minded their own business, and nobody asked anyone else much of anything. That's why we lived here. Nobody knew anything about us, and that was how we wanted it.

I took a deep breath and checked my mirrors like Dad had taught me to do. When I was sure there was no traffic coming in either direction, I turned the car around and headed home.

where they are now

In 2003, James Meyer confessed to Falmouth police detectives that he was involved in the attempted murder of John Busby. He told detectives he had been driving the car that night, while his brother, Raymond Meyer, leveled a shotgun at Busby's head from the backseat. Also in the car with them was Raymond's wife, Laverne. The shotgun had been borrowed from a friend and returned shortly after the shooting. The car had recently been purchased from a Falmouth police officer, Ahmed Mustafa, and had no plates; it was later destroyed at a junkyard.

Meyer's confession also included information about two unsolved murders and a disappearance, all linked to Raymond Meyer. The police report of his confession is unavailable to the public as it is currently part of the ongoing investigation into the murder of Laverne Meyer.

John and Polly Busby: Married for over forty years, John and Polly are now retired. They have four grandchildren. After his shooting in 1979, John underwent nineteen years of reconstructive surgery and speech therapy; he has partially recovered the ability to talk and eat solid food.

Eric Busby: Married for more than ten years, Eric and his wife live in the Pacific Northwest.

Shawn Busby: Lives in New England with his wife and their three children.

Craig Clarkson: Retired from the Falmouth Police Department, currently lives with his family in Falmouth, Massachusetts.

John Ferreira: Retired as chief of police, Falmouth Police Department, December 1979. Lived with his family in Falmouth until his death in November 2008.

Michael "Mickey" Mangum: Resigned from the Falmouth Police Department, 1977. Currently resides in Massachusetts.

Tony Mello: Retired from the Falmouth Police Department in 2007, currently lives with his wife, Kathy, in Falmouth, Massachusetts.

James Meyer: Confessed to police detectives in 2003 that he drove the car on the night of John Busby's shooting. Implicated his brother, Raymond Meyer, in the shooting, and also Raymond's wife, Laverne Meyer. As of March 2008, he is facing charges of malicious destruction of property in an unrelated case.

Laverne Meyer: Her body was found early on the morning of May 10, 2005, at her home; she had been shot once in the head and once in the chest at close range. Her murder remains unsolved.

Raymond Meyer: Charged by Massachusetts State Police in a bid-rigging scheme in 1984, acquitted in 1985 (his business partner Charles Cacciola was found guilty). In an unrelated case, Meyer was charged with assault, two counts of threatening to commit a crime, and malicious destruction of property in 2001; he was found unfit to stand trial and diagnosed with dementia. He has been incarcerated in the Taunton State Hospital since 2001.

Larry Mitchell: Former Falmouth police officer who refused in 1979 to take a polygraph test. In 1980, he submitted to a polygraph and failed. In 2003, James Meyer exonerated Mitchell by revealing that it was actually fellow officer Arthur Monteiro who gave Raymond Meyer the police department work schedule, something that Busby and others wrongly suspected Mitchell of for years. Died in October 2008 after a long battle with cancer.

Arthur Monteiro: Former Falmouth police officer, died in 1990. Implicated by James Meyer in the Busby shooting. James Meyer told police detectives that Monteiro was the inside source for information about Busby's work schedule.

Arthur "the Bear" Pina: Died suddenly of heart failure in 2007; he is survived by his wife and two daughters.

Don Price: Retired Falmouth police captain, currently resides in Arizona.

Rick Smith: Retired Falmouth police officer, 2008. Lives with his wife, Terry, in Falmouth, Massachusetts.

ACKNOWLEDGMENTS

John would like to thank:

Albert and Jean Santiago and family, who called for the ambulance

The EMTs and paramedics of the Falmouth Fire Department and the ambulance driver

Emergency room physicians and nurses at Falmouth Hospital, especially Dr. Gibbons

Massachusetts State Police escort to Massachusetts General Hospital

Dr. David Keith and the doctors and nurses at MGH who took care of me

The police officers who guarded me during hospital stays

Jim Alward and his wife, Carol

Bernadette and Dale Collier and my extraordinary niece, Kelly, for all they did to support us

Winny Woods

Businesses on Cape Cod that donated to our relocation fund

Jim McGuire and Phyllis Evendon, who formed the John Busby Road Race

My brother officers on the Cape for their contributions

Rick Smith, fellow officer and good friend, for keeping it alive

Newspaper reporters who kept digging for the truth:

Amanda Lehmert, *Cape Cod Times*

George Brennan, *Cape Cod Times*

Mark Sullivan, *Cape Cod Times*

Laura Reckford, *Falmouth Enterprise*

And last but not least—the guy who shot me, for opening my
eyes to what is truly important in life, and what follows life

Cylin would like to thank:

Thank you:

Damon, my love

August, our love

My brother Eric and his wife, Julie

My brother Shawn and his wife, Amber

My nephews Felix and Tabor (especially Felix for giving up his
room so I had somewhere to sleep during my research trip)

My amazing editor, Melanie Cecka, for saying yes

My fabulous agent, Barry Goldblatt, for not saying no

My early readers:

Nanci Katz-Ellis

Erin Zimring
Jean Ross and Betty David-Ross
Eddie Gamarra

My friends:
Eve, Shane, and Mary in Tennessee, for taking a chance on the
    new weird girl
Melanie, Blue, Pamela, Cecil; Jenny and Rick, Jennie and Ken,
    Israel and Dane

Falmouth police officers—especially Rick Smith, Craig Clark-
    son, Don Price, Mickey Mangum, Tony Mello, and Tom
    Mountford—for their protection, research help, and every-
    thing else. Terry, for the apple pie and a place to stay. Arthur,
    you are missed. Thank you for making me feel safe

James Alward and his family
Dr. Lisa Garber

The teachers of the SIJCC and Ruthie Shavit for giving my
    son a wonderful place to spend his days while I was writing
    this book

And Sister Celine Martin, for my name and for all the prayers.
    Thank you.

A CONVERSATION WITH CYLIN AND JOHN BUSBY

What made you want to write about this experience—and why as a memoir and not fictionalize it?

Cylin: I had been encouraging Dad to write his memoirs for a while. A couple of years ago, he finally sent me his notebooks and journals to see if I could shape them into a book somehow. As I was reading over them, I started thinking about how differently I remembered things, how our situation looked from my perspective—he was busy trying to survive his personal injuries and the threat on his life, while my brothers and I were going through something totally removed from that. I began to realize that there were two sides to the story of what happened to us—one from the perspective of a child and one from the view of an adult—and I wanted us to tell it together.

John: I had three reasons. First, everyone I have told about what happened to us would respond, "What a great book that would make—or a great movie." The second reason is now that the statute of limitations for my attempted murder has expired, the only justice for us is to put this out to as large an audience as we can reach to expose the people responsible and those who aided them by butchering the police investigation of the crime. The frustration of that only added to the hell we lived through. Last but not least, I wanted to make people aware that hate and revenge are wrong. They destroy you internally. Once I had decided to put my family first, I began to heal. It was not easy, it took some time, but it was definitely the right thing for us.

Cylin, how were you able to focus your childhood memories on that time without bringing your current knowledge and feelings into it?

For some reason—maybe the trauma of the events—that year of our lives is burned into my memory, and I have a vivid recollection of things that were said to me, the clothes I wore, even the food I ate for the weeks and months after my dad was shot. (But if you asked me what my teacher's name was the year after that, I honestly couldn't tell you!) Since the memories are still so vivid, it wasn't that hard to go to back to that time and write as my nine-year-old self. What *was* hard was keeping other people's personal memories out of my head, like my brothers', my cousins', etc. I did have to focus on what I remembered and not cloud my memory with other people's perspectives of the same events.

John, what was it like for you to relive that year?

Writing the book brought up many memories of the physical and mental pain, anger, and frustration. When these resurfaced, it was similar to the feelings I used to have when I had to shave off my beard for each surgery. I would see the scars of what they had done to me and would be enraged again. Like tearing off a scab will make a wound bleed—and this was a deep wound.

Cylin, when you began writing The Year We Disappeared you were the same age your dad was when he was shot. What's it been like for you as an adult and as a parent to see the events through your dad's eyes?

Now that I'm a wife and parent, I look back on what happened to us and I'm so proud of my parents, especially my mom, for having the strength to hold our family together. I don't know how she did it, or how my father endured all the physical pain and surgeries that he had to undergo. My dad also had to put his personal anger and need for revenge aside and focus on us—I think that's something he still grapples with every day. It's truly amazing to me that my parents are still together—over forty years of marriage. I think it's a testament to who they are as people and who we all are as a family.

John, what was it like for you to hear your children's perceptions of that year?

It was eye-opening. I was so centered on my own healing, I wasn't aware of the problems the kids were going through. I had a goal to reach and the people in my family were just innocent bystanders being swept along with me.

Cylin, your story captures your innocence, confusion, and grief; John, yours your anger, pain, and frustration. Have those emotions evolved, plateaued, or faded over the years? If yes, how so? If not, how have you come to accept and live with them?

Cylin: Since these events happened when I was so young, they basically shaped who I am today. People often ask me how I dealt with it or how I'm dealing with it now, and honestly, I just don't know anything different, so it's hard for me to explain. While I definitely see the difference in my childhood before my dad was shot and afterward, I don't know any other type of childhood than the one I had. The innocence was quickly lost and replaced with anger, confusion, fear. . . . Some of those feelings are still with me today, but I accept that as part of who I am and part of my experience.

John: My emotions have evolved and also faded. It has been thirty years; I'm sure if I had not decided to live my life this way, if I had continued to be in need of revenge, I would either have died long ago from some stress-related illness or I would be in prison for returning the favor. I am living a very happy, healthy life. I have four grandchildren, all of whom mean the world to me. I know I made the right decision because it has led to a life that includes and embraces my family, not merely the satisfaction of revenge.

How do other members of your family feel about you telling your family's story?

Cylin: I have two older brothers, and while they are happy that the story is finally being told, I think we are all wary of the repercussions that this book might bring. We grew up being told that what had happened to us was a secret, and that we were never to share information about anything with anyone. It's been very hard to put that type of thinking aside and reveal all the intimate details of our lives in this way, but I hope it will somehow bring closure, if not justice, for us as a family.

John: The reaction has been mixed. Some are concerned about the criminals mentioned in the book striking out in response (they are obviously prone to violence and have recently been involved in several violent crimes). But on the other side, this seems to be the only way we can get justice against them. All of the people involved on our side have given approval to print what we have written.

What was the hardest part of writing this for each of you?

Cylin: While researching the book, I came across the crime-scene photos of Jeff Flanagan (he's the seventeen-year-old whose body was found in the bogs). It's one thing to read about, or write about, his case, but actually looking at the images of him with the shotgun wounds, his hands tied behind his back—that was devastating to me. It's not so much that they were graphic, but more just seeing how young he was. He was wearing jeans and a T-shirt on the night he died, and he just looked like such a kid, such a teenager. I looked at those images of him and I cried, for him, for his family. Being faced with the injustice of his case and the other victims in this story is very difficult to handle, especially when you consider what his family must have gone through, and probably continue to go through.

John: For me it was going back in time to the pain, anger, and frustration. Being back in the darkness of hate and revenge.

Cylin, did you ever see *The Muppet Movie*?

No.

John, do you still play chess?

Chess is a daily activity for me. I do have some short-term memory problems since the shooting, so I keep a journal and also have an excuse for losing at chess now and again. No healthy chess player loses!

Why did you choose to use an alias for the man who was allegedly behind the shooting?

Cylin: When I first started working on the book, it was very hard for me to type his name—I know how petty that sounds, but it really was hard for me to give him the acknowledgment of typing his name. It seemed to legitimize him in a way that I just couldn't bear. After the book was vetted by a lawyer, we learned that we did not have to change any names for legal reasons (since the story is true and fairly well documented in the newspapers). As we got closer to publishing the book, I realized that this book is my story, my dad's story, my family's story, and that I didn't want his name in it, period.

John: I would like the criminals to be fully exposed, including using their actual names. But I understand why others in my family want the names changed. There is no reason to glorify them and their actions.

Have you learned anything new about each other or the incident through the process of writing *The Year We Disappeared*?

Cylin: I had no idea how angry my father was after his shooting. He and my mother kept us protected from that anger, and I think my brothers and I assumed that the changes in his personality were due to his injuries and our circumstances. It wasn't until we were writing the book that I became aware of how carefully he had planned his revenge, and in what detail. I didn't know until very recently how close he came to being a murderer himself.

John: I learned what my family suffered while I was caught up in a self-centered hell.

What do you hope people will take away from their reading of The Year We Disappeared?

Cylin: We see so much violence, either real or imaginary, through the media that I think we've become desensitized to it. We forget that every act of violence has a ripple effect. In our case, my dad's shooting took only seconds, but the effects of that night have taken years to undo—and some damage can never be undone. I hope it's not too lofty a wish to hope that readers, especially young readers, will take away a better understanding of how every act of violence can impact others.

John: I'd like people to realize, like I did, that hate and revenge are a self-defeating disease we inflict upon ourselves. I have been in that dark place and my family saved me from it. I healed when I left that behind; it wasn't fast, it wasn't easy, but due to my love for my family and my self healing, it was necessary—I did it.

ABOUT THE AUTHORS

CYLIN BUSBY is the author of several fiction and nonfiction books for young readers. She is the former senior editor of *Teen* magazine and the author of numerous magazine articles. She lives in Los Angeles with her husband and young son.

JOHN BUSBY is retired and lives with his wife of over forty years, Polly Busby. He continues to fight for the extension of the statute of limitations on assault of a police officer.